HITACHI
WALK ALONE
ATHLETIC CLUB
LIVERPOOL
POOL
LIVERPOOL
YOU'LL NEVER WALK ALONE
umbro

TRANSFORMER

Also by Neil Atkinson

Make Us Dream:
The Story of Liverpool's 2013/14 Season (with John Gibbons)
Red Letters: Two Fervent Liverpool FC Supporters Correspond through
the Epic Season That Wouldn't End (with Michael MacCambridge)

TRANSFORMER

KLOPP, THE REVOLUTION OF A CLUB AND CULTURE

NEIL ATKINSON

CANONGATE

First published in Great Britain, the USA and Canada in 2024
by Canongate Books Ltd, 14 High Street, Edinburgh EH1 1TE

Distributed in the USA by Publishers Group West
and in Canada by Publishers Group Canada

canongate.co.uk

1

British Library Cataloguing-in-Publication Data
A catalogue record for this book is available on
request from the British Library

ISBN 978 1 83726 292 2

Typeset in Adobe Garamond Pro by Palimpsest Book Production Ltd,
Falkirk, Stirlingshire

Printed and bound by CPI Group (UK) Ltd, Croydon CR0 4YY

FSC
www.fsc.org

MIX
Paper | Supporting
responsible forestry
FSC® C171272

For Joan – an answer to the happiness question

Contents

The Warm-Up

Introduction

Why?

Nobody needs to write a book, sell a book or read a book.

So you (i.e. me) had best have a good reason to take the attention of the good people at Canongate, booksellers, librarians and whoever it is that has this thing in their hands at this moment. That is you. Thank you for holding and hopefully reading it.

Everything is eyeballs these days. You (the reader) could be playing Grand Theft Auto or Minecraft, watching/listening to *Homecoming* by Beyoncé, reading *Time Shelter* by Georgi Gospodinov. I am in competition with all these things, which is pretty scary because they are all really good: Look, there's *The Chase* with Bradley Walsh; wonder what's happening on Instagram . . .

I'm Neil, and I host *The Anfield Wrap* where we make podcasts and videos mostly about Liverpool FC and the city itself. When they first asked us in 2012 to do the radio live on City Talk at 5 p.m. I wanted to be the best thing on the radio at 5 p.m., out of everything there is at that time on the radio, including *PM* on Radio 4, because what's the point otherwise? People could be doing anything but they are choosing you. Love them for that by being the best version you can be. Love them with your best.

You are now entering into this very direct relationship with me instead of watching Alison Steadman in *Pride and Prejudice*, asking me to take your attention and show you something, remind you of something, find some way of taking this shared existence of ours in this moment into a place it wouldn't be were it not for these words on this page.

With a little bit of luck, we (the royal but eventually the actual) are going to do that in the context of Jürgen Klopp being Liverpool manager; we're going to start there and go on a journey together about a sport, a city, a global institution, a diaspora, and, well, you. We are writing about you. You are somewhere here in this story, I am sure of it, and you'll do your own heavy lifting as we go.

Jürgen took a shared existence that went beyond football and showed something, reminded us of something and took our shared existence into a place it wouldn't be without his efforts, and made a ton of people somewhere here in this story, made them do heavy lifting, made them think again, love again, be proud again, made them the best versions of themselves, at least for a moment. By winning, yes, because as we'll discover, winning always helps, but also by finding a way that would become ours.

Jürgen turned up and made me feel and think a load of things, and some of them are in the pages that follow. The most important of which is that the whole thing is a gift and everything that matters is best done together. And that's the why of the book and the task of this book for both of us. We are in this as a collaboration. A team effort.

Another why of this book is I don't see anywhere near enough people writing about happiness in general, especially within the realm of football where grumpiness has become the order of the day. We're going to do that on the precipice or remnants of a night out: a kiss with an added cuddle, an argument that becomes a dance, a great howling laugh which minutes later is an arm around the shoulder. Some of this is going to be rewritten and recontextualised from previous efforts of mine but mostly it is seen through the lens of the nine years and contextualised by what came before. There is a timeline and there are key games and there is how it all was in the round.

Thanks for the eyeballs – honestly, I couldn't appreciate it more. I will endeavour to waste none of your time, will remember you have other things you could be doing, presume you are smart and have a memory of your own but will remind you repeatedly that the whole thing is an act of love, that this is your party and you'll cry if you want to, that this is sort of a choose your own adventure because you probably had yours and the specificity of mine is just a kaleidoscope through which you find your own anew today, and in the years to come when you decide to reread this rather than watch *Bradley* on Challenge TV.

This means, at times, I am going to refer to people and places you may not know and we may not always trouble ourselves with descriptions. You don't need to worry. That's because these people, they are your friends. They are you. These places, they are your places. You know them even if you don't know them. Trust me like I trust you. Because the actual (not the royal) we are in this together. And if we haven't learned that bit then Jürgen really did waste his time, and we both know that isn't true.

Prologue

The Beginnings: the 2013–14 'Failure'*

The First Beginning

After Liverpool beat West Ham United 1–2 at Upton Park on 6 April 2014 I recorded a show at the top of the tower, St Johns Beacon, which looks out across the whole city. Liverpool had absolutely clawed their way to the sort of 1–2 victory that history has tried to pretend was beyond this side. Sam Allardyce had lashed Andy Carroll up top and hit the big man repeatedly, but Liverpool repelled them time and again. Two penalties. Steven Gerrard tucked away both and Liverpool saw it out.

Liverpool top of the pops. Two clear of Chelsea; four clear of Manchester City, though they had two games in hand. Manchester City up next at Anfield. It was the first time since 2009 that Liverpool had been top in April (then with a Manchester club being two points behind with two games in hand). That, in turn, was the first time since 2002. Liverpool two clear of Arsenal – who had two games in hand.

While recording the show, I was getting texts about where the drink was happening. The Saddle on Dale Street. I couldn't believe it. With Steve Graves, I walked across town. 'I mean, it's not a good pub this, Steve. There must be some mistake. Maybe it is a holding position boozer.'

* A version of this chapter first appeared in the anthology *From the Jaws of Victory: A History of Football's Nearly Men*, edited by Adam Bushby and Rob MacDonald, Halcyon Publishing, 2020

When we opened the door, it hit us. The heat. The sweat. The effer-vescent glow of smiles on faces. The joy making the light shimmer. And the noise. The wall of noise. Adam Melia and his brother Daniel glori-fying 'This is How We Do it' by Montell Jordan on the karaoke and an entire room chanting back at them. The room being as eclectic as it could be; the Saddle receiving the overspill of Liverpool's gay district, its karaoke led by Candi; Liverpool supporters and lesbians and lesbian Liverpool supporters chanting the chorus back at Adam and Dan. South Central does it like nobody does. People on tables, roaring, laughing, dancing, carousing. I couldn't have been more wrong.

This was the happiest I'd ever been in my whole life.

You can't tell the story of Jürgen Klopp and Liverpool without telling the story of all the other bits: the places where the ley lines meet and split, begin and swirl. For me, you can't tell the story of Jürgen Klopp without telling the story of 2014 without understanding what it awak-ened in the sense of the football at Anfield and in the sense of what football felt like and why. This is what football does. Football builds.

There are too many beginnings. Here are some more.

The Second Beginning

17 August 2013. Simon Mignolet saved a penalty in the last minute against Stoke City after Daniel Sturridge had given Liverpool a 1–0 lead. Kolo Touré had turned up in the summer and said this was a squad that could win the league. He'd been downright adamant about it, but there was a vague feeling somewhere that this didn't seem quite as strange as it should have – Manchester United had lost Alex Ferguson and replaced him with David Moyes, and we knew all about David Moyes and we knew what old footballers looked like. We'd been there.

The end of the 2012–13 season had seen Liverpool score a lot of goals and look very lively. What transpired to be the key positive transfer window of Brendan Rodgers' time had just happened. Philippe Coutinho and Daniel Sturridge were signed, the latter, especially, inspiring an upturn in form and, by the time the campaign had finished, Liverpool had been able to look genuinely dangerous, having gone just shy of two points per game for the second half of the season, which made them much of a muchness with Arsenal, Chelsea, Manchester City and Tottenham.

When Mignolet saved the penalty on his Liverpool debut, the ground exploded. A point against Stoke City on the first day of the season would have killed us. Gerrard grabbed him by the throat afterwards. It is possible Simon never entirely recovered. Steve Graves said out loud: 'We can win this league, you know.' He made his case. It was almost as good as Kolo's.

It was a punch in the face, the realisation that, yes, we could win this league, you know. A punch in the face I'm glad I got early. A punch in the face that every Liverpool supporter would get between August 2013 and April 2014. For the first time since April 2009, it was valid to say, 'We can win this league, you know,' and that became the only sentence ever worth saying.

Villa 0–1 Sturridge followed, and then Manchester United and David Moyes rocked up.

Sturridge 1–0. United looked devoid of ideas. Liverpool played three, won three. Kolo Touré was incredible in all three games. Let's do it. Let's win this league. These are our lads. You know who my favourite players are? The 11 who wear red.

The Third Beginning

You're at the Melbourne Cricket Ground, it is July 2013 and Liverpool are playing. This is obviously weird but an early example of something you call 'Mad Job Syndrome' and go with it. Last night, oddly, you were on stage in front of 1,000 Liverpool supporters at a hotel doing jokes and bits for literally five hours. Dr Karl Kennedy of *Neighbours* fame and Craig Johnston were both there. Mad Job Syndrome.

There are 100,000 present in Melbourne to watch your football team from your wonderful but frankly weird city in the north-west of England play against Melbourne Victory. They put the lyrics to 'You'll Never Walk Alone' on the big screen and in the section put aside for 'active' supporters, you drink your white wine for which Australians have mocked you and you've smiled politely because their beer is frankly awful and no one needs telling that. You think to yourself: 'This all has to mean something. You can't be this big and just trundle. This has to have some sense of purpose to it. This cannot just become a nostalgic roadshow.'

There has to be something more. There has to be another adventure. Something has to start. You think, definitively, 'Fuck nostalgia,' and you never stop thinking it because, say what you want, the whole decade of the 2010s supports that conclusion. You think it has to be a joy to be alive in the now and, if anything is worth working towards, if any story is worth telling, it is that one. Please let the story be that one, you plead . . .

The Fourth Beginning

When Liverpool made Brendan Rodgers manager, I didn't really know what to think. 'Let's see,' I thought. 'Let's just see.' And, I thought, it will also be nice to have a manager I don't wake up in the night anxious about, you know, like the bloke who nearly died, or the bloke who fought for the soul of the club, or the bloke who, closer than anyone else alive, personified the soul of the club. I thought maybe this will help. A bloke coming in from outside who no one knows much about. Someone not infected with our nonsense. Maybe he'll get us playing a bit. And if he doesn't, well, we just get rid of him. Whichever way it goes, it'll be nice to get a full night's sleep . . .

The Fifth Beginning

On 3 October 2010 Liverpool faced Blackpool at Anfield. Roy Hodgson was in charge. The club was owned by Tom Hicks and George Gillett.

I didn't go in. I went to the ground but when push came to shove, I just couldn't face it.

They came back into the upstairs of the boozer I was in in their dribs and drabs. The first was someone called Kev Walsh. He arrived back on about 30 minutes. We watched the game and we talked.

Three days later Liverpool were sold to FSG (then NESV). Not long after that, the court case decided it. Then Roy Hodgson took us to Everton. We got beat 2–0 and he said to win there would have been utopia. Lad, we win there when down to ten men.

Before Christmas I met Kev in Pogues and we watched a Chelsea game. We agreed that Chelsea were our big team now. We go to the football, we watch Liverpool, but it's nice to see Chelsea do well and win things. We'll watch the cup final if they are involved. We were joking, of course, but . . .

The Sixth Beginning

I was in a boozer in London when they sacked Rafa Benítez. Me and the filmmaker Daniel Fitzsimmons were attending some meetings about some film work. Dan's phone buzzed. My phone buzzed. His buzzed again. The people we were meeting said, 'Don't you want to check your phones?' 'No, mate.' But Dan did. He looked at me. He nodded.

We wrapped the meeting up and went elsewhere and stared off into space. Both upset. Both, frankly, exhausted. What Benítez had shown . . .

The Seventh Beginning

When Kenny Dalglish resigned as Liverpool manager, when Liverpool were reigning champions, after an epic 4–4 draw against local rivals Everton at Goodison Park, no one imagined that it would be two generations before . . .

The Eighth Beginning

It's December 1959 and Bill Shankly arrives at Melwood. He calls it a bloody shambles. There was work to do.

The beginnings. Beginnings of thinking about this differently. Beginnings of wanting it to feel different. Beginnings of having the time and the focus to think about football quite possibly far more than anyone should. All these beginnings lead to endings of a sort, but endings are as trappy as beginnings when seasons come thick and fast.

There are things that have to be said here: that this was the moment when having a wonderful time began to make so much sense, despite the fact that in 2013–14 they didn't win the league. This moment was the starting moment, a warm-up for Jürgen Klopp to come. Despite it being 24 years since the title.

Time is unreliable, regardless. Liverpool hadn't not won the league for 30 years in terms of feel. For me they hadn't won it since 2002, since Emile Heskey went to Leeds and destroyed them, since Vladi Šmicer scored in the last minute against Chelsea and I was convinced, only to be crushed. That was my first time not winning the league. That was my year zero. For others, they maybe hadn't won it since Istanbul. For some it may have been 2009, and for others it may actually be this prologue season of 2013–14.

But also, frankly, it is insulting to the vast majority of football supporters to act as though it was 30 years of disappointment. I mostly had a lovely time and Liverpool won everything else in those 30 years. It did gnaw, though. It did gnaw at you. It did grate. Just one. Just give me one of those things those old bastards had 18 of. Just give me the one. I'm begging you. It grew obsessive.

You know when I didn't have a lovely time? From about 2007 to about 2010. Supporting Liverpool, going to the game, talking about the game meant having an argument, a perpetual argument. Over ownership, leveraged buyouts, protests, net spend, Benítez, our place in the world and our direction of travel. Liverpool came to resemble a thoroughbred racehorse laden with baggage. Liverpool's title charge in 2008–09 mostly wasn't an enjoyable experience. It was fraught. It was stressful. It was about sticking it to people. Not about the adventure and not even really about sticking it to people who didn't support Liverpool. It was about sticking it to people internally, sticking it to fellow Liverpool supporters about the manager, about Lucas Leiva, about Dirk Kuyt, about whatever was going. It's an amazing thoroughbred, Benítez's 2008–09, because it was carrying all sorts. Mostly weaponry either stuck in it or thrusting weaponry back. It was laden. It was fettered.

I'd never go back to 2008–09. Not for a second. Not for a moment. Not even for 1–4 at Old Trafford. It was thoroughly unpleasant, waking at 3 a.m. wondering if tomorrow would be the day Benítez ridiculously got sacked, arguing in the ground every other week. But I'd do 2013–14 again; I'd live those nine months over and over and over again if I could. Groundhog season. No one was looking to stick anything to anyone. Not when you could give them a cuddle instead. I'd go back in an instant. Back to waking at 3 a.m. excited that it was Saturday, Saturday, Saturday and still being up at 3 a.m. on Sunday, Sunday, Sunday. I'd go back in the blink of an eye. I'd do it mostly so I could see my friends that happy again: faces moist with sweat, improbability and delight.

The past is prologue. The past is practice. This past was practice for Jürgen Klopp.

So 2013–14 continued. Luis Suárez got back from his bite and his attempt to move to Arsenal. Not quite sure which of those two things was the more irrational. And then Suárez happened and just kept happening. Transfer requests easily forgotten, biting people easily forgotten, the Evra incident all too easily – and shamefully – forgotten. What made it easier to block the negatives from your mind was that Luis Suárez, from October '13 to March '14, happened more than any top-flight footballer in England ever had. It was like playing with 12 men. Possibly 13. He was both a 9 and a false 9 and he did bits out wide as well. He scored a header from 18 yards, and every brilliant performance he put in, Daniel Sturridge strived to match. The day Suárez headed home from a mile out as part of a hat-trick, Sturridge somehow lobbed a keeper who wasn't off his line. Suárez got two at Stoke, Sturridge made it five by doing keepy-uppies on the goalline.

Luis Suárez scored four against Norwich City at Anfield. Let me tell you about the weakest goal – it was reminiscent of Peter Beardsley's volley against Everton at Anfield in 1987. The third best was a 25-yard free-kick. That same night, Everton won at Old Trafford and Manchester United were none of our business. This was the first time since 1990 that it was due to their shortcomings rather than ours.

A week and a half after Norwich at home, they went to Tottenham Hotspur – 4 p.m. on the telly. No Steven Gerrard, he was in the studio. They battered them 5–0 – Suárez a pleasure, but Jordan Henderson and Raheem Sterling were incredible. It was quite possibly Liverpool's best away performance of the decade. After the game, Gerrard remarked he was worried he wouldn't get back into this team. Everyone laughed because they didn't understand Gerrard. He was worried he wouldn't get back into this team.

Over Christmas, they lost twice. Once at Manchester City, once at Chelsea, and, in the long run, there's an argument that these results were what cost us the title. There was harsh officiating in both matches – Raheem Sterling opened the scoring at the Etihad only for it to be given offside. It wasn't by a million miles. Samuel Eto'o threw a shocking tackle in early at Chelsea but you can do what you want in the first five, can't you? Suárez had a late equaliser chalked off. But Liverpool had gone ahead in the game, so what can you say? Liverpool ended the calendar year six points behind Arsenal.

In mid-January Aston Villa came to Anfield and Liverpool played Steven Gerrard at the base of the midfield and it was difficult to put into words how hard he found the game. It finished 2–2 and my God did Gerrard struggle. We hosted a resurgent Everton the following week, Ross Barkley in fine form, and everyone hoped Rodgers wouldn't pick Gerrard there. If Everton won, they'd go above us.

Rodgers picked Gerrard there. He scored the opener, the sort of header that thunders home. Then Sturridge got a quick-fire brace, the second a lob in front of the Blues, which was just unreasonable. Suárez made it four immediately after half-time and then we got a penalty. Steven put his only foot wrong all night. He handed Sturridge the ball. Sturridge missed. Had we made it five, we may have made it ten. We were that good. Steven resplendent. Steven the king of all he surveyed.

Steven was suddenly that good. Steven was incredible in interviews. Steven was Liverpool captain like he never had been before. Steven said: 'If you want to play two on two against these two, all the best.'

All the best.

Liverpool drop points at West Brom. Kolo Touré makes a mistake and the side is punished. Then they have Arsenal at Anfield. Arsenal are top of the pile, eight ahead of Liverpool. It's 8 February. It's Saturday, 12:45, and I have powered into the ground. This is it. It is now or never.

It is now.

It will never, ever be more now.

Liverpool go 4–0 ahead on the 20-minute mark and, my God, is that flattering to Arsenal. It genuinely should be six. You have never seen the like, not before nor since. Liverpool win the ball back through Henderson and Coutinho and turn Arsenal around so quickly. They can't keep track of Suárez, Sturridge or Sterling. Everywhere, there is a runner. Liverpool cut them to absolute ribbons. Liverpool press Arsenal to death. They destroy them. It's thrilling, visceral stuff, another harbinger of what is to come.

After the fourth goes in there's a sound I've never heard in a football ground before or since, and it is that of thousands of people just laughing in disbelief. After the game, Steven says: 'I'm trying to think of a performance I can remember in the last 15 years. Maybe one or two in the Champions League got close but that was as explosive as it gets. That is right up there. That's definitely in the top-three performances I have been involved in. You are talking about a side that is top of the league with world-class players, ones who are worth £42 million. Jack Wilshere, one of the country's big hopes. [Santi] Cazorla, a World Cup winner. We have absolutely demolished a top team from start to finish.'

Steven understates it. The first half is the greatest half of football any

Liverpool side has played since 1990. It could be the greatest ever. Liverpool punching everyone in the face.

We were out after, out all day, hanging out for *Match of the Day*, staying out for a massive dance. By February of 2009 I felt like an old man. I had seen too much, lived too much. I was strung out. Roll on five years and Liverpool 5 Arsenal 1 makes me feel like a teenager, even just thinking of it now. It makes me want to drink in the park. It makes me want to neck. It makes me want.

Suddenly, everywhere you went in the city, everyone you spoke to, everything that happened, had a buzz. Everyone was talking football, talking The Reds. It helped that Everton were playing well too. The whole city was alive. Suddenly, Liverpool was having a pint. Even more of a pint than normal. The Saddle tableau wasn't unique. All over the city parties were being had every weekend. Boss were putting on Boss Nights which were boss. The whole city bounced to the weekend's rhythm: boozers packed for almost every game that had any sort of an impact at the top, boozers spilling over before, during and after when The Reds played. This wasn't limited just to the city of Liverpool. The worldwide diaspora were going out and watching it together, and we knew that because we were doing *The Anfield Wrap* and they were telling us so. Suddenly, it was football that made you want to be with your mates, football that made you want to make new mates. Because these Reds. Suddenly it was a joy to be alive. Suddenly everyone had been punched in the face. We can win this league, you know.

They go to Fulham. Kolo Touré makes a mistake but Steven plays the greatest through ball to Daniel Sturridge you have seen in your whole life for the equaliser. Regardless, though, it is 2–2 last minute and Liverpool get a penalty. Steven steps up and scores and he wheels away and takes his top off. Look at him there, just look at him roaring at the away end, top whirring, Jordan Henderson in relief behind him. Look into his eyes. This puts Liverpool fourth but Steven has seen Liverpool fourth. Steven knows fourth. Steven doesn't take his top off for fourth. Steven has been punched in the face.

This is here and this is now. Steven's carried this burden, Atlas-like.

The broadest shoulders in Liverpool. Steven's been this man who looked around and lacked players who could make it happen with him. Not now.

All the best.

They didn't stop. Four against Swansea, three at Southampton, three when they dominated David Moyes's Manchester United, Steven drawing Marouane Fellaini's actual blood, Liverpool making United metaphorically bleed. Liverpool swanked around Old Trafford that day in a way they hadn't for at least 30 years – but would again soon with Jürgen Klopp. Steven missed a penalty for his hat-trick. It didn't matter.

Six at Cardiff. Four against Tottenham – Liverpool's season aggregate against Spurs being 9–0. Then came Manchester City at Anfield, and Liverpool battered them for half an hour. It was only 2–0 but it should have been more. It needed to be more. Anfield was a bear pit. I can't tell you. It was the most vociferous it had been for a league game in years. I'll never forget it – it was the moment Anfield found its voice which it had mislaid. We never knew it was just, in and of itself, a warm-up. It was a practice but we didn't know that; all we knew was that we needed more than wanted, that we wanted for all time and all we knew was that we needed to get right on top of Manchester City. Manchester City had walked into absolute fucking hell, indescribable fucking hell, the like of which they walked into again in January and March 2018. In November 2019. It was no way to play football. It wasn't fair.

And then they were ace. Let me tell you about Manchester City for the 20 minutes after half-time – it was among the greatest performances by an away side at Anfield. They penned us not in our own half but in our own penalty area. It was terrifying, and every single one of those Manchester City players stood up in a way that left you deeply impressed. They had us living on our nerves, and they got the two goals back.

The game settled and then Philippe Coutinho scored one of his few goals of the season and Rodgers dipped his knees on the pitch after an arcing drive into the corner and it was bedlam and I couldn't stop crying and the last ten minutes were as unbearable as I have ever seen in a football ground and Martin Škrtel appeared to handball it 16 times and I mean it when I say I couldn't stop crying and while it would be fair to say we'd all had a drink it would also be fair to say people could barely watch and Jordan Henderson got sent off and finally the final whistle went and then Steven got them all in and got them in a big circle in front of the Kop and Steven told them they were on the verge because they were and then Steven told them that this doesn't slip now and I couldn't stop crying and the ground didn't stop roaring while Steven told them that this does not slip now.

We went out. The 'we' there is practically everyone in Liverpool. It was a Sunday afternoon, Liverpool is a big city, a big drinking city, and every pub was bursting at the seams. It was unbridled. It was unfettered. It was freeing. It felt like new life.

But it was a beginning. It was a practice, a dress-rehearsal. We just didn't know.

They went to Norwich on Easter Sunday. Won 2–3, Sterling magnificent. But they missed Henderson, you know. They missed him massively.

I had a lot of thoughts about Chelsea at Anfield and Crystal Palace at Selhurst Park. A lot of thoughts:

- Liverpool weren't trying to go hell for leather against Chelsea when Steven slipped. If anything, they were too patient, Steven too deep, Liverpool too settled for half-time.
- They did though suffer through not getting the early goal then anxiety setting in.
- Luis Suárez had gone off the boil by that game at Anfield. In part, because of tiredness; in part, because footballers do.
- In the second half Liverpool completely lost their heads and this was where Chelsea's frustration tactics worked. Steven had about 100 shots, all of them never going in.
- One of the greatest nights of the season was when Liverpool went to Selhurst Park and tried to score ten for the goal difference, which was by then the only way they could win the league.

- Liverpool had an attempt every three minutes the ball was in play and a load of them were good efforts, unlike Steven's from the weekend before.
- The greatest moment of that season was when Suárez got the ball out of the goal at 0–3. Nothing has ever summed a football team up more. The snides and the greybeards will say that doing that and then drawing 3–3 summed the team up better, but those people are wrong – and no one wants to dance with them, drink with them or kiss them.
- Honestly, let me tell you about him getting the ball. We celebrated it more than the goal, celebrated it like it was two goals, celebrated it like our lives depended on it, celebrated it as it was the greatest release and relief imaginable, celebrated it because it was unzipped, unfettered, unbridled; celebrated it because what else were we in it for but this?

It is important not to forget what 2013–14 felt like. There is a history of football that is handed down to us through record books and television. It's a history that is predominantly written by the grey-bearded and the distant and by the cynics. Some of these dwell within our own parish, a darkness in their souls uncleansed, consistently unable to forgive Brendan Rodgers for one sin or another, perhaps even for bringing the party but perhaps for not being the bloke who nearly died or the bloke who fought for the soul of the club or the bloke who closer than anyone else alive personified that soul of the club. Or, now, for not being Jürgen Klopp. Which isn't fair because no one else is Jürgen Klopp either.

For many of these, the hard facts of the matter will always prevail. Hard facts can't dance. Hard facts have no rhythm. No one wants to get off with hard facts. The football history that really matters is about the stories, the collective experience, the days and the nights, the nights, nights, nights. Remember not the hard fact of the 3–3 draw, your side losing a three-goal lead, but instead remember that they were trying to score ten. Remember they were trying to do the impossible. Remember how proud you were of how close they came.

Remember too, loving footballers. We learned to love footballers again in 2013–14 under Brendan Rodgers, because at his best, he so clearly does. Footballers doing amazing things, making children of us, is a wonderful thing. We learned that goals are paramount to proceedings, and learned that, without them, nothing can be achieved. These might seem like straightforward and obvious enough virtues, but Anfield had been a dark place for far too long. Rodgers brought Delusion. Delusion turned to Hope and then became Belief. We hadn't had Belief for what felt like the longest time. Without what we had then – without those reminders of what it was meant to be, how it was meant to feel, the how and why of being happy, of being joyous and loving footballers – Jürgen Klopp would have had a steeper mountain.

What we learned, what this had awakened, put us in far better stead – made us ready to believe that it could all change.

It had begun. All the best.

The Normal Ones

'Does anyone in this room think I can do wonders? No. I am a normal guy. I come from the Black Forest. My mother is probably sat at home now watching this, not able to understand a word of what I am saying, but very proud.

'I am the Normal One. I was a very average player, became a manager in Germany at a special club, Mainz, then I had a great opportunity to take Dortmund, a special club, for seven years. For both parties it was best to leave, and now I am here. I hope to enjoy my work.'

Jürgen Klopp, 2015

One of the less remarked-upon remarkable things about Bill Shankly in his job at Anfield was that his backroom staff – the mythical Boot Room – were mostly in place when he got there. He didn't bring anyone with him, he didn't recruit anyone. He worked with the people he had, and it would be fair to say he got the best out of them.

Shankly feels like a superhero, in a sense, when you are born in Liverpool in 1981. The shirts were always loud, the jokes were always cutting, the charisma was off the charts. I mean, just listen to his voice. Everything passed down about him feels larger than life, sprung from the pages of a comic. Him, Matt Busby and Jock Stein were grown in a lab in the central belt of Scotland, with the incredible Hugh McIlvanney their similarly larger than life Lois Lane or Dr Watson.

Shankly was followed by Bob Paisley, who does not in any way seem like a superhero but who was unbelievably successful as Liverpool manager. When you go to Sunderland away the Lord Mayor of Hetton-le-Hole invites Liverpool supporters to go to a little service, a little tribute to Bob, of whom they are so proud. They say a few words and lay sandwiches on and we buy drinks in their very reasonably priced social club bar.

Because Bob was normal. Hetton-le-Hole is normal. But Bob won three European Cups and one UEFA Cup; six league titles and three League Cups in nine years. Bob cut a swathe across Europe, changed the way the game was played – with forwards who defended like demons or played like midfield maestros, or both at once in Rush and Dalglish – but Bob wasn't a superhero, and Bob didn't write anything down. He just saw the potential in his players, saw the potential in prospective signings, got the best out of them and encouraged them to get the best out of each other.

There was a BBC documentary that went behind the scenes for Paisley's final season as manager. Prior to Bob's final home game as manager, when his final league title will be presented, he and Ronnie Moran talk about that presentation as 'the palaver'. The palaver! Ian Rush elaborated: 'Ronnie Moran would put the league winners' medals in a box in the middle of the dressing room and say, "Take a medal if you think you deserve one."'

Bob Paisley, Joe Fagan, Ronnie Moran, Roy Evans. These were the normal men Shankly worked with, inspired, got the very best out of, and these were the men who would deliver four European Cups after he stood down.

Ultimately, this is one of sport's greatest tricks: to take ordinary people with ordinary upbringings and let them showcase their extraordinary talent. What's striking about Bob, Joe, Ronnie, Roy – and Jürgen – was that while they all had some footballing talent (Ronnie won the league as a player), it was their talents elsewhere that marked them out. Their understanding of the game and their belief in people, which meant they contributed to the achievement of wonders would delight millions.

Their belief in people. Shankly believed in the backroom team he arrived with at Anfield, found Ronnie and Roy Evans as players and added them in. Shankly saw something in them, saw their capacity for excellence and growth, their desire for hard work, their belief in the growth of others.

Belief in normal people is a gift, and being able to show it is a gift too.

In the work we do at *The Anfield Wrap* everything is about people. We have over 100 different contributors from across the world – though the majority are from Merseyside – and essentially we encourage ordinary people to say interesting things about supporting the club from the heart of the city. Funny things. Odd things. Stupid things. Heartfelt things. We take people who have never spoken into a microphone before, or written before – whether in general, or about football – and say, 'Go on. You can do this. We believe in you, and, anyway, what's the worst that could happen?'

Part new media business, part community asset and part volunteer organisation. But, ultimately, to do what we do you need to believe in people, believe they can help and believe they can be the best versions of themselves. It's an act of the deepest care done right, and I hope we have got it right more often than not.

Doing it since 2011 and doing it as a full-time job since March 2015 meant we got to see close up what Jürgen did over and over again. But, more than that, we got to work closely with a wide cross-section of people while producing media content predominantly (but not solely) about football; predominantly (but not solely) about Liverpool. Some of those people (for example, Caoimhe O'Neill, Dan Morgan, Harriet Prior) have gone on to work in football media full time. Some work in football already and take the time to come and work with us because we do it differently. And some – most, I hope – do it because it is a laugh, an opportunity, a way to run some ropes and show off and tell jokes in front of a warm audience across the globe. We love them all, every different type, for it. It's a way to be Liverpudlian with a dollop of glitter. It's that belief in one another, that care for one another and that idea of collective joy unconfined which underpins all of this – and by 'all of this' I mean the whole game and possibly (because we have a chapter called 'Games Make Us Human' to come) life itself. Normal people taking the opportunity to be not so normal here and there makes the world go round. It makes you fall in love.

Jürgen was normal, and still is. He made it clear in his arrival and is, in 2024, leaving because he wants holidays and wants time with his family, because it has been a slog, because normal people run out of energy. Go back, and it's worth understanding what FSV Mainz 05 was while he played there, and even most of the time he was managing. It was a second-tier German side, getting crowds of about 15,000, and he went there from amateur football and did his sports science MSc equivalent in his spare time at the age of 28 while still playing.

He isn't a superhero. Nothing was inevitable about any of this.

Of course, Bill was normal too. One of the things David Peace's excellent *Red or Dead* does a good job of is puncturing that superhero myth, grounding Shankly back to sheer, mundane normality: a life pockmarked with incredible moments but ultimately a grind. When he discussed his retirement Shankly said, 'Whilst you love football, it is a hard relentless task which goes on and on like a river. There is no time for stopping and resting.'

Take a medal if you think you deserve one.

Being Liverpool

Sometimes people ask me for help with a bit of writing or a speech. 'I'm finding it difficult to say what I want to say,' they say. So I ask them, 'What is it you really want to say?' Then they write the sentence without artifice, without any flourishes. Then I say, 'Just say that, then. Up the top. Just say that. Then you've said it.'

This is the last mini-chapter we're writing. I know it comes in the early going but you aren't an idiot, you know how writing books works. I think the only book ever truly written from start to finish was *The Spy Who Came in from the Cold* and, let me tell you, I am no John le Carré. Sorry to disappoint. There is no secret world here, no twist. I wanted to see where the rest of the book went before writing this chapter because I needed to know what to say and then just say it.

So just say that then . . .

What's important, for the story to work, is to understand that everything around the club, the city and the wider supporter base didn't organically just occur when he turned up. Loads of it was already in place, full of potential, including the city itself. It just needed the spark. In the same way that Klopp had Pep Lijnders, Jordan Henderson, Adam Lallana, James Milner, Joe Gomez and Roberto Firmino – and he just needed to help them all make sense of themselves – all the constituent parts were in place.

Close to the action there was already a supporter infrastructure that could, for instance, organise a walkout. There were YouTube channels and there were podcasts and there was BOSS Night putting on great events, before and after games, and Spion Kop 1906 organising the flags, and Spirit of Shankly organising the supporters, and Kop Outs, Liverpool's LGBT+ group. All of this was there, and all of it was full of energy and light and love.

The worldwide supporter base was there. The supporters' clubs were there. They'd been there for years in some instances, decades as far as Norway was concerned. They all had different numbers of members but had loads of people on the periphery, about to get excited, wanting to be part of something. You just went to the US supporters' clubs and games and you felt it. Everyone wanted to know.

There was also the city, the city as hub for the excitement was burgeoning and had been burgeoning since Capital of Culture in 2008. Liverpool was getting its sea legs as the destination for the country's big night out in a way that went beyond just Concert Square for stags and hens, however much that played and still plays a role. The city is one of explosions on a global scale, and has been since the Victorian era. That has always come with its challenges and its shortcomings, but this is the way of it when matters are tumultuous.

This is called *Transformer*. That was author Kev Sampson's suggestion, and you are only reading this book because of him. It helps that it's a great one because Being Liverpool is about to be transformed. But to transform something it has to be there in the first place and the process is easier if every party wants that transformation.

We wanted it. Jordan Henderson wanted it. Spion Kop wanted it. The growth of supporters watching the games in pubs in the US tells you they wanted it. The city craved it. We wanted a change, wanted a party, wanted a celebration, and wanted to invite the world. Just give us a reason, any reason. This book is about that transformation, and this book is about the reason why – and the best thing is that Klopp didn't just give us any old reason, he made it a great one.

First Half

Timeline

Date	Event
23 June 2015	Roberto Firmino signs for Liverpool.
7 October 2015	President Obama personally apologises to Médecins Sans Frontières International President Joanne Liu for an airstrike that killed 22 people, including 12 MSF staff members.
8 October 2015	Svetlana Alexievich of Belarus wins the Nobel Prize for Literature.
8 October 2015	Jürgen Klopp is announced as Liverpool manager.
9 October 2015	Jürgen Klopp gives his first press conference as Liverpool manager. He says, 'We will try to play very emotional football.' He says, 'We play our own game and it's important the players feel the confidence and trust of the people.' He says, 'You want to see fighting spirit, many sprints, many shots, and the result is the result of these things. You can be as good as you want but you have no control over the other team. If they are really good you have to bring them to your level. On your level you can kill any team.' He says, 'It's not so important what people think when you come in, it's much more important what people think when you leave.'

17 October 2015	Tottenham Hotspur 0 Liverpool 0. In Klopp's first game as manager very little happens except everyone runs loads, especially Adam Lallana.
31 October 2015	Chelsea 1 Liverpool 3. Liverpool fall a goal behind to the reigning champions before dismantling José Mourinho's team in crisis.
8 November 2015	Liverpool 1 Crystal Palace 2. Jürgen Klopp feels pretty alone in this moment.
21 November 2015	Manchester City 1 Liverpool 4. A feast of transitional football sees Liverpool batter Manchester City in the first half before a Martin Škrtel 25-yard drive settles the argument in the second half.
13 December 2015	Liverpool 2 West Bromwich Albion 2. Divock Origi's late equaliser sees Jürgen Klopp take his players to the Kop at the end of the game.
23 January 2016	Norwich City 4 Liverpool 5. Adam Lallana scores a last-minute winner and Klopp smashes his glasses in the celebrations.
1 February 2016	Pep Guardiola is announced as the next Manchester City manager, starting 1 July 2016.
6 February 2016	Liverpool 2 Sunderland 2. Liverpool lead Sunderland 2–0 before a mass walkout protesting over ticket-price increases disrupts the last 15 minutes of the game. Klopp has appendicitis and isn't in attendance.
20 February 2016	British Prime Minister David Cameron announces that the referendum to leave the EU will take place on 23 June 2016.
27 February 2016	Farhad Moshiri buys a 49.9 per cent stake in Everton.
28 February 2016	Manchester City 1 Liverpool 1 (aet: penalties, 3–1). Manchester City beat Liverpool on penalty kicks in Klopp's first final with the club. It's fine. He is going to lose other finals.

10 March 2016	Liverpool 2 Manchester United 0. The first leg of a Europa League last 16 game is the first time Liverpool and Manchester United have ever faced each other in European competition.
14 April 2016	Liverpool 4 Borussia Dortmund 3. The scoreline is 2–3 when Mats Hummels gets his teammates into a huddle to calm them down in Anfield's maelstrom before a corner. Doesn't go well from there.
20 April 2016	Liverpool 4 Everton 0. Ramiro Funes Mori hacks down Divock Origi, seriously injuring him and getting a red card and undermining the significant progress made by Origi under Klopp. Everton cannot get near Liverpool: they barely kick the ball second half, underlining the gulf between the sides. It is the most remarkable way to win a Merseyside derby.
15 May 2016	West Bromwich Albion 1 Liverpool 1. Liverpool finish the season in eighth, which equals their lowest finish in the top flight since Bill Shankly got Liverpool promoted in 1962.
18 May 2016	Liverpool 1 Sevilla 3. The Europa League final. Daniel Sturridge scores one of the great Liverpool European final goals only to see the inevitability of Sevilla take his moment of glory away from him.
10 June 2016	Premier League academy teams will be allowed to play in the EFL Trophy.
16 June 2016	Labour MP Jo Cox is murdered by a far-right terrorist.
23 June 2016	EU referendum takes places and Britain votes to leave the EU by a margin of 51.8 per cent to 48.2 per cent. Liverpool votes to remain: 58.2 per cent versus 41.8 per cent.
28 June 2016	Sadio Mané signs for Liverpool.
1 July 2016	Joël Matip signs for Liverpool.
13 July 2016	Theresa May becomes British Prime Minister.

22 July 2016	Gini Wijnaldum signs for Liverpool.
14 August 2016	Arsenal 3 Liverpool 4. Sadio Mané picks the ball up on the right-hand side and speedily slaloms past three before arrowing the ball into the top corner. It is the greatest goal any Liverpool player has ever scored on his debut. He makes it 1–4. He runs to his manager and nothing will ever be the same again.
20 August 2016	Burnley 2 Liverpool 0. Everything crashes down to earth and this author speaks to his partner, saying, 'I'm just worried this fella won't be able to do it.'
31 August 2016	By this date Liverpool have let 13 players who have played for the first team leave in one summer.
10 September 2016	Liverpool 4 Leicester City 1. Liverpool beat the reigning champions and open the new main stand. Big Stand FC are born.
29 October 2016	Crystal Palace 2 Liverpool 4. The best invocation of Klopp's football to date sealed by a picture-book Roberto Firmino goal to make it 2–4.
19 December 2016	Everton 0 Liverpool 1. The fourth official puts the board up for injury time in the 90th minute and it reads '9' minutes. Goodison groans. Four minutes in Daniel Sturridge drives the ball off the post and Sadio Mané is first to the rebound. The away end erupts. There is a video of me and a curious number of my friends all in one place going absolutely insane and, for reasons that I've never really understood, so is South African world 400 metres hurdles champion Wayde van Niekerk. It is the most remarkable way to win a Merseyside derby.
31 December 2016	Liverpool 1 Manchester City 0. Liverpool win the New Year's Eve fixture with a Gini Wijnaldum header. They sit second. They will not win another league game until 11 February and then not another until 4 March, which will be only their third win of 2017 in all competitions.

22 March 2017	Ronnie Moran passes away. His was the greatest imaginable Liverpudlian life.
7 April 2017	Future Islands release *The Far Field* and it is a collection of the most direct love songs you have ever heard. Oddly, the lead singer is an Evertonian.
8 April 2017	Stoke City 1 Liverpool 2. An exhausted Liverpool bring Philippe Coutinho and Roberto Firmino off the bench, and the latter scores the second-best goal of Liverpool's season to win the game with a dipping volley.
23 April 2017	Liverpool 1 Crystal Palace 2. A Christian Benteke brace gives Crystal Palace the win. Liverpool won't lose another league game at Anfield until 21 January 2021, behind closed doors, and won't lose one in front of a crowd until 29 October 2022.
1 May 2017	Watford 0 Liverpool 1. The best goal of the season. On a dismal evening Emre Can scores a spectacular overhead kick to keep qualification for the Champions League in Liverpool's hands.
21 May 2017	Liverpool 3 Middlesbrough 0. Just at the moment the ground gets edgy, Gini Wijndalum opens the scoring as half-time approaches and Liverpool qualify for the Champions League.
22 May 2017	The Manchester Arena bombing, perpetrated by an Islamic extremist and aided by his brother, kills 22 people and injures 1,017.
8 June 2017	General Election. Conservative minority government is returned.
14 June 2017	Grenfell Tower fire in west London burns for 60 hours and results in the deaths of 72 people, with more than 70 injured.
22 June 2017	Mo Salah signs for Liverpool.
21 July 2017	Andy Robertson signs for Liverpool.

21 July 2017	Virgil van Dijk is made to train alone by Southampton after his Liverpool move falls through.
9 August 2017	Philippe Coutinho has a back injury which keeps him out of contention for selection throughout August.
27 August 2017	Liverpool 4 Arsenal 0. Mo Salah runs very, very fast and finishes for Liverpool's third. There is a video filmed by the club from Anfield's tunnel which looks like a cartoon.
28 August 2017	Naby Keïta and RB Leipzig agree a deal with Liverpool that he will join the club in the summer of 2018. Everyone will argue about him until he leaves.
31 August 2017	Alex Oxlade-Chamberlain signs for Liverpool.
22 October 2017	Tottenham Hotspur 4 Liverpool 1. Liverpool are torn to ribbons in the early going at Wembley, and Dejan Lovren is substituted after 31 minutes.
7 November 2017	Emily Wilson's translation of *The Odyssey* is published. She is the first woman to translate the epic poem into English.
2 December 2017	Brighton and Hove Albion 1 Liverpool 5. Liverpool, despite a depleted defence, dismantle Brighton through a Philippe Coutinho masterclass. He scores the fourth and goes on to get seven goals in December 2017.
27 December 2017	Virgil van Dijk stands by a Christmas tree holding a Liverpool shirt.
1 January 2018	Burnley 1 Liverpool 2. A 95th-minute Ragnar Klavan scrambled goal shimmers in the New Year's Day gloaming and delivers Jürgen Klopp his first win at Turf Moor.
5 January 2018	Liverpool 2 Everton 1. FA Cup third round. Virgil van Dijk's debut. He is the world's most expensive defender. He scores an 84th-minute winner. It is the most remarkable way to win a Merseyside derby.

6 January 2018	A £142 million deal is agreed for Philippe Coutinho to join Barcelona.
14 January 2018	Liverpool 4 Manchester City 3. Manchester City arrive at Anfield having, 22 games in, only dropped four points all season. They are the unbeaten champions elect. Early in the second half the crowd and Liverpool whip up such an aggressive furnace that City's players are reduced to kicking it out for throw-ins. It is one of the all time great Anfield atmospheres.
26 January 2018	Dream Wife's eponymous debut album is released.
27 January 2018	Liverpool 2 West Bromwich Albion 3. Fourth round, FA Cup. BBC1. The first time VAR is used at Anfield. I'd had a pint, but for long stretches wasn't clear on what the score was.
9 March 2018	The Hold Steady play their first Weekender Show in the Electric Ballroom in Camden; there is so much joy in what they do.
31 March 2018	Everton 1 Manchester City 3. In the Manchester City *All or Nothing* Amazon documentary about their season in 2017–18 Pep Guardiola is filmed in his Goodison Park dressing room fretting about Liverpool.
4 April 2018	Liverpool 3 Manchester City 0. First leg, Champions League quarter-final at Anfield against the favourites. Liverpool are 3–0 up by the half-time mark. They hold on.
6 April 2018	'One Kiss' by Calvin Harris and Dua Lipa is released.
10 April 2018	Manchester City 1 Liverpool 2. Second leg. Manchester City score in the first minute and what ensues is the scariest half of football any Liverpool supporter has ever seen; in years to come Virgil van Dijk will refer to the first half as 'hell'. Manchester City are remarkable, finding all angles and pulling Liverpool everywhere. Just before the break Alex Oxlade-Chamberlain gets in but Liverpool don't score. Pep

	Guardiola is sent off at half-time and then on 56 minutes Mo Salah picks a ball up in the penalty area from a Sadio Mané break, keeps his cool and clips it into the back of the net. It is his 39th goal of the season, and, as he runs to pose in front of a Liverpool away end he has sent beyond raptures, it is the most iconic goal of his career to date. He has claimed Liverpool as his own and Liverpool have claimed a Champions League semi-final place. They will go on and win the game 1–2.
24 April 2018	Liverpool 5 Roma 2. The day Seán Cox was seriously injured in a cowardly attack by Roma supporters. I was on the same road at the time and it could have been any of us. Liverpool dismantle Roma up to the 70th minute – to be 5–0 up at this stage of a European semi-final is unheard of. Liverpool will be in the final in Kyiv.
2 May 2018	Roma 4 Liverpool 2. Liverpool are in the Champions League final. After the game we are all kept behind for an age. Klopp comes out. Ben Woodburn and Trent Alexander-Arnold come out. But the whole squad comes out and celebrates and holds up a banner devoted to Seán Cox. Right there, right then, we are all together.
18 May 2018	*No-One Cares About Your Creative Hub So Get Your Fuckin' Hedge Cut* by Half Man Half Biscuit is released. Wounding.
24 May 2018	1.45 a.m. The *Anfield Wrap* bus leaves Mann Island, holding 14 in cramped conditions. By Birmingham the air conditioning has broken. In northern France we work out what we will do on the stage in the fan park at 2 p.m. on 26 May 2018. Tons of time.
26 May 2018	Arrive at the fan park at 1.50 p.m. having had to drive through Ukraine through the night, 16 hours behind schedule. The fan park is remarkable. Somehow it is as though everyone you have ever met is here. I speak in between my *Anfield Wrap* co-host John Gibbons playing absolute rammers and the place goes mad, about a third as mad as it will

	later for Jamie Webster. It's a remarkable thing, an assertion of everything we have wanted and everything we have missed – independent of the manager but created by him and supported by the club in an enormous act of trust. It is the riding of a wave and the most glorious party that the people of Kyiv have helped us put on, and that won't be forgotten. Then Dua Lipa plays before the game and everyone in our end goes berserk because 'One Kiss' is all it takes. This is different and new and young. New songs and a new attitude. Liverpool lose the game 1–3, Gareth Bale scores perhaps the greatest goal I have ever seen, Mo Salah goes off injured, but it doesn't matter because it's the start, because if you want to win big you have to risk losing big and what has been lost hasn't just been found but renovated and nothing will be the same again.
28 May 2018	Fabinho signs for Liverpool.
29 May 2018	The *Anfield Wrap* bus arrives back at Mann Island, having driven through Prague and Dortmund. Our ankles are the size of balloons. Never again.
15 June 2018	*Oil of Every Pearl's Un-Insides* is released by SOPHIE.
1 July 2018	Emre Can leaves Liverpool and signs for Juventus on a free transfer.
13 July 2018	Xherdan Shaqiri signs for Liverpool.
19 July 2018	Alisson Becker signs for Liverpool.
12 September 2018	'Tonite/Home/I Want Your Love' is released as a single by LCD Soundsystem from the *Electric Lady Sessions*.
15 September 2018	Tottenham Hotspur 1 Liverpool 2. Liverpool win the first five league games of the season, outclassing Tottenham Hotspur at Wembley, less than a year on from their humiliation in the capital.

18 September 2018	Liverpool 3 Paris Saint Germain 2. Liverpool demonstrate that the previous season was no flash in the pan, dominating the Parisians for the first half before falling to some Kylian Mbappé magic. Roberto Firmino comes off the bench still struggling with an eye injury to make it 3–2 in injury time.
29 September 2018	Chelsea 1 Liverpool 1. Chelsea lead as the clock ticks over the 90-minute mark and, like Liverpool, have won every league game to date before a Daniel Sturridge 30-yard thunderbolt levels the affair.
30 November 2018	Richard Scudamore retires as CEO of the Premier League.
2 December 2018	Liverpool 1 Everton 0. The game is heading towards a turgid 0–0 when, in injury time, Virgil van Dijk shanks a shot over the bar. Everton's end throw a purple flare onto the pitch to celebrate the point because they can't get fucking anything right, before the ball takes an odd turn, bounces along the crossbar and Divock Origi, introduced to muted acclaim ten minutes earlier, nods in at the back post. It isn't just the greatest goal in Anfield's history but it is up there with the finest achievements produced by humanity, should be on any *Voyager 3* golden record alongside the work of van Gogh, the 130th of Shakespeare's sonnets and 'BIPP' by SOPHIE as the best we have to offer. One day it will be found by aliens and watched and one alien would say to the other, '*Hhhheeemmmmpp, qua?*' and the other will reply, '*Brrrip, bweeen, bar.*' (The first will be saying, 'How did that go in?' and the second answering, 'He's only got little arms.') It is the most remarkable way to win a Merseyside derby.
4 December 2018	The May government is found in contempt of Parliament due to failing to publish the legal advice on Brexit.

11 December 2018	Liverpool 1 Napoli 0. A magnificent late Alisson Becker save from Arkadiusz Milik ensures Liverpool qualify for the last 16 of the Champions League.
3 January 2019	Manchester City 2 Liverpool 1. Possibly the greatest game I've ever seen in person at this point in my life.
24 January 2019	Hugh McIlvanney passes away. Hugh's passion to tell the story of ordinary men capable of brilliant things on the biggest possible stage came through both screen and page.
1 February 2019	*Russian Doll* by Natasha Lyonne, Leslye Headland, and Amy Poehler is released on Netflix. In the second series a character will say, 'We can't spend our lives so scared of making the wrong move that we never live at all.'
10 March 2019	Liverpool 4 Burnley 2. Liverpool will win every league game from this date until 20 October 2019.
13 March 2019	Bayern Munich 1 Liverpool 3. After drawing the first leg 0–0 Liverpool need to go to Jürgen Klopp's *bête noire* to continue their European run. They dismantle the German champions, Sadio Mané scores two great goals, including rolling Manuel Neuer for the opener. It is a performance and result which pins Europe back by the ears.
31 March 2019	Liverpool 2 Tottenham Hotspur 1. An injury time own goal returns Liverpool to the top of the table.
17 April 2019	Beyoncé releases *Homecoming: A Film By Beyoncé* on Netflix. It is the greatest demonstration of relentless brilliance until the start of the 2019–20 season.
1 May 2019	Barcelona 3 Liverpool 0. Liverpool are the better side on the night but are mugged by Leo Messi's exceptionalism. European campaign is over. Now it is all on the league and we need City to drop points somewhere.

4 May 2019	Newcastle United 2 Liverpool 3. Evening kick-off, Saturday, May Bank Holiday weekend. Newcastle away and Liverpool need to win, and Newcastle turn into Brazil 1970 under Rafa Benítez. The game gets out of hand; Mo Salah goes down with a head injury at 2–2 and I look at everyone I am watching it with. One is in tears. Another isn't looking at the screen, back to it, head in hands, three are just holding each other, and then Divock Origi, introduced from the bench, rises in the 86th minute to make it 2–3 to Liverpool. We are still alive.
6 May 2019	Manchester City 1 Leicester City 0. City have been running out of gas and are up against a Leicester side looking at a Champions League push. Vincent Kompany scores a 30-yarder. Are you messing?
7 May 2019	Liverpool 4 Barcelona 0. The greatest night in Anfield's history. And I wasn't there.
12 May 2019	Liverpool 2 Wolverhampton Wanderers 0. Liverpool win but so do Manchester City. They have 98 points and Liverpool finish on 97. Liverpool's is third highest points total in the history of the top flight at that point, and by some distance the most points any side have ever accrued coming second.
17 May 2019	Megan Thee Stallion releases the mixtape *Fever*. It is her perfectly realised breakthrough into the mainstream.
24 May 2019	Theresa May resigns as Prime Minister.
29 May 2019	1 a.m. The *Anfield Wrap* bus leaves Mann Island. It holds 14 in cramped conditions.
31 May 2019	Arrive in Madrid in good time. This is not our first rodeo.

1 June 2019	The fan park is enormous. At least 60,000 people are here by the time we finish, and it must be in excess of 100,000 by the time Jamie Webster hits the stage. I end our part saying, 'If they don't win, this isn't Kyiv, never speak to me of this again. This one, today, is about winning. Just winning. This team needs its big trophy.' Then Gibbons does 'The Anfield Rap' with John Barnes while I did the travel announcements to get people to the ground. Liverpool 2 Tottenham Hotspur 0. Everyone cries. Everyone is overwhelmed. Everyone got what they came for.
24 July 2019	Boris Johnson becomes Prime Minister.
17 August 2019	Southampton 1 Liverpool 2. Liverpool suffer but win on the South Coast, but the key thing about this day is that finally Manchester City break. At home that evening against Tottenham Hotspur they draw a game 2–2 they have the chances to win. It's a sunny day in Liverpool and the city absolutely comes alive on this Saturday night.
5 October 2019	Liverpool 2 Leicester City 1. Liverpool batter Leicester but the game is tied going into injury time. Sadio Mané wins a penalty that James Milner converts – Liverpool have won their first eight games of the season. City are eight points back with a game in hand.
20 October 2019	Manchester United 1 Liverpool 1. Liverpool fail to win in the league for the first time since 10 March.
2 November 2019	Aston Villa 1 Liverpool 2. Both Liverpool and Manchester City trail at half-time in a rare weekend when both kick off on Saturday at 3 p.m. By the 83rd minute Manchester City lead, but it takes until the 87th for Andy Robertson to finally kick the door down for Liverpool and equalise. Seven minutes later Liverpool have a corner and Sadio Mané – who wants

	to win the league more than you — stoops to head the ball home and Liverpool have set up the following week's game against Manchester City as a potential title decider, and it is only the first weekend of November.
10 November 2019	Liverpool 3 Manchester City 1. It is all over by the 51st minute. Sadio Mané adds to gorgeous goals by Fabinho and Mo Salah, getting on the end of Jordan Henderson's cross to put Liverpool three ahead and completely in control of the title race. Liverpool are eight clear of Leicester and nine clear of City and they are not looking back any time soon. No one wants to get turned into a pillar of salt, after all. Not when there is a league title to be won.
27 November 2019	*Knives Out* is released, meaning Sadio Mané has competition for most flamboyant performance from a Liverpudlian in the calendar year.
4 December 2019	Liverpool 5 Everton 2. Liverpool make a series of changes for this midweek game against their local rivals. Fabinho is injured. Liverpool rest Salah, Firmino and Henderson, while Alisson Becker is suspended. They are 4–2 up at half-time, goals from Mané, Xherdan Shaqiri and Divock Origi all underlining Liverpool's dominance. Gini Wijnaldum makes it five and Everton sack Marco Silva, arguably their biggest on-pitch mistake during Klopp's tenure as Liverpool manager. It is the most remarkable way to win a Merseyside derby.
12 December 2019	General Election. Conservative majority government is returned.
21 December 2019	Liverpool 1 Flamengo 0. For the first time in the club's history Liverpool become world champions, the winner scored by Roberto Firmino in extra time.

26 December 2019	Leicester City 0 Liverpool 4. The world champions go to the league's second-placed side and decimate them. It is only 0–1 at half-time but Leicester City can't land a glove. In the end the King Power has to stop and admire the greatest Liverpool team there has ever been.
27 December 2019	Wolverhampton Wanderers 3 Manchester City 2. Manchester City go down to ten men, go 0–2 ahead before losing 3–2. They are now 14 points behind Liverpool.
5 January 2020	Liverpool 1 Everton 0. FA Cup third round. Liverpool only start one player wearing a squad number from 1 to 11 and that is James Milner and he has to go off due to injury in the ninth minute. He is replaced by Yasser Larouci, squad number 70, on his Liverpool debut. Everton are full strength and managed by Carlo Ancelotti. Liverpool have Nat Phillips at centre-back, having brought him back on loan from Bundesliga 2 side Stuttgart to solely play in this game, his Liverpool debut. Neco Williams is at right-back. It is his second appearance for the club. It is Harvey Elliott's fifth, Pedro Chirivella's ninth, Curtis Jones's fifth, and Takumi Minamino makes his Liverpool debut. Minamino must have been knocked over by the Adam Lallana masterclass in the heart of the midfield. Lallana puts in one of the all-time great Merseyside derby centre-midfield performances to keep Liverpool competitive and involved and let Everton slowly lose their minds. This is a game they should win. The clock ticks and Liverpool's band of merry men grow in confidence and then in the 71st minute Curtis Jones picks it up on the left side of the box, gets it out from under his feet and curls it beyond Jordan Pickford's despairing arm to make it 1–0 to The Reds. It is the most remarkable way to win a Merseyside Derby.

19 January 2020	Liverpool 2 Manchester United 0. Liverpool ought to have made more hay while the sun shone in the first half but they end the game under the cosh. Alisson Becker claims the ball, looks up and sees Mo Salah on the move. He sends it. Salah latches onto it, holds off Dan James and slots it between David De Gea's legs then takes his shirt off, basking in front of the acclaim of the Kop. Becker runs the length of the pitch, urging his exhausted outfield teammates to run with him to celebrate with Mo Salah while the ground shakes to the sound of Liverpool's massed support for the first time singing what has been apparent since November: 'We're Going to Win the League'. The gap is 16 points with a game in hand and maybe, just maybe, this is the only way it will ever work. But look at those Liverpool players Becker runs past. They are exhausted. They are drained. They have given everything. And now you are going to believe. Us.
23 January 2020	Wolverhampton Wanderers 1 Liverpool 2. They don't stop. They just won't stop.

Key Game 1
Liverpool 2 West Bromwich Albion 2
13 December 2015

On 13 December 2015 Liverpool played West Bromwich Albion at Anfield. Liverpool drew 2–2. But football matches never happen in a vacuum, are never played without context. On 8 November 2015, less than a month after Jürgen Klopp's first game as manager, Liverpool had lost 1–2 at Anfield to Crystal Palace, a header from big Scott Dann in the 82nd minute settling the argument. Liverpool poor against a mid-table side. Liverpool beaten. And loads of people left, not even bereft. Not even surprised. They left because they were sick of it, had seen it all before. After the match Jürgen Klopp said: 'After the goal on 82 minutes, with 12 minutes to go, I saw many people leaving the stadium. I felt pretty alone at this moment. We decide when it is over. Between 82 and 94 [minutes] you can make eight goals if you like. They have reasons [for leaving] and maybe it is easier to go out, I don't know. Don't make a big thing about this, but we are responsible that nobody can leave the stadium before the final whistle because anything can happen. We have to show this and we didn't. Everything is OK, but we can do better.'

Liverpool took to the field against West Bromwich Albion having not scored in their previous two games but did manage to hit the back of the net first before big Craig Dawson equalised. The game was a pretty squalid affair, short of quality. Then Liverpool's divisive centre-back Dejan Lovren suffered a terrible tackle from Craig Gardner – a red card if ever there was one – only for the referee to show a yellow. Anfield was incensed. Klopp was incensed. You expected a reaction and got one.

Yep, big Jonas Olsson made it two and Anfield had seen it all before. Liverpool poor against a mid-table side. Liverpool beaten. But people stayed, incensed. They stayed and they roared. Mad as hell and not going to take it any more.

Liverpool plugged away. I'd love to say they were good, but they weren't. They were willing. And finally Divock Origi had a shot as the clock ticked to 97 minutes: the shot deflected, taken in and there was bedlam.

After the final whistle Jürgen Klopp rounded his players up and took them, Teutonic style, to the Kop where they saluted and were saluted in return. They lined up. They waved and perhaps even danced, Klopp himself delighted after having murder with Tony Pulis.

And the world was angry. The grey-bearded, the distant, the cynical Reds disappointed, so many of them with columns in the newspapers and hotlines to the phone-ins. Did Jürgen Klopp not realise what an insult this was to Liverpool's heritage? To this great club? That day I wrote for *The Anfield Wrap* about the game:

Where do you end up? A manager and a team in front of the Kop end saluting them after a 2–2 draw against West Brom? Well, I was proud of them. Proud they kept coming, proud of Liverpool's collective roar. I want that. I want Jürgen Klopp's Liverpool to commune. Not to troop out separately but to commune. What is this thing but something from which people come together? Come together before games, come together after games, but come together during games? Come together to get behind this thing?

If it isn't a collective glorious thing then my mother is right and it is just 22 men kicking a ball around a pitch.

Where does that get us?

Where does that get us?

The manager understands this gets us nowhere. The manager parades the players at the end to tell them this: 'These supporters, they are you. And they are proud of you. Because you ran till you dropped.'

The manager understands this gets us nowhere. The manager

parades the players at the end to tell us this: 'These players, they are you. They are imperfect like you are. They are flawed like you are. But they gave themselves for you.'

You can have a million different things to say about a football match. You can have interesting things to say, things to notice, talking points. You can learn five things. You can find a million ways to say things about 22 men kicking a ball round around a pitch, and I know we are going to on *The Anfield Wrap* this week.

The final whistle went and I left that match roaring and hoarse. Heart pounding. I left that match sweating and twitching. Prepared to fight the world. The final whistle went and I thought, 'Liverpool. Liverpool.'

I left that match seeing a million different possible stories. It's 2–2 against West Brom. It's not good enough. It's nowhere near good enough. It's more than anything.

A million possible different stories. This book is about the story we got to live. And, you know what? It was a million-to-one shot. Let me tell you, 13 December 2015 Neil would never have believed it, nor would 44,146 other paying customers. Promise.

From the Walkout to Dortmund, and What Next

In 2016 Fenway Sports Group, Liverpool's owners, wanted to vary the prices of regular seating at Anfield far more than had ever been done before. It would have netted them, year one, an increase of approximately £2 million across the course of the year, shifting the price point of the most expensive seats from £59 to £77.

It's 18 quid. It doesn't seem like much to some minds, but from the moment Jay McKenna, who had been part of Liverpool's Supporter Union, Spirit of Shankly, since 2008, laid it all out to me upstairs in Leaf it was clear that it was step one in something which, in years to come, could well have set Liverpool on a very different path. Crucially, it created over 15 tiers of pricing across the ground.

What seats are worth is fascinating. I love where I sit now. I like the people around me. I am on the aisle and I can stick my legs out ('you are taller than I expected') and I am bang on halfway but 30 rows up. Great view. I have no emotional connection to it as it stands, but elsewhere in the ground people do. They have lost loved ones, shared moments, lived a life in their seat. Its value cannot be calculated solely on a transactional level – but attempting to bring US-style variable pricing does exactly that.

I always love relaying tales of Jay McKenna in ticket meetings with the club, present on behalf of Spirit of Shankly. Once he asked a Liverpool executive why they didn't sell tickets for Liverpool versus Manchester United for £200 a pop when that would see the ground sell out. When the response came that that 'wasn't right', McKenna said, 'Then we agree in general, in principle. All we're arguing about is where the line is.'

This shift into heavily tiered pricing, topping out at £77, was over the line and was a pathway to more things over the line. That much was clear and fuelled the desire to take some serious action – then the walkout stemmed from conversations between Spion Kop 1906, which arranges the flags at Anfield, and Spirit of Shankly.

There was murder about it. We did a live YouTube thing for the first time with Spion Kop 1906 and Spirit of Shankly, and we had people who subscribed to *The Anfield Wrap* in the US cancelling their subscriptions. There was a fear it would lead to anti-US sentiment around the match and there was, in some places, this idea from a North American context: 'You don't know how lucky you have it; you don't know how cheap it is.' Tickets for sporting events in the US routinely run into three-figure territory – worse on the secondary market. This isn't to generalise – there was negativity about the action in Liverpool too, because there always will be.

It is fair to say that a lot of activism around football is a magic trick, really. You need to be able to convince the powers that be that you can achieve a lot – but, in reality, you mostly can't. Going public, going direct, going to the media is all better as a threat, because once there is a lived reality there can be message management, calm responses and the realisation that, actually, what the supporters threatened to do wasn't that bad. Therefore calling for a walkout was a risk. It was playing the de facto biggest card you had, and organising something like that is very difficult. It would have been easy for it to fall short, look lame – and mean that you'd never be taken seriously again.

I was a bag of nerves. I was concerned it would fall short of expectations. I was concerned it'd do well enough it would cut through, but not so well that it'd make a difference and therefore become our lived reality for months. I was concerned there would be bedlam in the ground, as there was during the Hicks and Gillett protests in 2008, everything degenerating into arguments and fights. The moment came. You held your breath. It was a mass exodus. A reasonable estimate was that at least 10,000 people walked out on the 77th minute as Liverpool led 2–0 against Sunderland. It finished 2–2. It felt, in the moment, enormous. It was such a visible symbol and such a successful protest it led to Liverpool reversing their position and offering a number of £9 tickets for people with an L postcode, alongside adding to a climate which led to football clubs across the country freezing their prices (at least until the pandemic), and it massively buttressed the Football Supporters' Association's campaign for set prices for away tickets for Premier League games.

Quiz question. Who was manager for the game with the 77th-minute walkout at Anfield?

You've got this book, but ask your friends.

It's this odd thing about the walkout. It feels like it happened before Jürgen arrived, because how could such a thing happen when he was in charge? How could it be?

But that day he wasn't in charge. That day he had appendicitis. It is the luckiest bout of appendicitis in Liverpool's history. Prior to the game Jürgen replied ambiguously when asked about the walkout, gave himself plenty of wriggle room, and then the appendicitis hit.

The appendicitis and walkout occurred on 6 February 2016. On 14 April 2016 Jürgen Klopp was firmly in the dugout when his former club, Borussia Dortmund, arrived at Anfield full of vim and vigour and excellence but found themselves on the end of quite a night: the future signposted, and then some. In the end all of this probably strengthened the hand of Jürgen Klopp. By the time we got to the summer of 2016 he could say to FSG something approaching the following: 'What do you want? Do you want more of things like Sunderland? Or more of things like Dortmund? It's not a complicated question, and shouldn't require a complicated answer.'

Indeed, when we were lucky enough to interview Klopp for the first time in the summer of 2016, he called the Lovren winner 'Anfield's goal'. He said he'd been happy to settle in his own mind that the performance had made a point to and for these players. But Anfield demanded and got the winner. His view was that it was the prime example of what we could achieve when in harmony. You could see in his eyes at that moment what the goal lit up in him, and it wasn't difficult to imagine him taking that energy into any conversation with FSG.

And, in a business sense, what Dortmund gave FSG for the first time was the taste of it when Liverpool could go global. What it meant not just to have Brendan Rodgers' 2013–14 season of a toddler running down a hill that never quite falls though you constantly expect it to (to quote the excellent Andi Thomas), but the potential of what this could be were it to become a juggernaut . . . The walkout showed that we could stand together in extreme circumstances, and Dortmund showed what could happen if we all truly stood together when opportunities arose. The questions were as simple as these: with us or against us? What do you want? You want them to pay more? Or them to show it means more? Do you want 50,000 representative screaming maniacs with you, or do you want them against you?

Sense prevailed. Things weren't perfect. They couldn't be. This was Liverpool: a series of constant negotiations and compromises with the present, the past and the future, to name but three, and nothing is ever permanently solved. Yet there was a way home for us all as one.

Everything worth doing is worth doing together. Everything.

Key Game 2
Liverpool 4 Borussia Dortmund 3
(Europa League)
14 April 2016

There were three renditions of 'You'll Never Walk Alone' across this tie. The first was prior to the game in Germany, and, let me tell you, it was beautiful. It was a soft rock ballad. It was Journey. It was lighters in the air. Going across to Germany, my God, they were lovely. They were delighted to see you, delighted to share in football and Jürgen Klopp and historic occasions and iconic stands and 'You'll Never Walk Alone'. They were delighted because they knew they were better, had it better, had it bigger, had their football culture blossoming and here were Liverpool to drink it all in, to frame their success, exalt their majesty. They were telling us that Tottenham had hammered it in the squares and then lost their voice in the ground while losing it on the pitch. So we all sang 'You'll Never Walk Alone' in the standing sections and we roared as we watched Liverpool fight for their lives to get a deserved 1–1 back to Anfield, but the prevailing view from the grey-bearded and the German contingent was that Dortmund would prevail. They were outscoring Bayern Munich on their way to second place, going at 2.3 points per game. They had marvellous players, whereas Liverpool were a ragtag contingent held together by Jürgen Klopp.

Then there was a second 'You'll Never Walk Alone' before kick-off at Anfield, and it was more of a snarl. Our ground. Our manager. Our team. Our song. Not yours. There was an air of menace about it, a snarl; a burning ring of fire rather than lighters in the air. No soft rock, nothing lovely, instead an urging, a wanting, a needing. This was Liverpool in Europe and there hadn't been enough of it for eight years and this was our song and our manager and we were claiming both before a ball was kicked.

The song finished, the whistle went and the grey-bearded and the German contingent were right. Dortmund were magnificent. They raced into a two-goal lead playing some of the best football Anfield had seen in years. Julian Weigl, Shinji Kagawa, Marco Reus and Pierre-Emerick Aubameyang verged on unplayable. They were the better side and Liverpool got into half-time having limited the damage to only 0–2.

Second half in the early going Emre Can found Divock Origi, who found the back of the net, and suddenly Anfield woke again only to be answered by a delightful Marco Reus goal to make it 1–3 and, given the away goals rule, the de facto end of the contest.

But there was so long left. Reus scored on 57. And James Milner had other ideas.

Two early gifts of Klopp's were, firstly, the reiteration that matches go on for absolutely ages, secondly, the power of other ideas. The latter had been lacking, despite both the madness of 2013–14 and the spine transplant that had been the return of Kenny Dalglish, since Rafa Benítez left town. James Milner was the essence of 'other ideas': he simply didn't stop, as though he realised before anyone else this was a Dortmund side that could be got at as long as you were prepared to try every different angle and keep working.

When Philippe Coutinho, fed by Milner, made it 2–3, suddenly Anfield had other ideas. The place became a furnace, but the other oddity was the time. Coutinho scored on 66 minutes. On 78 minutes Liverpool won a corner, there was that huddle and the ball came in. 3–3. Three. Three. Mamadou Sakho.

Seventy-eight minutes. That's ages until the end, and Dortmund were the better side. Sense should still have prevailed. But sense had left town and Dortmund couldn't escape. They couldn't breathe. A furnace burned off all available oxygen and the Dortmund players just couldn't get it into their lungs as Liverpool pinned them back. In injury time Liverpool delayed putting a ball into the box twice – because there was loads of time – and that magnetically drew all the Dortmund players towards the ball before Daniel Sturridge played it through some legs (as only he could) on that side to James Milner who sent it to the back post and there was Dejan Lovren at the Kop End to make it 4–3, and the only majesty getting exalted was that of Anfield.

There was the final whistle and then there was the third, valedictory 'You'll Never Walk Alone', the joyously moist-eyed 'You'll Never Walk Alone' as players and manager went around the ground, the 'You'll Never Walk Alone' sang to crown a truly great Liverpool night, to have the manager be confirmed as ours, not theirs, the song as ours, not theirs, the historic occasion as ours, not theirs, and the goal that mattered scored in front of our stand, not theirs.

No crowd in the world does moments like that, has other ideas like that, makes ten minutes feel like an eternity or be over in the blink of an eye. They sing constantly in Dortmund, you know. A lovely crew. But no one ever needs a huddle to get over it.

As a postscript, the headline on the *Guardian* sports section the next day read: 'Liverpool stir the memories with a famous European come-back.'

The memories, indeed. What was. What had once been. What we used to have. The headline writers, they missed the urging, wanting more than needing, needing for all time. They mistook what was reclamation for reminiscence, but there, then, in the moment, singing that third 'You'll Never Walk Alone', it felt entirely as though something had been realised. We had other ideas.

The Gossip, the Circles, the Shape and the Challenge

There is always the secret world of football.

Men gossip.

Football people gossip.

Football supporters gossip.

Men and football people and football supporters love gossip.

It is gossip that powers the secret world. A key football truism is that everyone knows everyone. Before Liverpool played Fulham in the Carabao Cup semi-final in 2024, in the press conferences it emerged that Pep Lijnders had worked with Andreas Pereira when at PSV Eindhoven. When the latter was nine. Everyone knows everyone.

The whole thing runs on information which may or may not be 100 per cent true, but which the public barely has any real sense of other than, mostly, when someone in the secret world decides they'd like it out in the real world. That doesn't make it true either – once I spoke to a journalist who had to run a double-sourced transfer story which he was 99 per cent sure was never ever going to happen. But he had the story, and people would respond to it.

This doesn't really matter – it's football, for God's sake. Not politics. Indeed, there are times it can be concluded it is mad that Jürgen Klopp, Mikel Arteta, Eddie Howe – hell, John Coleman – have to face the press more often and in more directly emotionally charged circumstances than any prime minister.

The gossip is part of it, and the gossip is now more mainstream than it ever has been. Transfers are everything in terms of how football is discussed and covered, and the transfers arguably run all year round. Because men gossip, and they love it.

It is an obsession which is deepening and, at times, feels like it skews brains, takes people away from the pitch, from the game, and turns everything into a near future which may not actually ever be, but if it isn't then someone will be to blame.

There is also both a relief and a democracy to it. Wherever you are in the world, however badly it may be going, you can get involved, and your stake and influence is the same as any other supporter anywhere else. You don't need to worry about getting a ticket, getting to the ground, doing anything at all, in fact. It's an all-access domain.

Doing *The Anfield Wrap* for years it's become clear that gossip matters a lot to people, and that it also has a shape – has a code and an innate logic to it. You work out that a Sadio Mané link is real but a Henrikh Mkhitaryan one just doesn't ring true, yet both can excite people.

When Jürgen Klopp took the Liverpool job in October 2015 he knew that Pep Guardiola would be Manchester City manager from the summer of 2016. It wasn't even that well kept a secret. But what Klopp also knew, which no one else has quite worked out yet, was just what it would take to go head to head with Guardiola's Manchester City.

At Borussia Dortmund Klopp had won back-to-back Bundesliga titles against Bayern Munich before Jupp Heynckes won not just the league by a mile but also a treble, beating Klopp's side in the Champions League final. Heynckes was then replaced by Pep Guardiola, and no one else in Germany, not even Klopp's Dortmund, for a variety of reasons, could get anywhere near them. Klopp had the lived reality and could add that to his knowledge of a Manchester City setup being crafted for Guardiola to slot into perfectly. Arguably players were being bought for Guardiola before his arrival, along with everything else in the backroom environment. From the minute Klopp arrived he knew that if he was to succeed his biggest obstacle was to be one which didn't even exist yet. Every decision Klopp made in terms of approach, recruitment and timing should be seen through this lens. He started there, with this awareness. This is part of what made him able to make the decisions he did.

The best example of this came when Klopp made a priority of and then waited for Virgil van Dijk. Liverpool made a mess of recruiting van Dijk in the summer of 2017. The gossip was that Liverpool were desperate for him, but Liverpool's approach antagonised Southampton. They refused to sell to Liverpool. Klopp had needed a new starting central defender but hung on and backed the existing players to the hilt, even when he had to substitute Dejan Lovren in the first half against Tottenham Hotspur in October 2017.

This antagonised those who love the gossip, love the transfers, because things needed to be better and needed to be new immediately. Players needed to be bombed out and others added because it had to be better – and better now. There was a period where people argued that Jürgen Klopp, or the club, were negligent, because the gossip demanded action. You had to do something. To wait, to commit to a strategy, looked like doing nothing, and doing nothing was negligent.

But from minute one Klopp knew the scale of the task, and there was no time to indulge the gossip machine. Better right now wasn't the KPI; 100 points was to be the KPI. The rest of the league either had no idea what they were going to be up against, or effectively chose to give up once Guardiola's Manchester City hit their straps in the autumn of 2017. But Klopp had always known, and Klopp wasn't going to give up because the day he signed his contract at Anfield, he knew that this was what he had signed up for.

Thereafter, every medium- and long-term decision the whole club made was in this context: 'We may well need 100 points.' It wasn't that Liverpool had a cheat code (far from it, quite the opposite), but they at least had an eye on the shape of the future. Look back now and see the principles set, the players prioritised, the quick decisions on sales in the summer of 2016 which arguably left Liverpool light (as they ran out of centre-midfielders and starting strikers the year after you could feel that Joe Allen and Christian Benteke could have done a job here and there); the stepping-stone decisions such as Ragnar Klavan and the big calls; that first window where we see Joël Matip, Gini Wijnaldum and Sadio Mané, who would all play a major part in eventually winning 26 out of 27 league games. Liverpool were so efficient in their approach. The manager had identified who could challenge for a 100-point season, and began to shed those who couldn't.

There was no wasted effort. No wasted motion – because we would be up against a behemoth backed by a state, who would eventually receive over 100 charges for financial irregularity from the Premier League. We couldn't afford a litany of mistakes. We couldn't suck it and see.

The irony of it all was that it was bad for business. Football supporters love gossip. Transfers are engagement. Engagement is good for clubs. Hell, it also means subscribers for things like *The Anfield Wrap*. But being the only club who understood what taking Manchester City on would require, and then doing it, was good for the soul – and Jürgen Klopp understood all of that too. The reality was that at times the rumour mill had to grind against itself. Liverpool would pick their moments, would not be scattergun and would not give themselves problems to solve down the road once the cull of 2016 had been completed.

The first part of the job made them immediately more physically imposing, because the intensity was about to ratchet up. That first full season under Klopp – 2016–17 – wasn't always pretty, especially not towards the end, but there were no passengers on the journey to Champions League qualification. Once that qualification had been achieved only Lucas Leiva, with his 346 Liverpool appearances, wasn't going to go on and contribute the season after. In one summer Klopp had got Liverpool battle-ready for many a season to come.

Key Game 3
Liverpool 2 Tottenham Hotspur 0
11 February 2017

I want to go dancing.

Presume all of this book is written by someone who wants to go dancing and doesn't manage to do so anywhere near enough.

I want to go to football matches and I want to go drinking and I want to go dancing. Ideally, with you.

There is an oft-cited online meme of Kurt Vonnegut's where he goes to buy an envelope and does a million other heart-warming, real-world tasks and ends by calling humans dancing animals and is, ironically, often approvingly quoted in its long form by people who are choosing to be snide about modern technology. The thing about being snide about technology is that once modern technology was a hammer; modern technology was once the mass-produced brick. And only an idiot would be snide about a hammer or a brick. Modern technology is just a tool and, done right, it can aid the desire and ability to dance, the sounds to dance to, the people you get to dance with, the days of dancing and drinking and being beautiful and getting up and going to do something. Were it not for modern technology and it aiding people to be dancing animals I wouldn't be writing this book, you wouldn't know who I was and your shelves on which this book will live long term wouldn't stay up.

The key part, though, is the dancing. Which brings us to Liverpool 2 Tottenham Hotspur 0 on 11 February 2017.

Liverpool had been appalling for an extended period. There was nothing to dance about and it all felt like a slog – they hadn't won a league game since New Year's Eve and hadn't looked like winning a league game in that time either. They'd been poor in the cups, and football looked and felt hard in the bleak winter. You had just begun to wonder. For the second time in this season – the first being the early defeat at Burnley – you had just begun to wonder whether or not Jürgen Klopp at Liverpool was going to really happen.

Now there is a general feeling that Jürgen Klopp was inevitable. That it would always have come together. That league-winning season, when they won 26 out of 27, there is almost a retrospective complacency about it now: 'Of course they were going to win the league. I mean, they won 26 out of 27. Of course Jürgen Klopp was going to be successful. I mean, look at him. He's Jürgen Klopp.' This overlooks the work and worry – the worry most of all. It overlooks the kitchen sink drama of January 2017 and instead recalls the blockbuster sci-fi of May 2019. It overlooks that every building block, every brick, was hard fought, and all of them existed to be celebrated.

Liverpool had been appalling for an extended period, had lost touch with the league leaders Chelsea, had gone from likeliest to stay with Chelsea to being in a pack with the rest of the Big Six – it was this season where the idea of the Big Six was actually brought into being because football changes constantly – and by early February, after a sole victory over Plymouth in the cup in January, looked the least likely to qualify for the Champions League for the second time in the decade.

Doubts were perfectly plausible. Only an idiot wouldn't have them.

And then Sadio Mané blew Tottenham Hotspur away in the course of 20 minutes in a game which kicked off at half-past five on a Saturday. Sadio, Liverpool as a team and Anfield as a place blew Tottenham Hotspur away in 20 minutes.

The metaphor about building blocks largely works but is occasionally insufficient because when we consider building blocks we conceive of them appearing all the same from minute one, delivered off a pallet. Bricks. You have a number and you build.

But Jürgen Klopp also had to create the bricks themselves. He had to remind everybody what they looked like as he knocked them into shape. There had been a slight precursor the season before against Manchester City, but the idea that a rival side would arrive at Anfield and get bent out of shape in a brief period, get put in the washing machine, as Mikel Arteta would call it in 2023, hadn't yet truly happened. Against Spurs in February it happened for the first time.

The washing machine is everything working in harmony: the team's approach working; the selection working; the nuts and bolts working. And then the crowd coming in in the most wholehearted way because we were sick of not winning for six weeks, we were mad as hell and we weren't going to take it any more.

It was zipless, seamless, overwhelming, and the miracle wasn't that Liverpool were 2–0 up by the 20-minute mark but that it wasn't five by half-time. Tottenham didn't know where they were and were begging for that whistle. Second half they came out and basically kicked Liverpool. They had no other answer, just tried to match Liverpool's aggression but couldn't match Liverpool's quality and focus on the night.

This would be repeated at the next league home game, that one against Arsenal, also half-five on a Saturday night, also against a direct rival, also Liverpool being 2–0 at half-time and that flattering them.

That night, after beating Tottenham, we went out. The game finished, the work needed doing and by the time I got out it appeared that everyone in Liverpool had gone out. So too had The Blues. This matters. Everton were unbeaten in eight and it gave the city an extra dimension that night.

That night: ending up in Newington Temple, where we just took over, took over the music, took over the drinks, took over the atmosphere of the whole place. Every time I looked up there was dancing, there was Roger Sanchez, there were people on tables and there was bedlam of the best kind, the kind that exists on the edge of no longer being the best kind but where the border will remain foxtrotted upon.

Everyone I wanted to see was there and I am sure one way or another you were there too. Everyone had this combination of joy and relief, everyone had somehow seen the way home, seen another building block created in front of us and knew that every little thing was going to be all right.

In Kurt Vonnegut's *Timequake* everyone has to relive the same ten years but do it all exactly the same, knowing the same outcomes, for better or worse, and go through it all relentlessly. The whole day of this game I wish I could have again, do again and see again, make all the same choices, end up with all the same outcomes.

When Klopp confirmed at the end of January 2024 that he was going to leave Liverpool there was a slew of articles, rightly, but the finest I read in the mainstream press came from Tottenham supporter Jonathan Liew in the *Guardian*. He wrote: 'Football has never been purely an intellectual exercise and it has never been purely a professional pursuit. At its best it is the background music to life, the backdrop to nights in and nights out and comedowns and breakdowns and hook-ups and break-ups. Not everybody in the navel-adoring world of football really gets that. Somehow, you always felt Klopp did. Liverpool are not my club and Klopp has never been my manager, but perhaps the greatest tribute you could pay him is that sometimes I wished he was.'

It was that night I knew this to be true, knew more that it can come on any occasion, at any time, in any game. Everyone knows what the massive games are, the ones that happen in April and May, but from nowhere Jürgen Klopp football could change your whole weekend, could change your whole life – I knew that it was, in fact, the real deal in all the ways the real deal needed to be; that life was worth living; that we are dancing animals and that it was beautiful to get up and do something as long as that something was communal, collective; as long as we could do it together and as long as I got to do it with you.

Two quotes from *Timequake*:

'I say in speeches that a plausible mission of artists is to make people appreciate being alive at least a little bit.'

'You were sick, but now you're well, and there's work to do.'

Not every football manager has to make the building blocks from scratch, has to knock them, people and ideas into shape with a hammer, has to put shelves up, has to remind people what they are meant to look like, what they are meant to do and make people appreciate being alive at least a little bit. But this one had to.

We were sick, sicker than we should have been, made sick due to a history which had become a nostalgia for what had been and was gone, rather than, yes, adoring the cathedral that had been built but instead using it as a reason to just keep building new magnificent things together for ever.

That night, after Tottenham, we were suddenly, weirdly, oddly well. And there was work to do.

The Minimum Requirement

When Liverpool beat Middlesbrough at home in the last game of the 2016–17 season it meant Champions League qualification for only the second time since 2009, and at his post-match press conference Jürgen Klopp was asked by Rory Smith of the *New York Times* about what Champions League qualification meant. He went back to Rory, who clarified and made the point his question was sporting, not about money, not about transfers. Klopp's response is slightly paraphrased, but only slightly: 'It's the sports thing that is interesting. Of course, for the club there is money. It's the best tournament in Europe, there is nothing better, maybe in the world (I never played in South America) . . . for me, it is the best competition, you want to be there, Liverpool needs to be there consistently, all the time. I love the perspective. We will be really strong. We will fight for it. Last ten years, Liverpool was not part of it too often – two, three years ago, once, maybe. We should try everything to change this, you have to make steps and the step is for us to be around the best teams in the world because we are in one of the best clubs in the world, and that's it.'

Managers arrive in England from abroad and we think they will know everything about us and about our football. Then those managers themselves get told, pay attention, are smart people and switched on, and they think they have picked it up. But, truly, until you have played Tony Pulis's West Bromwich Albion, or at Kenilworth Road, or football in December; until you have experienced it, lived it, do you know it?

Klopp had had the Europa League season, so he knew what European football meant to Liverpool, but he hadn't had the Champions League. He knew what it meant in a usual sporting sense, but until he had seen Liverpool strut about in it, he couldn't learn what we all intuitively somehow know: it is the minimum requirement, not because of what Liverpool means, but qualification for the Champions League is the minimum requirement precisely because it gives Liverpool meaning, gives Liverpool focus, gives Liverpool fuel and force. It makes seasons bounce and fizz. It offers constant belief and something to look forward to through the winter.

Klopp sort of knew that in 2017, but he hadn't, metaphorically speaking, played Tony Pulis's West Brom yet. He hadn't seen what it gets like across the board when Liverpool truly pin Europe back by its ears, how that gets the domestic juices flowing too. That never happened properly in 2016, but it would in 2018 and beyond. It is a reason the opposite of the swagger – the Covid European campaign, the humiliation by Napoli in 2022 – hurt harder too, withdrew that hope. Your greatest strength is so often your greatest weakness. Cut that oxygen flow and the flames die out all too quickly.

We have to be around the best teams to be the best version of ourselves. The sporting is everything. Rory intuitively knew that, and it is why his question was the right one. The money, the transfers, they take care of themselves. But the sporting and the strutting and the swaggering . . . well, we will be really strong. We will fight for it. Because it is the minimum requirement in this thing of ours.

Key Game 4
Liverpool 4 Manchester City 3
14 January 2018

Manchester City hadn't lost a domestic game up to this point in the season and had only lost their sixth Champions League group game after winning the first five. They looked invincible when they arrived at Anfield in January 2018.

But here's the thing: Liverpool were unbeaten in 17 prior to kick-off in this one. This is important because what happened in this game in part happened precisely because it wasn't just out of the blue. It wasn't some rambunctious team of scamps rattling the champions elect. And what went on to happen across the rest of 2018 didn't appear from nowhere and wasn't conjured into existence solely because of this game. The building blocks, the bricks, they were being fired in the winter of 2017.

In a way this was Klopp's great gift. There was all the preparation, all the hard yards in training, all the smart choices in recruitment and selection and approach, all the experience being garnered through playing and playing well and winning . . . but then there was the explosive moment when Liverpool felt like far greater underdogs than they actually were and managed to harness all the energy of that and ally it to their own excellence.

This could sound churlish: Manchester City had only dropped points in two league games in their first 22. They were so, so good. But this was also part of the thing: they were being admired. No one was ready to do anything against them but purr in adoration.

Jürgen Klopp and Liverpool were ready to take them to the cleaners.

Manchester City had been outrageously good against Tottenham Hotspur at the Etihad on 16 December 2016. They had played some exceptional football and they played it here in the first half but Liverpool were able to stand firm and get in at 1–1, Emre Can exceptional against the ball. There was the break, and it was there in the air as the sun set; now it was a night game, now it was under the Anfield lights.

The 25 minutes immediately after half-time were the best seen at Anfield since the opening of the Rodgers 5–1 against Arsenal – in actual fact, better, because Manchester City had played 22 and won 20 and no one had really landed a blow.

Liverpool landed a million. It was all blows. The noise and the intensity and the intelligence of both Liverpool and the Liverpool crowd after the interval was off the charts. There is a romantic and now European version of what a crowd should be at a football match: a (yellow) wall of constant song, regardless of what is happening on the pitch itself. So often sides come to Anfield and sing, '*Where's your famous atmosphere?*' off some notion that it's meant to be exactly that: witty chants about players and unaccompanied rinky-dinky folk music.

Anfield, for 25 minutes, was a roar. Sometimes it was a louder roar. Sometimes it was a roar that suggested we were happy about a turn of events; sometimes it was a roar which wanted people playing in sky blue to fuck off. But it was just a relentless roar. No songs were sung. No ditties were repurposed. It was a roar which said we can win this game and win it now. It was elemental and unified in a way I struggle to imagine in domestic games prior to Klopp's arrival. None of that is to say that Anfield hadn't had magnificent atmospheres, hadn't sucked the ball into the net, hadn't intimidated the opposition. It had, on so many occasions. But this felt like we'd been part of the half-time team talk. 'Bobby, if you drop here you can isolate John Stones. Oxlade, great goal first-half, son, but get it forward quicker when you can. And if you 50,000 lunatics could just scream at the top of your lungs when-ever anything happens then that could create a bit of space for Mo to operate in.'

We all duly obliged. Liverpool were first to everything and then vertical with it. They hounded every single Manchester City player to within an inch of their lives. At one point Kyle Walker just kicked it out for a throw and turned to Pep Guardiola as if to say, 'What am I meant to do?' And Pep, perhaps for the first and only time in his professional life, appeared to respond with, 'Fuck knows, lad.'

The goals came: Firmino's was teasing and delightful; Mané's powerful, inevitable; Salah's a punchline, a custard pie, a glorious gunging. Liverpool couldn't keep it up beyond that point – at some point the songs must return and the roaring must cease.

Ultimately, when I try to frame that second half, and especially the first 25 minutes, into a football context the first thing I think of is Graeme Souness planting the Galatasaray flag in the middle of the Fenerbahçe pitch. It was Liverpool saying to Manchester City, 'We are real, we are here and we can live with you, stretch you and break you.' It was the throwing down of a gauntlet. But remember the start of this. It hadn't come from nowhere. It had, in fact, been on the cards, but simultaneously came to be another brick fired into shape. We all knew what we could do. Klopp's gift, you see.

The Summer Tours

The first summer pre-season tour we went on was in July 2013 in Australia of all places, shifting from the idea of being in a studio speaking into microphones doing podcasts into speaking in front of crowds on the other side of the world. The essence of going big. It was ridiculous. Now – when podcasts are selling out parts of arenas on the one hand, and when football clubs' summer tours are full of peripheral events on the other – it doesn't seem ridiculous, but back then nobody had got near to trying this sort of thing, and we were doing it about as far away from our houses as possible.

We did three live shows: one in Sydney and two in Melbourne. Prior to the season before – 2012–13 – we'd been doing *The Anfield Wrap* and talking about the side going to the US, and I'd been cynical. So cynical. I could see the value of the tours as a money-spinning exercise, but surely it would be better for the players to go and do an intensive summer camp to get ready for the season. Why drag them around time zones? Why exhaust them? Why not get them proper time together? Why not make them camp, or something? Days and days of drills. There could be something in it, there really could. But in 2013 we saw the other side for the first time, and came to see it every year since. It was all Andy Heaton's ridiculously ambitious idea, the essence of Andy's ambitious ideas being a key reason I am in the position to write this book.

That time, when we were in the Melbourne Cricket Ground in front of 100,000 and they put the lyrics to 'You'll Never Walk Alone' on the big screen, my response wasn't that of cynicism or 'why this time-wasting?' but of wonder. The absolute size of this. Why are we knocking around in sixth? It would have been completely understandable for the players and the manager to come to the same conclusion. It would have been the correct conclusion.

When we were in Melbourne, or in Singapore, or in Boston, or in Michigan, that was the main takeaway. That, and the fact that people aren't stupid. They know the matches aren't competitive, they know they're glorified training sessions; but they love their moments, they love having the eye of the Liverpool-supporting world on their country, on their town. They love that people come to their place to commune with Liverpool. They want it all and they want it with the people they have met through supporting Liverpool. Which I completely understand, because I want it all too.

Everyone is always desperate to tell you how early they get up or how late they go to bed in order to watch The Reds; everyone wants to tell you how they started supporting Liverpool; the ex-pats want you to know they are clued up, and the locals want you to go to the right gaffs for your drinks, your cheese steaks or your dim sum. Everyone wants to feel part of it. And you have to be both hard of heart and, frankly, wrong, to say they aren't. They are. Because, 'The absolute size of this.'

What we have got to see is the behaviour of the support. Prior to the game at Ann Arbor against Manchester United in 2019 we walked right around the stadium and while there was about a 50/50 split in terms of pure numbers it was striking how many of the Liverpool fans were in big groups while the United fans were in ones and twos. Anecdote isn't data, and we need to be careful to not only see what we want to see, but it was visible.

Then, when you were in the ground it was like being in the ground – that first time in Melbourne we were in the active area and, I can assure you, it was active. I know more and more fans who live in Liverpool who now take the chance to get over and do the tours, go to the bars, watch the games that aren't competitive but enjoy the journey and the trip because everyone comes home and talks. It makes you love the city more, getting to go to these other places, getting to have those conversations and see the tailgates, see every supporters' club bar.

When there, you say to them, 'You should get over to Liverpool, if you can, you know. You should come once, just get to Anfield once, come and see it, and get your stories, get your anecdotes.' And it makes you want them to make the ground bigger and bigger. Being global isn't something to be cynical about. It's something to be proud of.

Klopp, Football and Brexit

In an interview with the peerless Donald McRae of the *Guardian* in April 2018 Jürgen Klopp spoke up with his views on Brexit:

> When Mr [David] Cameron had the idea [of a referendum] you thought: 'This is not something people should decide in a moment.' We are all influenced by the way only some of the argument is given, and once the decision is taken nobody gives you a real opportunity to change it again. The choice was either you stay in Europe, which is not perfect, or you go out into something nobody has any idea how it will work. So you give people the chance to make this big decision. And then it's a 51–49 [51.9 per cent–48.1 per cent] vote and you're thinking: 'Wow, 49 per cent are not happy with the decision that's going to change the country.' For the 51 per cent, I'm sure they realised pretty early after the vote: 'What have we done?' . . . The EU is not perfect but it was the best idea we had. History has always shown that when we stay together we can sort out problems. When we split then we start fighting. There was not one time in history where division creates success. So, for me, Brexit still makes no sense.

You read it in Klopp's voice. The 'wow', the rhetorical questions, the idea of seeing other people's positions but them rethinking their own, the need for thoughtfulness, not thoughtlessness. Its tone of 'this is just how I see it'.

There was something similar in the tone of Klopp's desire to replay the Tottenham match after the VAR collapse which led to Liverpool not being awarded a goal: give human beings the chance to do something again and they'll do it better, get closer to it being what it needed to be. Give people the chance to correct a mistake and sense will prevail. He believes that. It is at his core. In that same interview with Donald McRae he said, 'But then, come on, let's sit together again. Let's think about it again and let's vote again with the right information.' It'll be better this time. We'll do better. We'll improve. We'll grow. Let's give ourselves the chance at least. Klopp fitted a strand of Liverpudlian optimism – which it is important to say isn't homogenous, but which is often in opposition to much of the rest of the country.

One of the oddest things about living through the Klopp era in this England was witnessing how he naturally juxtaposed against England's 52–48 trends and the overall mood of the time but still found he spoke to and for an enormous constituency of people across the whole country. There was always at least a 48, and Klopp ended up going wider than just the sports pages in terms of his impact precisely because of how he spoke and how few spoke like him.

Klopp believes in people, in experts, in community, in acknowledging things are hard but can be better, in correcting mistakes. He came over as sensible and practical and happy to acknowledge what he didn't know, but happy to answer questions too. Comedian Laura Lexx's book *Klopp Actually* reimagines him as the most ideal, no-nonsense husband and is a strong example of how the rest of the country viewed him. He transcended the game in a way no other intelligent figure managed this century.

The day he announced he was leaving Liverpool, the extent to which Klopp's departure was considered genuinely national news was astonishing: his press conference was carried live on both Sky News and BBC News. (Not the sports channels. The news channels.) Sky came over to me for my immediate live reaction at the end of the press conference. It was unbelievable. But then football holds such a place in the collective cultural imagination in Britain – and across the last ten years we've seen all of this country's problems and woes be, at some point, viewed through football's telescope.

So reimagine Brexit through its lens.

For too long, debate, acknowledgement, discussion of simply 'Europe' in the UK came in two main forms. The first was the political: predominantly the Conservative and Unionist party's constant psychodrama fed by a vicious press unable to discuss the matter with nuance – and between the two parties there was casting about to make a pro-European position be considered elite. Not something for the working, ordinary man, but something they like in their cities.

And the other was, well, football. European football. Not European music or European art or European theatre, and certainly not European politics and policy. (We can barely cover our own outside pantomime.) Instead, football. And the thing was always this: European football is for the elite. The best. And the best tend to be the richest.

There are 92 teams and only ten of them can ever dream of European football, and we know all about the big clubs, don't we? Big clubs in their big club. What's Europe to me? Waste of time. Not even on ITV any more. Doesn't matter to the likes of us. Their business, and they probably don't even support their local team.

Since the 1970s Liverpool supporters have had the most astonishing relationship with the continent. It wasn't just football but instead a style of dress and a way of life, a creation of new businesses.

But you just can't say that for most people, and if one of the country's main cultural reference points turns Europe into something that is perceived to work for only the few rather than the many then why be surprised if people take against it, especially without there being much other cultural outreach. Europe was other. Happened to, and for, them. The idea of European football being a good thing for the country, representative of the country, was long gone. It belonged to a different era.

The point is that Jürgen was right about the facts and he was right about the rationale and he was certainly right about togetherness. But, currently, in England, division wins. People picking fights tend to win the war, if not the battle, because division is its own success, and Jürgen Klopp stood out because he both believed in and talked about togetherness and expertise and its importance at precisely the moment it was being dismantled in every sphere.

2018 Was the Most Fun Ever

Liverpool didn't win anything in 2018. They get knocked out of both domestic cups at home in the early stages. They lost a Champions League final in contentious circumstances, got beat in Belgrade and Napoli. They lost at Old Trafford and played out a pretty dire 0–0 at Goodison Park. Yet it is impossible to conceive of enjoying a year of football more. Not just 'in that context'. Not 'given what hadn't been won'. Just impossible to conceive of enjoying a year of football more.

It started at Burnley, on New Year's Day, a game which when I was lucky to interview the manager in the summer, he said was 'his game'; played in the daytime but in the dark, a scrap settled by a last-minute Ragnar Klavan winner which was celebrated so hard it gave me a blistering headache. After the microphone was switched off during that interview it was this goal, this celebration, this day and its attendant hangovers he wanted to talk about and relive, laughing his head off about the headaches and the celebrations. It was that moment in the summer of 2018 I realised that of all the Liverpool managers I had interviewed it was this man who'd most love everything around the game were he not in it. This man who would revel in the away days and nights.

Me, you and Jürgen weren't always at Turf Moor slogging it out, though. Instead, we were watching the fastest, most intense, high-quality football imaginable; football to thrill every soul, and it was cutting a swathe across Europe, and every game it felt possible that Liverpool could score four or more and leave an opposition side crawling off the pitch.

It hadn't appeared from nowhere, but it didn't feel far away from nowhere. Mo Salah was going to finish the season with 44 goals in all competitions, Roberto Firmino with 27 and Sadio Mané with 20. Virgil van Dijk, even by May 2018, looked like he could be in all-time Liverpool XIs. Andy Robertson was establishing himself. Trent Alexander-Arnold was breaking through. You could see it in front of your eyes. You could believe, and every game gave you more reason to believe.

It had both ends of the spectrum: they'd harass the life out of the opposition, not allow them a second's room, and then pounce, show such silk with such speed, with partnerships everywhere.

Those partnerships flexed and shifted. There was a triangle down the right, a triangle down the left, and then the hinge of Roberto Firmino going where he was needed to offer that bit more. They scored two lightning goals at Southampton where Firmino assisted Salah and Salah assisted Firmino, and Southampton just had no answer because the question was unreasonable.

All of it was being led by the most charismatic figure in the Liverpool dugout since Bill Shankly, and you felt his masterplan coming to fruition, almost running away from him at times with its risk-taking.

The first Champions League knockout game since April 2009 and Liverpool went to Porto and won 0–5 wearing bright orange. Five–nil away. Who does that? How does that happen? Had anyone ever seen the likes?

They were 5–0 up against Roma in a Champions League semi-final at Anfield in 70 minutes. Again, who does that? Where did that come from? Even now it dazzles to think about it. There are more outrageous and surprising scorelines in Europe these days, but they all feel inspired by that Klopp way of playing which can put one side into turbo-charge and leave another with no game to speak of in just ten minutes.

In the summer of 2018 when I was placed on other media platforms and asked for a season prediction, mine was that Liverpool's would be record-breaking: they would get more points than any side before in coming second. Like everyone in my game, I get asked to make a lot of predictions and mostly think it to be a fool's errand. What'll be the score at the weekend? Christ knows, to be honest with you, Brian. But this one felt right. Liverpool had clearly, by the summer of 2018, been the second-best side in the country by a mile despite coming fourth. They'd lost fewer games than second-place Manchester United, had scored significantly more goals and had done so while getting to a Champions League final.

And then we were on the march into the following season after a summer of adding Fabinho, Alisson Becker, Naby Keïta and Xherdan Shaqiri. There was a mini Daniel Sturridge revival that coincided with beating a Paris Saint-Germain side at Anfield which contained Neymar, Cavani, Mbappe and Ángel Di María, and a Sturridge 30-yard last-minute equaliser against Chelsea at Stamford Bridge.

Off the pitch there was a continuation of all the noise and colour around the run to Kyiv, which itself had culminated in Shevchenko Park, that explosive afternoon where everything crystallised and showed the way forward: murals began to appear, hotels around Anfield full of music and delight were popping up, the drums were pounding and they were never going to stop.

Divock scored against Everton in the 96th minute on the first Sunday of Advent and nothing had ever been so good, no one had ever laughed as hard as we did that night, but then Liverpool were going to go on and win every game for the rest of December as though we were opening a calendar.

The nearest corollary to this in my adult life supporting Liverpool had been the treble season of 2000–01 under Gérard Houllier, but that was almost entirely defined by trophies. This was the opposite. It was defined by seeing people and the city before, during and after, and loving them in the context of just watching this football and this football team. My heart swells to think of it, to think of you, to think of the nights and the hangovers and the texts and the plans and the dancing and the waiting for the next one, because we had it all, because we had hope and we had hope which could and would be realised. We had never been more on the march, and being on the march is the only thing which truly matters. Everyone should get a go.

Key Game 5
Wolverhampton Wanderers 0 Liverpool 2
21 December 2018

Bold as brass after the game the manager says, 'You will probably need 105 [points] to be champions at the end of the season, you don't know.'

Liverpool had won 0–2 in the teeming rain of Wolverhampton, the lashing, pissing, drenching rain, and he says this. Liverpool on 48 from 18 and he says this. It was what he had always known. It was the head start he'd had from his time battling Guardiola's Bayern Munich. It was his insight from day one, and after Liverpool won this muscular encounter he just went and said it out loud. Everything he had seen that night was probably part of why he said it when he did. Because Liverpool had looked like champions. They had looked like 100 points was in their gift.

It was our first time at Molineux in years and they'd had a DJ on the pitch beforehand, and loads and loads of fire in a startling battle of the elements, because the rain would simply not stop. Wolves were good; seventh before kick-off, having won their last three, and it was their last game before Christmas: a Friday night, a DJ and Nuno's back five which became a three . . . they were a big side.

Looking back on the game now, what's interesting here is the Liverpool approach. So much has rightly been written down the years about Liverpool's front three, Klopp's 4–3–3 and how it brought glory for Liverpool. But on this night while all three started, he played a 4–2–3–1: Sadio Mané off the right, Mo Salah through the middle, with Roberto

Firmino behind, and Naby Keïta on the left. That meant Fabinho and Jordan Henderson in a double pivot.

Klopp was constantly capable of this. He had more than one way to skin the Premier League cat, and the emphasis on that front three is actually reductive. During this game he tweaked his shape to pose different questions of Wolves, or to give support to his side. It had been 4–2–3–1 the game before against Manchester United too, and would be something more akin to 4–2–2–2 the week after against Newcastle United. In the second half of the season it would be 4–3–3 far more often than not as Liverpool sprinted the second lap and as Fabinho settled into the demands, but the point of Klopp's 105-point shout at the top is that there was, in his mind, no run-in. There was a run, an 800 metres, two laps as quickly as you could, take no prisoners. You had to win.

This drenched, sodden night was one where Liverpool took no prisoners. It was a game defined by Fabinho and Jordan Henderson in that midfield two. They dominated proceedings, the rock on which the whole thing was built. Indeed, the whole thing was about rocks – rocks everywhere in that back seven: James Milner getting selected ahead of Nathaniel Clyne at right-back; Virgil van Dijk brilliant at centre-back, snatching a goal; and Dejan Lovren solid as his partner. And Alisson Becker looking for all the world like the best goalkeeper you could dream of.

'Rock hard' was what you came away with. That Salah, Mané and Firmino were brilliant had been the story of 2018; it now went without saying, whatever the shape. But suddenly Liverpool looked big enough and strong enough and serious enough about their business to go anywhere, in any weather, and to make the weather. Liverpool were no longer solely one brilliant, exciting, dramatic blast of exuberance – they could dial it up or down; they could win 0–2 somewhere like Molineux and have it be never in doubt. This was the essence of managing imperfection, managing the elements, managing the moments.

They had to be able to look like 105 points for the manager to come out and say it, and they did. There were two more games in the year of 2018, in the most fun year you have ever had in your life, and Liverpool would score nine goals at Anfield. But it was this game at Molineux which was the important precursor for 2019, the best year any football club would ever manage to have. You need to be able to get 105 points, boys. And you can. So don't you forget it.

Mo Salah and How Nans Missed Out

I love Clive Tyldesley. There is something always so deeply evocative about just hearing him for a split second. I worried that was nostalgia, that nothing was ever as good as when you were 18 and knew what was number one and perhaps even cared, but then I met and interviewed Clive Tyldesley.

Because of this, because of his text messages and his jokes, and both his pride and his humility; because he'll help anyone who asks; because late in life he has become a party politically engaged activist opposing gambling advertisements around football; because, ultimately, he cares about people, I love Clive Tyldesley.

And interviewing him, talking to him, you hear that was always there in his commentary. Clive didn't and doesn't commentate to people who know and perhaps even care what a *regista* is, Clive commentates for the people who have come in from a long day at work and want to watch a game of football and know what's going on right before their eyes. On ITV Clive commentated for everyone. When he did the Champions League on ITV he wanted everyone to be in the midst of the game, in the midst of the adventure, of the likely and unlikely. He had no interest in being niche. After all, people's nans were watching this. And football belongs to them as much as the rest of us.

This is precisely why, in a wonderful period for Liverpool Football Club, in a time of mostly stupendous highs and incredible moments, the greatest shame is that the Champions League ceased to be on ITV. Jürgen Klopp would have been a draw, sure. But let's be clear: nans were meant to love Mo Salah. In 2017–18 there had never been a more nan-friendly player. Salah crisscrossed Europe, being at the centre of so many Liverpool goals with speed and directness, playing football with a smile on his face, hair up, blazing a trail in red. He both was and looked electric: like a rock star, like Beyoncé had suddenly turned up. And like Beyoncé he was simultaneously all frills and no frills. He had come from nowhere and he played with a simplicity which carried everyone who saw him.

None of this is to say nans are stupid. Nor, for that matter, that Mo Salah in 2017–18 was stupid. The aim is to take the ball and get it in the goal and ideally do it as quickly as possible. Nans aren't stupid because they mostly aren't wasting their money on subscriptions to football channels, and they mostly aren't messing about with VPNs. But that isn't to say they can't love the game. Nor, indeed, love a story that doesn't have a natural conclusion – that Liverpool didn't win in 2018 after Salah's injury in the final would have led to a nation of nans willing them and him on in 2019. Whacking the final on YouTube or indeed making it free-to-air in other ways is not the same as building a story over time.

And so many a nan missed him, missed the highs, the crushing low and then the glorious second adventure. Missed Clive describing him and all that. We lost that moment when everyone watched the football, watched Liverpool score three in half an hour against Manchester City, five in an hour against Roma, and everyone got to share in it – and at the centre of it all, a man who transcended everything and belonged in every living room in the land, narrated by a man who understood he was talking to every living room in the land.

Key Game 6
Southampton 1 Liverpool 3
5 April 2019

It's important to be clear about this: an answer to the question, 'Have you had the best night out of your life yet?' is, 'Quite possibly, Friday 5 April 2019.'

It came from nowhere. It was a game Liverpool should have won – away against 16th in the league. It was a game Liverpool had to win, going blow for blow with Manchester City at the top of the pile. And suddenly it was the greatest night I have ever had in an away ground in the league. Under Jürgen Klopp this was so often the case: the straightforward on paper would become the spectacular to live through.

It came from nowhere. It had been a lovely day, drinking in Friday London sunshine with two friends Paul Senior and Dan Austin, who'd taken the afternoon off to relax and enjoy. London is the best city in the world to drink in between 12 p.m. and 6 p.m., and that counted double on a Friday in 2019, before getting a train to Southampton and wandering to the ground. To see the side on the march, easing their way into this run-in with bigger challenges on the horizon. And then. God. From nowhere it became the toughest challenge of them all. Liverpool were dreadful. Southampton started brilliantly but Liverpool were dreadful. The first ten minutes was Liverpool's poorest of the season. The second ten was Liverpool's second poorest of the season. The third ten was Liverpool's third poorest of the season. So they were improving. Just from a very low base, and not by very much.

It was like watching an intense psychological thriller, not because the football was awful (the clichéd 'horror show'), but because of the sheer amount of peril, the staring at the abyss, the walking of the tightrope. They had to win. Being one goal down meant they needed two. In the away end hearts were pounding. I can't remember singing, just the sheer agony that Southampton's one would become two and that would be the end of everything, and we were just not ready for everything to end.

Southampton stopped hurting us on about 25 minutes. They began to run out of steam. This made a massive difference. And then ten minutes before half-time Naby Keïta nicked one and we were suddenly all square, which we did not deserve to be.

You ride your luck in this game. Something about this iteration of Klopp's Liverpool made them brilliant at riding their luck. Everyone gets lucky – it's what you do with it that defines you.

Second half Liverpool were better but not actually good. The manager brought Jordan Henderson and James Milner on around the hour mark to play right-hand side and Liverpool improved again, but the need was for the goal.

The goal, when it arrived on 80 minutes, came from Mo Salah running through the middle of the pitch on the counter, reaching the edge of the area and not using Roberto Firmino, instead arrowing it home off the inside of the post. Mo Salah hadn't scored since 9 February. Two months in that year of years and then he did that.

The explosion in the away end was the biggest I have ever known. It was overwhelming, the sheer tension of watching Salah carry the ball, knowing this was it, that we should score, that it was now or never, and then it being enormously, staggeringly, now, that after 29 years it was goals like this that would win league titles, that this was our time, that our history was being written, all of it collapsed down onto that moment . . . and sharing it with Paul and Dan was just the most special thing I can imagine.

Salah wheeled away, taking his top off, looking the bedlam he had caused dead in the eyes. Salah was so bonded to that end in those moments. Henderson would deservedly make it three and remove any doubt.

There are away ends that more than anything you wish everyone could have been in. An oddity of this thing of ours is that half the time only about 3,000 of us can be part of it at any given time, and it feels so, so significant that the 3,000 feels like nowhere near enough. I wrote this on the train back to London: 'When Mo Salah stares at the whole end with his top off and loves it, when Mo Salah milks every last bit of his own brilliance, when he comes back up after praying, after putting his top back on, when Mo Salah turns back one more time and urges the roar from the travelling Kop, I wish we all could have been there to respond. I wish you could have looked right at him, our slightly frayed superhero, I wish you could have acclaimed him.'

On that train, on the way to the capital, trying to write about the game and getting overwhelmed with the momentousness of it all, what kept hitting me was that they'd only win their first league title in 29 years once, that this feeling had a shelf life. It would be a 19th league title but a first, and you only get one first. I'd had some of this feeling before – Emile Heskey at Leeds United in 2002; Yossi Benayoun at Fulham in 2009; Raheem Sterling at Norwich City in 2014 – but this was the greatest and the rawest. This had to be it. They had to do it. I wrote:

I want this not to stop. I'll remember this end, I'll remember how much it wanted, craved Liverpool winning the game. We needed more than wanted; Henderson wants for all time. Longing on a large scale is what makes history. The history Liverpool can make is not the history happening elsewhere in the country but it is the history of a city, the history of a state of mind, the history of thousands of people in one place, the history of millions around the world, the history of our lives and our moments and our rhythms, our needs and wants. Perhaps we shouldn't long for this as much as we do, but we do and these are the facts of the matter. The scale of the longing overwhelms but liberates, there is something about them on the grass doing what they do that frees us from mundane concerns. They give us life. Heart-thudding, hormonal life. This is what it is to be alive, in the blood and the bone.

I want this not to stop.

Of course it wasn't going to directly lead to the league title, not that year, and of course it wasn't the best night out of our lives, precisely because we went back to London, the worst city in the world to drink in on a Friday after 10 p.m. It couldn't satisfy our blistering needs, but then we were exhausted. Spent. Tired and oh so emotional. That night all those feelings came from nowhere, and it was everything and it always will be.

You Don't Always Have to Be at – or Watch – the Game

Gini Wijnaldum made it three against Barcelona at Anfield. I turned around to the people behind me in A&E and said, 'It's three.' I was reading the *Echo*'s live blog on an iPad set up for under-12s. I'd had to half hack the thing to get it to put the *Echo*'s website on.

I was there because of a heart scare brought on by stress (job, not football), pulled muscles in my left shoulder and arm after having moved two tons of gravel, and general exhaustion (job and football), and the good people at A&E had just wanted to check everything twice given family history. The checks came back all good, but this meant I wasn't at the greatest night in Anfield's history.

The sky didn't fall in. I still host *The Anfield Wrap*. Canongate are still letting me write this book.

The start of the following season against Norwich City – a Friday night – I was at a wedding. I was a best man for my Evertonian friend Greg, and that took priority. I'd missed the 0–4 at Bournemouth for something to do with him in the previous season as well, but I love Greg and we've all seen Norwich at home.

I wasn't at Anfield for the 3–1 against Manchester City in 2019 but instead watched it at the Tokyo supporters' club and met some great people. On the plane home I watched Crystal Palace 1 Liverpool 2 via German television and got to make the fantastic observation that it was perfectly legal to do that in international air space but not to have watched it in Britain as it kicked off at 3 p.m. on a Saturday afternoon. You can always find the positive, even if it is just grist to your mill.

I like to be at the match, and am lucky to be able to go to as many as I do, but it is OK for other things to take priority; it's OK to miss out from time to time.

Furthermore: it's healthy. I lie to myself about how many books I read. I don't see family anywhere near enough. I should watch more films, go to more clubs, see more plays. And I do do some of those things, but they all require making an effort. We need to want to be well-rounded humans.

In a way, the Liverpool argument is: you can't just define football supporters by one thing, but if you don't want to be defined by just one thing, you need to do and be more things. Why is that a Liverpool argument? Because in a city the size of Liverpool, with a vibrant cultural life but dominated by two football teams, the people who make things happen will probably number among them football supporters. None of that is unique to Liverpool, but it is more pointed here precisely because of the small size of the city and the pervasive nature of the game. Two things are true: 1) it is worth checking the fixture list before putting something on or committing to go somewhere; 2) it is absolutely fine to miss a game.

You can't do everything, and the good things about seasons are they come back around — Shankly's ever-flowing river doesn't stop. Even the greatest night at Anfield won't be the greatest night at Anfield for ever. Inter Milan gave way to St Etienne which gave way to Chelsea which gave way to Barcelona. A better one is on the way. Has to be.

Key Game 7
Liverpool 2 Tottenham Hotspur 0
(Champions League final)

1 June 2019

The video of everything Jürgen Klopp did after the final whistle, after winning the Champions League, starting with a handshake with Mauricio Pochettino through to crying with Jordan Henderson, is a work of empathetic genius – both his and the filming of it. It tells you everything about him, how much he understood the moment for everyone involved.

It builds through his commiseration, his waves, his hugs and soft words into him seeing his own players and responding to each in kind. It reminds you that he saw Alisson Becker as a wizard, adored his squad players, but ended with him seeing Jordan Henderson and being overwhelmed by the sight of him.

The two of them had been unlucky generals. They had lost. Lost big. Lost big in the league. Lost big in all their cup finals together. Henderson had lost big in 2013–14. Klopp had lost a Champions League final in the last minute at Dortmund. They knew about winning and winning and winning and then, at the very last, losing on the biggest stage, in the biggest, most public way.

Yet they continued to believe in winning to get into the situation to win the biggest of them all.

But it had been a day when losing big was never on Liverpool's agenda. This was the change from 2018 to 2019. Liverpool, in the late blistering heat of Madrid, were simply never losing this game. They were only ever winning the big one, and it helped they had the opponent they did: a Tottenham team who had finished over 20 points behind in the league.

Saying that now, and what they went through to do that, are two different things. It was a game of moments in my mind. The penalty hammering home. The Becker save from Son. The Divock Origi goal to clinch it. What they went through is in that moment: Virgil van Dijk collapsed when the ball hit the net. His legs just went from underneath him. That's what the moment meant, what it did to us all.

After the fact, after the whistle, while Jürgen was being filmed with Son Heung-min, James Milner ran to our end and held six fingers up and, honestly, in the whole run-up the idea of six European Cups hadn't occurred. One for them: that team. Just one for them, and one for us, one to crown everything since the manager had arrived. Since Sadio Mané had arrived. Since Mo Salah, Virgil van Dijk, Alisson Becker had arrived. Just that one.

The tears and the hugs and the worldwide emotional outpouring was the equivalent of Virgil collapsing. There. This.

My day had been out of hand. It started with me losing and then finding my passport, still drunk from the night before, and from there led to getting onstage to do all the fan-park nonsense. This feels like an exaggeration, but it isn't. That ended with me and Dan Austin singing 'Believe' by Cher, which had become a weird city-centre anthem for the season.

Then a lovely afternoon was spent eating an industrial quantity of Spanish ham, before having a nightmare (on my own) getting into the ground courtesy of the Spanish police hating my bag but offering nowhere to put it and getting thrown through a turnstile. When in and settled I was surrounded by so many friends from *The Anfield Wrap* it was incredible to be able to share the win. It was perfect, and when Origi scored the whole end couldn't stop crying.

Coming out of the ground we were overwhelmed with thirst, but then I had the best drink of my life with Paul Senior, with whom I'd gone to so many games throughout this period, and the drink was two pints of Coke from a takeaway. We then met back up with Phil Blundell, who contributed to so much of our work, his mates, Fuad Hasan, who was to go on to direct our Jürgen Klopp documentary, his dad Nasser and a host of others, singing 'Believe' again, before bumping into journalist and author Simon Hughes, who was with then Accrington Stanley manager John Coleman, Rory Smith and *Irish Times* writer Ken Early, with whom I did a podcast as we walked the streets looking for a bar still open at 2 a.m. and found ourselves in a Madrid gay bar.

That bar was brilliant, but then Gibbons rang Fuad to say he could get four of us into the players' party where he was DJing. Off we went – me, Fuad, Nasser and Phil – and stayed there till 7 a.m. It was hell sharing a dancefloor with Virgil van Dijk, but he accepted with good grace that he was nowhere near as cool as me and Fuad. It was hysterical watching Daniel Sturridge DJ through John. Every three songs he'd be over to John telling him what the next three needed to be.

So many dynamics were at play but the footballers seemed so joyous. People, especially us, mostly left them alone to share the night with each other and their friends, and it seemed if anyone got too close Adam Lallana was there to gently usher them away, full of class.

It was at 7 a.m. that I went to the airport to get back to do some work around the parade. I have a picture with the cup at the party with Fuad and Nasser, and that picture (alongside one taken later that summer, posing with Rakel Mjöll of Dream Wife) is probably my favourite picture of this period. It marks that day, that triumph, and all the attendant weirdness – but also that love for (and with) the collective; as a day, it had everything because it had everyone. Everything worth doing is worth doing together. It transpires that includes winning the biggest prize in club football.

Winning Helps

My Uncle Robert – when I was about 20 and we went to away games and settled back into some cracking pub, post-match, in, say, Boroughbridge (having been ferried there by John the Driver) – would settle into his first pint and say, 'A win always helps.'

A win always helps. It was true of every away game. You can have a great day without the win, and up and down the country every weekend many of them are had. But a win, my god, a win always helps. It is the key truism of sport whether playing or spectating.

There is no end to the contexts in which winning helps. I'll always remember when we were in a Midlands boozer and Robert came back from the bar where a woman had said something wild to him about Hillsborough. I said, 'What did you say?' 'Oh, I just said, "Well, at least we got a win today, and we're all on our way home," and smiled.'

Winning makes things easier.

This was as true for Jürgen Klopp as for any football manager. Klopp can be an impressive communicator, as thoughtful a man, as funny as you like – but if his teams didn't win, or didn't win often enough, then it all fell apart.

If, as a football manager, you challenge the crowd to buck its ideas up, or you speak publicly about Brexit, or you grasp the nettle of LGBT issues in football, it helps if you can point to success. Perhaps that shouldn't be so, especially where the LGBT aspect is concerned, but it simply just is. Winning helps. It lets you do the other stuff and gets you a fair hearing.

This is true in our work as well. It is easier for me to spend an afternoon with the team covering Cash for Kids or Hillsborough Law if *The Anfield Wrap* is a success in terms of its bottom line, if you don't have to worry about keeping the lights on. In everything we ever do, having an element of success means we can try to do more, try to be more. In fact, I'd argue the relationship goes the other way: if you are fortunate enough to be successful you should be trying to do more, trying to be more. That's not to be onerous onto people; rather it's just an aspect of being human which matters – we are, after all, dancing animals.

Winning also helps, though, because it makes you feel more upbeat, more likely to be successful again. It firms the ground under your feet and makes you feel able to go again, win again, take a chance here and there.

Winning helped Jürgen Klopp because he was good at it. What I mean by that is, with the possible exception of the very end of his very last season at Liverpool, Klopp, like all great football managers, could harness momentum and work with his team to create a rhythm for success. Victories begat one another because they could all be learned from and built upon, because they found a groove.

The thing that happened to Liverpool after winning that Champions League, after winning 30 out of 38 league games, after getting 97 points, was that they knew they could win. Liverpool's run at the start of the 2019–20 league season remains the longest stretch of games any football team has ever won in any of the top leagues in Europe in any era. By the end of February they'd only dropped two points. They went past halfway: when they finally lost to Watford there was less than a third of the league season left. It batters all other English sides into a cocked hat.

Not only has no one ever won more, no one has ever won like it. It is an achievement under-discussed, in part because of the pandemic but, also, because of its purity. Liverpool were often good, rarely great, but they won. They gritted their teeth and they won. They waited until the winning was there and they took the winning in their stride.

Winning will always help. Everything. Everywhere.

Of course, sport is different to life in general. In sport, for you to win, someone else always has to lose. What needs to stop is the losing hurting quite as much. In English football, and in life. English football's issue is that the consequences always seem so dire but we can change that easily: the leagues, the structure and the financial frameworks that have been created by people in the last 30 years or so can easily be changed if the will is there. None of this has been handed down on tablets of stone.

In our wider lives, across these last nine years too many have felt too defeated for too much of the time. When Jürgen Klopp spoke to Paul Amann, founder of Liverpool's LGBT supporters' group Kop Outs, for a Liverpool FC video about offensive chants he demonstrated that, yes, winning helps but also helping wins. Nothing makes sense on your own; why would we hurt one another when we can help one another?

The Opinion That Dare Not Speak Its Name on My Watch

Everyone gets to have a say. Everyone gets to have an opinion. This matters. The game collapses as soon as we act like some opinions are beyond the pale.

But some opinions wind me up more than others, and some therefore deafen me to almost anything the person who spouts it has to say.

The biggest of those is an oft made argument that both at the time and in hindsight Liverpool's transfer business in the summer of 2019 was negligent. Liverpool signed no players for the first team, just Harvey Elliott for the long term, and two substitute goalkeepers on free transfers. The line went (and has never stopped going) that Liverpool choosing to add no first-team players was the sign of a badly run club who were risk-averse and who couldn't be trusted at the ownership level – something that perhaps filtered down, all the way to the manager. Liverpool had just won the Champions League, and the time to strengthen was from a position of strength.

The issue is that the argument acts as though what would happen next was inevitable, that Liverpool were always going to become league champions. It was inevitable because they won it by such a distance.

It wasn't inevitable. Liverpool had become a finely calibrated winning machine, and across the first 14 league games of the following season they would win 13 but would win eight of those 13 by just the one goal. It was in getting off to a strong start that they set the tone, and the idea that those games, those tight games, would always have been won had there been additions is tenuous.

It really wasn't. Liverpool hadn't won a league title for 30 years and had flopped in every season after they had become runners-up in that period.

It forgets the opposition. Liverpool were up against the most relentless winning machine in English league football history and needed to break them to stand a chance, but breaking that would take some doing.

What happened instead was a football manager knew a group of players would continue to sprint for the line, would start a second 800-metre race immediately after finishing second in the Olympic final against the world record holder, knowing this time they'd do it.

It was actually one of the bravest and most self-confident acts of management the football world has seen, especially in an era where the transfer is king. Klopp believed that they could keep on in a way and at a pace which seems inhumane, and they didn't just keep on but they went beyond and won 26 out of the first 27 by backing themselves and one another and knowing that if they held their nerve they could bend any game to their collective will.

The achievement in the end feels like the only way we could do it, the only way it could ever work; taking what they did against Tottenham in the Champions League final in Madrid in terms of winning as ugly as it possibly could be and then doing it at Bramall Lane, because it needed a jammy goal to open the scoring deep in the second half and we needed those points. It needed two late goals against Aston Villa to kick the door down.

But because of City you had to win every single way winning was done. Beautiful, ugly, lucky, late, ground out, glorious. Because you lose a league with 97 points you need to take everything else out of the equation, make any obstacle look tiny because the burden was so great.

And then there was Covid.

We'll get to that, but now, looking back, it has been slightly lost because of Covid, in the lack of a parade, a party, a shared moment, a dance; in Virgil van Dijk's injury in the autumn of 2020, in the timeless slog on the pitch behind the closed doors.

If the argument goes that that season could have been compromised for three new faces and some more squad longevity then there needs to be an awareness of the stakes of that counterfactual. The stakes:

Everything.

Because that league title was everything.

And if you want to gamble my everything with your talk you'd best have some serious chatter. Adding Tanguy Ndombele is simply not it.

Other unsustainable opinions across the last nine years:

Letting players leave on free transfers was always negligent.

Željko Buvač was the brains of the operation.

Nathaniel Clyne shouldn't have been allowed to leave when he was.

Pep Lijnders writing a book is why things went wrong.

The manager should never talk about the weather.

Why Would Anyone Go to a Live Podcast?

There is this look on LCD Soundsystem lead singer James Murphy's face during the concert video of *Shut Up and Play the Hits* as Reggie Watts finishes his part. It goes into 'Sound of Silver' with the choir and he smiles in a manner that is transcendent. This is what he got – what he won. New York City, Madison Square Garden, to do this in, with all these humans watching, with this cast of thousands onstage, with all of his friends tonight. He can do what he wants. He can do what he always wanted.

Shut Up and Play the Hits is marvellous and liberating. Obviously there's the music – it's three hours of one of the best bands of the last 20 years doing what they do – but there is something more.

Imagine the process: the thought, the glee and the sadness that went into the execution of this concert. Summing up ten years of your life; ten years you might have thought you would never have with people you loved. Ten years where enough people you didn't know came with you so you never had to compromise. Ten years when you could mostly do what you wanted, ending in this final blowout of being able to really do what you really want. Watching *Shut Up and Play the Hits* makes me think of twin titans of twentieth-century culture: Orson Welles and Sid Waddell.

It reminds you of Orson Welles because of his line that a film set was 'the biggest electric train set any boy ever had!' And to paraphrase Sid Waddell: when Alexander of Macedonia was 33, he cried salt tears because there were no more worlds to conquer . . . Murphy was only 41.

When *The Anfield Wrap* started doing live shows in earnest, regularly touring, believe it or not, I had a deep reluctance. I'm not – and I know people won't believe this – particularly extroverted. I found it hard, found it awkward, but also found I didn't enjoy them enough for everything that went into them. They were podcasts that weren't recorded: a bit drunker but mostly just far, far more draining. And it begged the question why.

So for a while I watched as much spoken live performance as I could, for form – everything from political speeches to *Morecambe and Wise* to Hannah Gadsby and all points in between – to try to find what it was I wanted us to be without it straying too far away from the honesty and authenticity.

It was music that helped the most. It always has been around *The Anfield Wrap*, both in terms of being onstage, and when recording, but also when thinking about how to create a community in both a local and a global way – all of which exists online, in the ether, until it very much doesn't – and when walking around the city, or Anfield especially on match days, or when doing the live shows.

It was there in the intense guiding intelligence of things like *Homecoming* by Beyoncé, and LCD Soundsystem married with the quasi-Black Flag but synth-direct love songs of Future Islands and the snarl of Fontaines DC, and seeing Lizzo at Sound City in 2014 and then The Hold Steady with all their joy, and Megan Thee Stallion building a community in an amazing way and Charli XCX's illuminating but deliberately dissatisfying fragments and then Yves Tumor's glamour and Fred Again's adapted speech and images . . . and then in the clubs that we found a way to do it, that idea of making it be joyous and inclusive but on terms that suit you and your people. You are putting the party on, managing it, leading it, but you have invited all of these people with you.

It sounds odd and pretentious – because we're small scale and tend to be in such small venues, and it is just talking about football – but you've got to care about everything you do, find something special on every night, because it doesn't matter that not many people are coming. What matters is those who are coming are gifting you not only their money but their time. Their attention.

There is no greater gift.

And if you respect that gift, if you've invited them to your party and they have brought their gift, then you need to give them a gift back. You owe them that, at the very least.

It is important to be self-aware precisely because it is talking about football (and what do you know, really?), but it is also talking about shared spaces and sharing something of the place you are from but often in their supporters' clubs, the one that belongs to them, where they commune. They have given you their place, their space. Getting to do that there as well as we can is what we won; the spoils to be enjoyed.

A reason the LCD Soundsystem comparison stays with me is down to a criticism often levelled at the group that they were 'self-aware' – which is, frankly, just a nonsense criticism. If you are over 30, you are constantly self-aware, aware of how the self is letting you down on an almost hourly basis, aware of how the self has let you down already, and aware of how you are trying to piece things back together in some way. If you are over 30 and you aren't self-aware, you are doing it wrong. You shouldn't be so certain. Being crippled by self-doubt is precisely why I have to think endlessly about the live shows.

Look at the state of you. There's a lovely Jeffrey Lewis line from 'Roll Bus Roll' about not being designed to go fast, to have so much past.

What we talk about on our shows as podcasts, in our live shows, what we want Liverpool to offer is joyousness in every possible and available moment and to encourage everyone to do that. A unified scene. To milk those moments dry, to leave them cherished with friends you'll have for ever because you got to share in one another's most glorious seconds, and they become minutes, those minutes become hours, and then there are nights out.

There is a responsibility. The last time I interviewed the manager my first question was, 'What do you feel you missed out on?' 'Oh,' he said, quick as a flash, 'the city.' He told stories about people coming to stay and getting to go out and then the morning after telling him all about it and him being jealous. He said he had only been into Liverpool five times, twice on open-top buses.

After we beat Newcastle 2–1 with a last-minute Fabio Carvalho winner I absolutely hammered it on our after-match video. Gave it the big one – a ridiculous clown. Our bench had had it with their bench when the winner went in. Months later, I found out that pretty much when the video had been released Pep Lijinders messaged someone behind the scenes at Liverpool and said he wanted to go and find me in a bar and get on it.

We share that explosion but we get to take its propulsive force into the night. They can't, the coaches and the players: for them the next game starts immediately. But we get it, that great endorphin thrust into one another's arms for hours to come.

All of this is why the influence of the music looms larger than the spoken word: cascading, momentous and overwhelming, grabbing the moment and being pulled by it. The whole process of music, of football, throws open this:

Have you had the best night out of your life yet?

Have you? Think about this. It is an important question. The best night. Everyone was funny, everyone was pretty, everyone was heading for the centre of the city. Has it happened? Has it gone, lost in the ether, half remembered, face sore from smiling the next morning, head sore from excess? It's the question LCD Soundsystem ask you over and over again, and the one we ask over and over again. Has it happened? Are we the other side of it? Is it all downhill from here?

Absolutely not. We can't ever give that up – after all, look at what came from nowhere after this Swabian fella turned up in October 2015, over and over again. Being honest, for it to happen, the moment it hits, we'll be almost too old. Almost. Not quite. Not quite too old but nearly. Nearly there. We'll need to have ways that we can show our age. But we need one more night. Give me that one more night; I always want one more, I want that greatest night out of my life, I want that this Saturday and next Saturday. I want one more big dance. One more big, transcendent dance with you.

All that said, I do sort of hope the best night out James Murphy ever had in his life was at Madison Square Garden.

Key Game 8
Leicester City 0 Liverpool 4
26 December 2019

They had been invited to Qatar because they were Champions of Europe. While there they became Champions of the World. They returned with one last question to answer: would all the travel and disruption undermine the quest to become Champions of England.

0–4; 13 clear of second-placed Leicester with a game in hand; 14 clear of Manchester City having effectively broken them by continuing the pace from the previous season's run-in, with the same number of games played. Liverpool had played 18, won 17, drawn one. They had blown the league to smithereens. They had last lost in the league at the start of 2019, away at Manchester City. They were going at a rate which no one could live with.

Second-placed Leicester. Everyone knew that Manchester City were the second-best team in the country, but, nonetheless, Leicester held the spot, a good 19 games into the campaign. They weren't mugs. They were just made to look like them.

It was another game where calling it 4–3–3 wasn't quite right: Roberto Firmino came so deep in possession, Naby Keïta pushed right on, and Sadio Mané and Mo Salah played so narrow it looked more like a 4–4–2 diamond or even 4–2–2–2, with Jordan Henderson and Gini Wijnaldum holding the fort.

But the key thing was Trent Alexander-Arnold, who played so advanced on the right-hand side with Salah narrow that he was a one-man flank who led the charge, putting in his best performance for Liverpool to date; man of the match in Liverpool's most significant away win of the season.

For the one and only time in this book, let's do the stats from StatsBomb:

Leicester had three shots with an xG value of 0.09 cumulatively. Liverpool had 15 with 2.85 xG generated; the biggest difference in xG at the King Power from the start of the 2018–19 season until Leicester got relegated.

In the first half Leicester didn't muster a shot.

The possession was 59 per cent–41 per cent in Liverpool's favour, but Liverpool still put in more pressures than Leicester (222 versus 194) and they also had more pressure regains: 44 to 29.

Leicester did win one more tackle than Liverpool, but attempted nine more for that one better.

Leicester had two corners to Liverpool's eight.

It was the biggest win in a game between first and second since 2011 when Manchester City beat Manchester United 6–1. That day Manchester United went down to ten men, Jonny Evans sent off on 47 minutes. Coincidentally, he played for Leicester City in this one. Post match Brendan Rodgers said, 'People were trying to put us in a race with Liverpool but we know where we are.'

Liverpool won the league well before the pandemic hit. The first time the Kop would sing 'We're Gonna Win the League' came when Mo Salah scored Liverpool's second against Manchester United in four league games' time; four league games Liverpool won without conceding a goal.

But a question to ask is: when did you know it was done? When couldn't you ignore the evidence of your own eyes? My only remaining concern had been coming back from Qatar. That had been it. My last remaining slightest doubt. I first thought it was extremely likely around the time of the home win against Leicester City, truly believed after the home win against Manchester City. After this, though? We had watched the champions put in the performance of champions. Any remaining doubt dispelled.

I started the post-match audio in the ground, talking to Paul Senior about the quality of the display as the crowd noise swelled and fell behind us, as though it had a team of sound designers working on it. It was the acclamation of the Champions of Everywhere. It was the sound of majesty.

The next night Manchester City lost at Wolves, having been 0–2 up. It was done: 2019 was Liverpool's. They had won it all, won the run-in that never stopped, won the first league title since 1990. They had battered the Premier League in a way that no one else had before or perhaps ever will.

2019 Was Liverpool's Greatest Ever Year

I just want to lay out the facts to start.

On 27 February 2019 Liverpool beat Watford 5–0. Next game, they would draw at Goodison Park. Liverpool then won their following 17 league games across two seasons. Then they drew at Old Trafford on 20 October 2019 with a late Adam Lallana equaliser. Then they won every remaining league game that year – and the run would go into 2020: their next 18 league games in total.

Eventually, across 38 games – a full league season – they won 36 and drew 2.

P38, W36, D2.

It's a scandalous run, the sort of run which should not be possible.

After that game against Watford in February 2019 they went to Bayern Munich and dominated them 1–3. They eased through against Porto, lost at Barcelona and then produced the greatest night Anfield ever saw to make it 4–3 on aggregate.

They won the Champions League.

In December they went to Qatar to play in the Club World Cup, beating Flamengo in extra time. It was the first time Liverpool had ever been crowned World Champions.

Football is seasonal and crosses years. Them's the rules. Normally, the work done in the first half of a year builds on the work done, the second half of the year before, and so on.

Except the rules don't really work on this occasion. There are two reasons why it's rare to see this transcended, but, firstly, in 2019 Liverpool managed it by virtue of being so good, so spectacular they smashed the rules into smithereens. The second reason why is less uplifting: there wouldn't be a meaningful 2020 to get to build through; 8 December 2019 was when the first hospitalisations were confirmed in Wuhan.

But for now, let's accentuate the positive: 2019 was Liverpool's greatest ever year, and within it Sadio Mané was Liverpool's greatest player, with Virgil van Dijk and Jordan Henderson a couple of steps behind.

Sadio Mané was simply incredible. He showed up in every type of game and scored every type of goal. He was relentless in his desire to see Liverpool get over the line; livid with his teammates for over-celebrating the Lallana equaliser at Old Trafford. There was a game to be won.

Of course, all of this was because of where Manchester City had placed the bar, going all the way back to the start of the year when 11 millimetres separated Liverpool from the lead. In the final reckoning it is reasonable to conclude that was the difference between zero points and three that day. Liverpool were just better, but Manchester City showed such courage and fight to clinch their 2–1 win.

It was as if Sadio stored that 11-millimetre frustration, kept it, and used it as raw force, raw fuel for the year. In that game against Watford in 2019 he sparked the rout, scoring a goal with a chipped backheel. He wasn't messing. He wanted to win more than you, more than me, me being a grown man who used to brush his teeth and say afterwards into the mirror, 'That was the tooth-brushing of champions'; a man who offered to lose his thumbs to win the league; a man who saved the image of the league table on his phone in November 2019 and kept updating it just to see. Just to make sure.

Sadio Mane scored his 14th goal of the season on 29 December, against Wolves in a 1–0 win. His 31st goal of the calendar year.

Sadio Mané wanted it more than me. And we'll never be able to thank him enough.

The greatest. In the greatest year.

Despite It All

Despite it all. Despite Sadio. Despite Bayern Munich. Despite Southampton. Despite downing the wine and despite the leisure activity. Despite Barcelona. Despite Leo Messi getting flicked the Vs. Despite the stage in Madrid. Despite that seven-minute video of Jürgen ending with him and Jordan crying. Despite the little legs. Despite the greatest pint of Coke with Paul Senior. Despite the players' party. Despite Dream Wife at Glastonbury. Despite that cat being lost and found. Despite beating my wife at Greg's wedding quiz. Despite battering Norwich. Despite Adrian's full debut ending with him making saves to win a penalty shootout. Despite a last-minute James Milner penalty against Leicester at Anfield. Despite Villa. Despite a crazed 5–5 Carabao Cup game against Arsenal at Anfield. Despite podlife in Tokyo. Despite Mo Salah scoring one of the greatest ever goals at Anfield against Manchester City. Despite Divock Origi running amok against Everton yet again at Anfield. Despite being the Champions of Everywhere. Despite battering Leicester in their own ground. Despite sharing it all with you, loving you, adoring you, despite that. Despite the trophies.

Despite it all. It all.

Vonnegut/*Timequake*-style, if I could choose, I'd relive 2018 over 2019.

Every single time.

I'd relive the heady, hormonal teenage energy of it, relive its pogoing punk, its clicks and hisses, its raw potential and endless promise, its clarification of what we should always be, what it should all always be, its pounding peppermint beat of the club, its head thrown back, raw howling laughter, the manager on the pitch in the goalkeeper's arms after Divock and the purple flare.

Every single time. Despite it all. Because we had it all. We knew we had it all. He and they gave us that certainty; 2018 was as brilliant as it was because 2019 was just there, and we all believed. 'Believed' isn't the half of it. We were Zealots. And the only thing better than the promised land was the gift of going there all together as the best version of ourselves.

Key Game 9
Liverpool 1 Shrewsbury Town 0 (FA Cup)
4 February 2020

In December 2019 Liverpool got to the quarter-finals of the EFL Cup and something that was apparent to anyone paying attention happened: Liverpool had a clash between that fixture and the World Club Cup in Qatar.

Every year at *The Anfield Wrap* we create a season-long schedule with all the available data. We tend to do this in May. Immediately, with all the dates that were out there, it was clear there was a problem.

In the end, Liverpool played a youth XI managed by under-23s manager Neil Critchley and got soundly beaten by Aston Villa – but won in Qatar.

There was another problem on the horizon. The Premier League winter break was scheduled to fall when a fourth-round FA Cup replay would be played. Again, at *The Anfield Wrap* we were aware of this one looming too.

The point here is that, on both occasions, football's authorities just sat tight and hoped for the best. Hoped it would go away. Hoped it wouldn't emerge. After drawing 2–2 against Shrewsbury Town away – a game Shrewsbury should have won and would have been favourites to win if it had gone into extra time – Liverpool got the replay. Klopp said,

In April 2019 we got a letter from the Premier League where they asked us to respect the winter break, not to organise friendlies and not to organise competitive games in respect of it. I have said to the boys already, two weeks ago, that we will have a winter break, so it means we will not be there – it will be the kids who play that game because they cannot deal with us like nobody cares about it.

It's about players' welfare and they need a rest – mental rest, physical rest. That's what the winter break is about, and then another competition tells us it's not that important. We had to make these decisions before, because the boys have famil[ies], and the international players like Jordan Henderson, Virgil van Dijk, Georginio Wijnaldum, Trent Alexander-Arnold, Mohamed Salah, Sadio Mané, all these guys, they never have time off.

Since his arrival into English football Klopp had been astonished at the state of the English calendar and had spoken out repeatedly about player welfare, not just in Liverpool's interests but in the interests of what he saw as the wider game. Therefore it came to pass that a Liverpool team fulfilled the fixture. There were five debutants. The average age was 19.6. The oldest player was Pedro Chirivella, making his tenth Liverpool appearance. And they won 1–0 in front of a capacity Anfield.

Immediately after the match this is what I wrote for *The Anfield Wrap*:

There is a variant of this piece which is just 1,000 words on everything Pedro Chirivella did after the final whistle.

A thousand words on his every move, his every word. Who he hugged, when, what he was thinking and feeling.

I was in the upper Kemlyn. The final whistle blows as he runs towards us. His arms are outstretched. His roar to the heavens is enormous. His joy is unconfined.

He looks again back at the Kemlyn. He bites his badge right in front of my usual seat, where I know my dad is tonight. My dad's three times Pedro's age, four times Harvey Elliott's, but I know he'll be as proud as I am, as overjoyed as I am of this Liverpool side who have managed this.

Pedro goes to his teammates, makes time for their manager, lifts his manager, goes to the Kop end, roars again, leads half a lap of honour. He's at the centre of the celebrations as he was at the centre of the team, at the head of the head of the celebrations as he was at the head of the team.

He spent the game organising them. Spent the game telling them. Spent the game prompting and probing, finding and sending, dropping and covering. It should, given the context, go down as a truly great Liverpool centre-midfield performance.

Chirivella, unlike Harvey Elliott, unlike Curtis Jones, is unlikely to make 100 Liverpool first-team appearances. But he should never have to buy his round in this city unless he insists upon it.

He will insist upon it. Tonight told you that. He does his share. He carries his weight. Because he is a Liverpudlian – and, like all the best Liverpudlians, he comes from outside the city – he will insist on getting his round in.

Anyway – in another universe there is 700 more words on all this. On who and what that five minutes after the game tells us. A novella on a walk. On a life. On a weird career. On what is next.

I need to leave this. Crack on.

Crack on with a side that just showed for one another. That were the most willing. That believed when those around them didn't.

I believed in Curtis Jones. He repaid my faith. I believed in Harvey Elliott. He repaid my faith. The two most gifted footballers on the pitch showed exactly that. They are making 200 appearances for Liverpool. They are present and future.

I didn't believe in Sepp van den Berg. In general, over the long term, yes. But not tonight. He made a mockery of me. He was first to everything, won every battle, passed every ball. His line was tremendous. He got every bit of playing centre-back right. It was a performance which came with a klaxon. That was what Liverpool invested in.

Neco Williams nearly scores first half and in the second nearly finishes a truly great Liverpool move. Williams is fascinating; he could easily become a deputy to Alexander-Arnold, but where the latter carries a constant threat of creativity, Williams looks like goals. He arrives in a manner similar to the way my dad speaks of Chris Lawler. Tonight showed that.

Adam Lewis grows into it. He finds his way. He's a footballer. Lively, physically and mentally. He finds little angles, loves it round the corner.

Clarkson and Cain never stop. Give, go, show, show, show feet. Liam Miller runs himself into the ground.

And then, as the clock runs down, the goalkeeper claims. As the time runs down, Liverpool lock Shrewsbury in the corner. The clock runs down and their shortcomings are clearer, and clearer, and clearer. Liverpool break them. Erode them down to a nub. Liverpool are everything.

You want the magic of the cup? It is here. Here where lifetimes are redefined, where Neil Critchley gets to give it the biggest of big ones in front of the Kop, where meaning and purpose collide, where Liverpool show an essence which is the envy of the country, the envy of the world. Jürgen Klopp didn't turn up tonight in person, but his essence, his value, is everywhere.

This, here, could well be his finest victory of the season. The glory is that it isn't solely his. None of them are, though. But the size and significance of the victory makes his smaller than normal slice bigger than ever.

We're left so deeply and profoundly proud of those footballers, tonight's coaching staff, the wider coaching staff, the senior pros who set the example.

Tonight is the best of us. Liverpool Football Club have done a lot in the last 12 months. They've done nothing better than tonight.

Chelsea next. Before then, a sweetheart bonus night in town and a Pedro Chirivella tattoo.

Getting to write the words is a privilege, handsome. A delight, gorgeous.

Days later we went to Ireland on tour. Three live shows. While I was in Dublin my phone went – a number I didn't recognise. It had called twice before in the week. It was Alex Inglethorpe. Liverpool's Academy Director. He was calling to say he had read the piece and shared it around internally. He thanked me for writing it as I did, told me everyone was very proud and said if there was ever anything he could do to give him a shout.

He'd already done what he needed to do. So had Jürgen Klopp.

Half-Time – A Pandemic

Timeline

9 March 2020	President of the regional government of Madrid, Isabel Díaz Ayuso, announced the cancellation of classes in the Autonomous Community of Madrid. Spain has 1,231 cases of Covid confirmed and 30 deaths.
11 March 2020	Liverpool 2 Atlético Madrid 3. To the backdrop of 3,000 Spaniards making the trip to Liverpool, The Reds crash out of Europe. Jürgen Klopp tells supporters in the main stand to put their hands away.
12 March 2020	Boris Johnson says, 'We advise all those over 70 and those with serious medical conditions against going on cruises and we advise against international school trips,' but stops short of any form of a lockdown and says, 'We are considering the question of banning major public events such as sporting fixtures. The scientific advice, as we've said over the last couple of weeks, is that banning such events will have little effect on the spread.' Games will go ahead at the weekend. Then Mikel Arteta is confirmed as testing positive for Covid. Games will not go ahead at the weekend. And everything stops.

Time Elapses	Everything stops. Time elapses. People, stuck in their homes, start washing their shopping. People pass away, unmoored from time, separated from loved ones in the grimmest circumstances, and no one quite knows what to do.

For us, for this, for our purposes: play stops. Play stopping in all its forms: playing on playgrounds, on school fields, on tennis courts, in snooker clubs, in pubs and bars and clubs and with each other.

The language around life returning to normality is around the dutiful things, and the dutiful things matter, of course they do, but it is play in all its forms which bonds us, gives our lives meaning and offers ourselves dates and context for all of our experiences, and it is this which unmoors us from time and from each other. It is as though, now, that this time didn't count, as though it happened in Narnia or perhaps more accurately in Punxsutawney.

Somewhere in Punxsutawney Liverpool win a league, somewhere in Punxsutawney Liverpool are champions for the first time in 30 years, and I am on a beach with Ben Johnson and Dave Pownall playing 'Nessun Dorma' on a bluetooth speaker in the dark, and with Adam Melia whom I have loved for years and James McKenna who helped found Spirit of Shankly, and he was the one who was the first to point out all the people who stayed for the last 20 years, who could have left, who could have lived elsewhere but who stayed for this, and this made me realise and remember I was one of those people, but it wasn't meant to be like this: Jordan Henderson crying in Formby Hall and us crying on Crosby Beach, but it is Punxsutawney, pal, and you'll be glad you made it and, you know what?, you'd have 'Nessun Dorma' again if you could.

They lift it at an empty Anfield, an Anfield like a theatre, a silent disco, after beating Chelsea 5–3. They party together afterwards and then you realise that the nature of sport is that this could well be the

	last time they are all in the room together, and that room is the entire ground and while that has a poetry to it, it is a poetry soaked in melancholy; we will never get to thank them, never get to thank each other.
	Another season starts and Liverpool have signed Kostas Tsimikas, Diogo Jota and Thiago Alcântara. The games begin just after the time you could eat out to help out but, much like that, are alien and odd, not play as we understand it but play in a laboratory. Liverpool lose 7–2 at Villa and Virgil van Dijk gets injured at Everton then Joe Gomez gets injured, but there isn't play as such, just tests every morning, terrible, scary news from a government you can never trust, and there is no dancing to be had because there are no dancefloors, and you worry there may never be dancefloors again. The laboratory matches can scarcely be remembered let alone contextualised, and that further reminds us what play actually is, because all this, this isn't it, this isn't real, this gives us nothing to hook onto.
	Play in all its forms – art, storytelling, food, sport, hanging out – is living. Everything else is existing, and this is a book about what it means to feel alive.
3 April 2020	Yves Tumor releases *Heaven to a Tortured Mind*.
29 April 2020	*Time Shelter* by Georgi Gospodinov is published in Hungarian.
14 August 2020	*Ted Lasso's* first episode is premiered on Apple TV.
11 October 2020	Project Big Picture is leaked.
14 October 2020	Project Big Picture is kiboshed.
16 December 2020	Liverpool 2 Tottenham Hotspur 1. In front of 2,000 spectators Roberto Firmino scores an injury-time winner and then runs, exhausted, towards them all.

27 December 2020	Liverpool 1 West Bromwich Albion 1. In front of 2,000 spectators Liverpool drop two points but, more importantly, Joël Matip suffers an injury which puts him out until the end of the season, alongside Joe Gomez and Virgil van Dijk. Liverpool are top of the league. This will not remain the case.
30 January 2021	SOPHIE passes away in Athens due to an accidental fall. Writing in 2024, I listen to something by SOPHIE at least once a week. I don't see that changing until she doesn't sound like the next thing.
22 February 2021	'Marea (We've Lost Dancing)' is released by Fred Again. Marvellous
18 April 2021	The European Super League plan is announced via a press release and a website whose designers had last worked in 2003.
20 April 2021	Liverpool players led by Jordan Henderson launch an online campaign about the Super League proposal: 'We don't like it and we don't want it to happen. This is our collective position.' Petr Cech tries to placate Chelsea supporters about the Super League on the streets outside Stamford Bridge. By 1 a.m. the next morning every Premier League club invited to the Super League has pulled out.
21 April 2021	John Henry apologies to Liverpool supporters for 'the disruption I caused' by signing up to the proposed breakaway.
22 April 2021	Tracey Crouch to chair a fan-led review into English football.
16 May 2021	Liverpool 2 West Bromwich Albion 1. The doors are again closed as Alisson Becker becomes the first goalkeeper in Premier League history to score a winning goal – a glorious arching header, which people could congregate together in bars to watch and celebrate – and it feels, firstly, like an end is in sight and, secondly, like Liverpool will play Champions League football again next season.

1 July 2021	Ibrahima Konaté signs for Liverpool.
22 July 2021	The *Crouch Review Interim Report* is published. It is robust around licensing and regulation and offers the beginnings of an overarching blueprint but rightly doesn't get into the detail of how leagues run themselves.
28 July 2021	Liverpool Crown Court coroner confirms Andrew Devine is the 97th victim of the Hillsborough disaster.

'When's the Parade Going to Be?'

'I still have no idea how you did it, but the sound level, keep it on one level, it was unbelievable. It was not like one person shouting, and then the other one shouting. It was all 'yeahhhhhh'. How does that work? So that was completely overwhelming.

It's for a person, too much attention. To be honest it's not, I think, exactly where I want to be. It's like, OK, all eyes on me, or stuff like that, so it's nice, but it's stress as well, because you cannot get all the eyes but you want to have eye contact. It's too much, but it's the best thing you can ever do, it was unbelievable.'

Jürgen Klopp, July 2019, on the Champions League Trophy parade of June 2019

'You cannot get all the eyes, but you want to have eye contact.' There are few things that tell the story of Jürgen Klopp in his own words more than that. It's stress, not being able to look at the people inter-acting with you in the eye. He wants to do it, finds it difficult, wants that moment with everyone, wants to make clear to everyone that this relationship is one of 'we', not of me here and you there. You cannot get all the eyes, but you want to have eye contact.

In early February of 2020, when Liverpool were a million points clear, we went to Ireland to do three *Anfield Wrap* live shows and the most common question we were asked by the Irish contingent was, 'When do you think the parade is going to be?' Everywhere we went, everyone we spoke to asked that question. 'When should I book my flight for?' 'What if they go out of Europe?' 'Will it be after the cup final?' 'Will they do one for the league and one for anything else?'

It was all that was on everyone's mind. The league title had been won. At some point it would be confirmed. But when, when will the parade be? When should the pilgrimage be made? When will there be the opportunity to say thank you, to congregate together, to celebrate?

There is something so democratic about a parade. Anyone can be part of a parade. Under Klopp we had two, and what was striking was the many different types of people who showed up. Liverpool's tickets are controlled by people who look and sound like me. White men aged over 40. They/we hold the tickets, and due to Liverpool's intense access issues they/we aren't giving them up any time soon. Not at Anfield, not away, and certainly not for European games. All of this is one of our next big rows, one which bubbles beneath the surface, one which will be intractable unless someone argues to abolish season tickets and makes themselves the most despised person in Liverpool.

But a parade – all you need is your bit of concrete. Indeed, people who are able to go to finals, who have the golden tickets, often aren't there at the parade. They can't get back and, in any case, they got their own parade scampering around the ground with the trophy.

The parade is everyone's, anyone who can get to Liverpool at the time of asking gets to be part of it, gets to share in that moment. And Klopp knew that, knew what they wanted, that moment of communion, and knew even then he couldn't quite give it as he would like.

Under Klopp we had two parades. It should have been three. People should have flown in from around the world to find their bit of Liverpudlian pavement to display their bit of love and respect and admiration and togetherness.

We lost this. Not because another side got one more point or because of a goalkeeping error or a fixture pile-up – the final parade with Klopp in 2024 was lost because we didn't quite deserve it. It was sporting; it happens.

Of course, it feels trite: over the last four years so much was lost. Lives. Friends and relatives were lost. Jobs were lost. Businesses collapsed. Time was lost; opportunity, education, confidence, belief. But so was the fun stuff. The games, the massive nights, the killer parties, the opportunities to fall in love, to celebrate. To have eye contact with each other.

Those nights in Ireland, when we had 750 people together across the three nights, they were the closest we got to celebrate that season, to celebrate together. We talked about the little gold trophy that they gave Arsenal when they went through the season unbeaten; we went out night after night after the shows and the world was all hugs and a wistful look for what was already here. We knew the league was done. But we didn't know precisely what was around the corner and, more than anything, I wish we had.

Klopp: the Vaccine, the Title and Null and Void

'There was talk that people wanted to declare the season null and void. So you thought, "Huh? We have played 76 per cent of the season and you just want to delete the thing?"'

Jürgen Klopp

No football manager, when doing his or her badges, has undergone training in what you do when there is a pandemic. It's not covered. It doesn't come up.

The videos that were put out by Liverpool (and by other teams) of stretches and team meetings in *Brady Bunch* squares were comic in one sense, not least in the players themselves speaking to each other. The videos being released were acts of kindness: football clubs saying to the world that they were still here, just waiting.

The thing about the 2019–20 season, though, from Liverpool's point of view is that those *Brady Bunch* players had achieved a cliché no one had ever managed before: 38 cup finals. Or rather, by the point of lockdown, 29 cup finals, with 27 won, one drawn and one lost. In Liverpool's last league game before social distancing James Milner practically broke his neck on the hour mark against Bournemouth to clear off the line to stop the game going to 2–2. And then Bournemouth weren't allowed another shot. It was, if not the moment of the season, then quite possibly the moment which defined the season.

The thing was they'd given absolutely everything in the pursuit of Liverpool's first league title in 30 years. More than everything. More than anyone else: imagine the emotional weight after 97 points the season before and not winning it and then doing this? And then, just as it was in sight, this happened.

Honestly, yes. I didn't think when we went to lockdown, 'Oh my god, that is our season, we are so close.' Because it was not important in that moment.

But that doesn't mean that certain things are of no importance at all just because they are less important.

I became worried when people started talking about 'null and void' . . . because I was like, 'Wow!!' And I really felt it physically. That would have been really, really hard.

Jürgen Klopp.

The null and void talk is now easily passed over but, in a way, it was the first very public fracture (or at least for a decade) in the Premier League's very public placid face. Up to this point most Premier League agreements seemed to be reached away from contested votes and any publicly aired disagreements between clubs. But suddenly 'null and void' was everywhere, and it feels like that lead to the constant claim and counterclaim we have today between the clubs, which has now extended into lawsuits against the league.

It isn't difficult for me to imagine being Jürgen Klopp when the null and void talk was happening, having to reassure loads of people remotely, because I'm the fella who hosts *The Anfield Wrap*. My messages in all categories were flooded with people asking for reassurance: 'They can't. On top of everything else going on, they can't. Can they?' 'They can't. I can't cope if they do.'

To say it was never likely because of the money is easy now. It happened in Holland. It happened all over the place and, yes, the money is different and that is why I never thought they would. But it is human to be scared, especially when at home staring at the ceiling during a pandemic with not enough to do and reading what West Ham United people were arguing about cancelling the season.

What was striking was that, at the same time as this, Klopp was becoming a public figure in matters pertaining to the vaccine. In one way, this was unsurprising: the history (and perhaps future) of Liverpool is marked with matters pertaining to public health, and being Liverpool manager is a complicated job – again, not something they walk you through when doing your badges either. A landmark city-centre pub is named after Liverpool's first Medical Officer of Health, Dr Duncan. Matt Ashton, Director of Public Health for Liverpool City Council, hasn't reached that point yet, but he led Liverpool brilliantly through the pandemic, and one of the biggest advocates for the vaccine was the man who had become spiritual leader for two-thirds of the city, with a diaspora way beyond that. Also a man who loves answering a direct question with a direct answer, something he never stopped doing throughout the pandemic:

When you don't know, you call a specialist and the specialist tells you. That's why I took the vaccination because I am in an age group [mid-fifties] where it is not that easy any more, the virus could be tricky, and I was really happy when I could get [the jab]. The specialists out there say the vaccination is the solution at the moment.

If I say I am vaccinated, other people say: 'How can you tell me I should be vaccinated?' It is a little bit like drink-driving. We all probably were in a situation where we had a beer or two and thought we still could drive, but [because of] the law, we are not allowed to drive so we don't drive. But this law is not there for protecting me when I drink two beers and want to drive, it's for protecting all the other people, because I'm drunk, and we accept that as a law.

I don't take the vaccination only to protect me, I take the vaccination to protect all the people around me. I don't understand why that is a limitation of freedom because, if it is, then not being allowed to drink and drive is a limitation of freedom as well. I got the vaccination because I was concerned about myself, but even more so about everybody around me. If I get [Covid] and I suffer from it: my fault. If I get it and spread it to someone else: my fault and not their fault.

There is something relentlessly Klopp here. You can imagine him privately reassuring the players. The league will come. The time will come. The situation will clear. The smart people will work it out. But you can also imagine him feeling it physically in his own time, imagine him tearing his hair out at decision-makers in his area of expertise, finding the football hierarchies infuriating and finding the idea that he had come so close and that it could be taken away by vindictive, selfish idiots during a time of far greater human loss difficult to process. Because it was.

The Loss of Play and Why Games Matter, Why Games Make Us Human

I love an ancient toy; most recently I saw a photo of a wooden cow on wheels which suggested that some craftsman had realised that while cows are good, children pulling them back and forth is far more satisfying.

The oldest extant chess set dates back to the eighth century. Ludo is probably older – it was originally an Indian game called Pachisi and variants on it in India go all the way back to around the time the original Olympics took place, which was 776 BCE. In *The Iliad* Achilles organises funeral games for Patroclus, and in *The Odyssey* Odysseus absolutely batters the Phaeacians at the discus. Just rocks up to their gaff and makes a show of them. Gives it the big one in front of their end.

For as long as there have been people there have been games. Playing. That playing tends towards the sporting variety, and that the sporting variety are often done for an audience is another fascinating element of humanity. It isn't enough just to play, something in some of us wants to watch others do it.

What happened during the pandemic stripped all of that away. It remains one of the greatest oddities of the period. It took play away, the play you see as you go from A to B. It took the rhythms of the year away. The tennis wasn't when the tennis should be. The snooker disappeared. These things, they become comforts, certainties, and they were gone, along with everything else.

There are people who don't like any sport and, while I want to be clear we are not calling them inhumane here, I am just shocked at how they know when anything happened. How on earth do they remember when the exact date of their young brother David's christening is if not for Ray Houghton's header against Everton in the fifth round of the FA Cup?

After all, the ancient Olympics being four years apart became a way some Greek cities measured time. This makes total sense to me, intuitively. The oddest thing about football behind closed doors during the pandemic was how unmoored to time it was, how unmemorable it was. This wasn't solely or even primarily because it was on television, but because the other hooks we arrange the events of our lives on in our own mind had been knocked asunder.

The sport, the play and the events of our lives themselves tangle up. Without the play it felt like lives fell into stasis, and it is why it is striking that it was the moment when Mikel Arteta tested positive that everything changed in this country. The games had to stop, and with it everything stopped.

The games, the playing, is how we work ourselves out in a given moment, how we emote, how we congregate and commune. Even the missed game because of a wedding has a positive capability. We loved our friend enough that we chose her over Wigan Athletic away. It was a close run thing, but Wigan Athletic aren't going anywhere whereas Andrea will probably not have a third marriage. And do you remember when Tony was checking the scores during the service?

For playing, we can take almost anything cultural or communal because they boil down to the same thing: telling ourselves stories about who we are and how we want to exist, to be. There is a lot to be said for the experience of writing and reading a book, but almost all other forms of that process require contact with other humans. Even eSports draws real-life crowds into the thousands; people wanting to watch others play twists in terms of what the game itself may be but remains, at its heart, a communal experience.

None of this is luxurious. Getting to do or watch play at elite level comes with its trappings, but it is what we are, a pure conception of what we can be: dancing animals. But brilliant ones and attracted to seeing and sharing other brilliant ones in action.

Winning the Right to Play

One of the things that happens when you get to write a book like this with good people is that it goes through a process with notes and edits and suggestions. Where and what is the essence of the book? What, precisely, are you trying to achieve? They want the best possible book, which is perfectly understandable. It is, after all, their job, and it is the sort of job you only excel at if it is really a passion.

These people have more experience than me and the very best of intentions. Yet here we are.

Repeatedly when working through the material sent and returned with edits and comments came, 'This is a whole other book.' I didn't entirely agree with that. There is more than one reason why.

Firstly, the era of Klopp at Liverpool had seen him, the fan base and the whole of the club involved in controversy about:

- The women's team being relegated
- The relationship between the game, television and kick-off times
- PGMOL
- The players and their welfare
- UEFA in the context of the European Super League
- UEFA in the context of Paris and supporter welfare
- Ticket prices
- What does or doesn't make a good ownership group
- The Premier League in the context of the pandemic and the fraying of relationships between clubs

- The Premier League in the context of its rules, including but not limited to Manchester City and Everton
- The Premier League in the context of Project Big Picture
- The importance of the game and its leading figures in the national consciousness

Part of the reason why I wanted to write this book is because I find the wider discourse around issues in the game to be frustrating and limiting, and these reached a breaking point during the pandemic and haven't really gone away. This is a book about loving football and everything the game can offer – viewed through the lens of Jürgen Klopp's tenure at Anfield and commemorating that, but also wanting all that for more people and for more aspects of the game. Once, on an early *Anfield Wrap* podcast, I said I defined 'The Liverpool Way' as 'a Scouse boot stamping on the face of humanity for ever'.

What an idiot. What a loser. What a terrible notion. I should be ashamed. And what has made me ashamed of such a notion is the experiences we had under Klopp.

That's the first reason. We live and learn. Under Klopp we got the chance to do both.

The second is that missing from political discourse in Britain (and in most countries these days) is the core 'why' of politics. To make lives better gets some traction, to make lives worth living gets a little less. But ultimately this notion is (or ought to be): to make lives be able to be as brilliant as they can be. To give people every chance of happiness.

The why of football takes up the vast majority of this book. Falling in love with a manager, a team and one another. The incredible days and vibrant nights. The dancefloors. The finding of new places and finding of new selves. This book is just that why over and over because the brilliance of Jürgen Klopp was to understand that that was what we wanted for us all, and what he could give us all – if only we did our bit too.

But books about issues in football always gloss over that why and descend quickly into a how. How it came to this or how it should be. However, in missing that 'why' those arguments become remarkably sterile and often really rather small 'c' conservative and instead find themselves wallowing somewhere, often in an imagined past, occasionally in a theoretical framework but seldom asking what we want, in real lived terms from the game as it is now.

And they are always so very sure.

They should be, I suppose. They have chosen to write a book about it. Their questions and their frameworks never start from pure pleasure, though. And they certainly never end up there.

The third reason is to provoke, like Klopp himself in a press conference on a day of mischief, going down a tangent where he ends up saying this is what he thinks but you may think otherwise. Convinced, but not going to obsess over it. It's good to think.

Fourthly, it's also OK not to be certain. There was something I wanted to do here around fragments and wholes. I wanted to play with the idea of a text which took the emotional prism of the Klopp era and invited the reader (you) to be a live character and be able to choose or recollect adventures; and here I want you to be able to find their/your conclusion, to look in your own mirror, to find your own theory of what you think the game is and who it is truly for. I want you to agree with me because, come on (!), but I'm not going to insist upon it. I'll show you how I got to where I got to, and we can diverge at any time. This is hard to convey, especially while simultaneously writing the sort of massive shout this text revels in over and over again. But I'm backing us. You've come this far; you'll do for me.

Lastly, it simply just isn't 'a whole other book' as far as I am concerned. The reason it isn't is because I don't think it is entirely worthy of that. English football has more than enough money and has more than enough passion and more than enough energy. The answers don't need an enormous slab of text. It's a pamphlet at best, or rather a number of them, and I will write my one but, in my view, one just needs to be selected. But one won't be, because the truth is that English football not only isn't listening, but it doesn't want to; isn't creating but doesn't want to; isn't collaborating but doesn't want to – again, something Klopp said over and over. This begs the question of whether I am wasting your time, which I promised I wouldn't do.

But it's half-time. It's empty time during the pandemic, and it was during this empty time the idea of football looking in the mirror really hit. Let's do this again together. Let's do it better. And turn the well-intentioned doubters into believers. We'll start, though, by not being certain. We'll start with Liverpool Women being relegated, and everything since then.

A Nice Day Out?

At the women's Merseyside derby in October 2023 I felt on the verge of a breakdown at Anfield. I wanted to win desperately. Having been into Melwood in the week, knocked around, interviewed Niamh Fahey, helped publicise the game, having felt part of the process in a way I never am, I was suddenly in Anfield and I was desperate to win.

Those Liverpudlian women were desperate to win. Their record both in the derby and at Anfield is really poor.

Both me and they were debilitated by the moment. They started well. So did I. But the opening goal didn't come and we deteriorated from there.

My desire for a general roar or scream of support couldn't be sated, because it was a markedly different crowd to the usual one, not in my seat, not surrounded by people who know that a volley of abuse at the referee or a ballboy or the lower main stand's lax conduct is just punctuation, just a way of telling the time. Many, many more children. Instead, I just felt self-conscious and developed 16 nervous tics and generally shook back and forth and really sweated despite it being cold.

We got beat 1–0. I haven't entirely got over it at the time of writing.

There was a game in February 2023 when former Everton manager Willie Kirk brought then bottom of the table Leicester City to Prenton Park (where Liverpool Women played their home games until the summer of 2024) and they demonstrated unbelievably negative tactics around timewasting after they got into the lead. I was close to the dugout and rose to hammer Kirk with a string of gratuitous abuse when they took it to the corner flag on about 72 minutes. I was going to use all the worst words as much as humanly possible. I mean, we're trying to grow the game here. I rose and started and realised the horrified eyes on me. I shrank back down.

This, though, strikes at the heart of the problem. We're trying to grow the game here. I was especially appalled with Kirk because of that. He's trying to win a football match at all costs; being a good manager. Time-wasting is part of football. He's doing his job in that moment. Leicester didn't want to get relegated; they needed the points. They were deadly serious. But this voice is also in my head: 'We're trying to grow the game here. We want people to come and keep coming.'

This is one of the key conflicts around the women's game. It's elite sport. So it's serious, serious business. I want to win. I believe in the winning as part of the playing. But you run into this wall, which is also annoyingly made up of so many of my own mostly toxic behaviours around that energy.

When Liverpool Women were relegated during the pandemic, through a points per game calculation, there was a lot of criticism of the club – and the club deserved it. But at *The Anfield Wrap* we tried not to join in because we hadn't been good enough either. We hadn't given the women's game the focus we had in earlier years. We'd taken our eye off the ball. You can't criticise Liverpool Football Club if you can't look in the mirror when contemplating your own choices.

So we committed as much as we could. We got to games when the football came back, albeit in the odd but privileged position of it being behind closed doors. Rachel Furness became my third or fourth favourite player because she attacked everything – don't tell me she wasn't deadly serious: she was hewn from iron.

You could hear the players screaming at each other, see what a draw against Liverpool meant to Durham, be overwhelmed by a cup win against Manchester United. It was magic, despite the ground being empty. John Gibbons heckling then England manager Phil Neville. Philippa Smallwood having a pop at the linos from the press box. I genuinely look back on it fondly despite the results just falling short.

Every draft, every plan of this book has got me further away from writing about the women's team. This is sort of my last stand, my desire to at least have something in here at all costs, because the women's game has been part of the overall journey, and this is at least a bit of a memoir. The women's team is the only way we really work with Liverpool FC. We've a good relationship with many people at the club, in general, despite a few peaks and troughs, and I'm pleased with that, but the most meaningful way in which we work with the club is definitely around the women's team, in terms of how to help grow the audience for the games and awareness for the players through interviews and shows.

But it's hard. It's hard to fit the women in. It's harder to find a partner or sponsor for the work, and not just our work but that of others, and even the teams' themselves at times, despite all the fanfare about the money flowing into the game. It's hard to even just get to the games, because so many of the kick-off times have clashed with the men's, which means the work will get lost even if we can make it work, which we often can't.

It's what's struck me with the book, seeing the number of words written grow and seeing how it will hang together and being aware that writing about the women is going to seem odd, askew, even in a collection of mostly oddball nonsense. And that makes me feel I am falling short. There is not a key game during this period which is about Liverpool Women. I just needed to be honest about that. There is the work on Liverpool, and the work on Liverpool Women. I think this should not be the case. I think.

There's a core issue which has become clear across the time since the pandemic, since doing the work, asking the questions, doing the thinking, and that issue is this: many of the hardcore, match-going Liverpool support are going to find it difficult to support the women too. A key part of the reason why Liverpool and Manchester United supporters find engaging with the England men's team difficult is the time, cost, practical, physical and mental toll it takes supporting enormous clubs, which play so many massive games and have done for years. There are other reasons – political, aesthetic, having a supporter base of complex national mix – but a truth, not the only truth or even the biggest one, is that: you only have so much to give.

The same is true of support transposing itself onto the women's team. By support, I mean actual support. The active verb. Getting to a game when you can. Watching the matches when they are on. Not just checking the results from time to time. It ought not to be that hard, and it verges on offensive to our Liverpudlian women footballers and supporters to cast it as such, but I understand it. This is my job, and in doing my job the purest moments are the shirts on the grass. I really don't care who is in the shirts when Leicester or Everton shirts need vanquishing and I am in the ground watching it. Fucking into these.

But the idea of getting to Prenton Park or getting to the Totally Wicked Stadium on a Sunday when you just got back from Aston Villa to watch the men on a Saturday night, and you need to spend some time with your partner, is hard even for me at times. Takes some explaining. And this is my job. I don't think anyone should feel guilty about this.

A lot of those 'thinks' and 'don't thinks' aren't me stylising my opinion. They are 'I *think* I want the arrabbiata', 'I *don't think* I fancy dessert' and pulling a face. You know: genuinely unsure.

One of the striking things about the current movements and crisis in football (and I have listened to many a panel now) is how rarely women's football gets anything more than a cursory mention. 'Yes, yes,' they say. 'We need to do something about the women's game.'

The historical context of the women's game in Britain matters but rarely gets an airing because it is so deeply miserable. The women's game was effectively made illegal in this country in 1921. That lasted for 50 years. What restarted in 1971 didn't take the women's game back to 1921 but to 1861. Only now does its timeline approach 1921. Bear that in mind. Don't be a prick. I'm sick of it.

I'll be honest: I have been guilty of the same quasi-ignorance as those panels I mention, and I apologise for that staggering hypocrisy. You can read it in this chapter. Yes, yes, we need a bit about the women's game. Yes, yes.

The Totally Wicked Stadium. In the summer of 2024 Liverpool announced an agreement that they will play the next ten years of women's football at the St Helens Rugby League Club's ground, which is heavily sponsored by a vaping company. The Totally Wicked name was conspicuous by its absence from all the club press releases but try to google the ground without mentioning it and see what you get. It's one hell of a branding job.

As is Liverpool Football Club in all its ways, and it is difficult to imagine the men's team near a vaping company, if we are all honest.

There is the unspecified desire to get more women's games at Anfield. This will be good, though hopefully no derbies, as I may snap. The number is unspecified because it sort of has to be; there are so many variables, and they will always tilt in the direction of the men's team.

The direction of the women's team is good: in 2023–24 they finished fourth and won some big games. The direction for the whole game is good. The *Carney Review* into the future of the women's game could have done with a little more flesh on its bones, but is fundamentally strong and its intentions were to build a long overdue skeleton. The question of the flesh is where it touches the whole game: pitch provision at grassroots level, corporate and on-pitch dominance by big clubs at the highest level. Elsewhere the question is begged: precisely where is the space in calendars, stadia and TV schedules to show and encourage attendance to the game, with all its other tensions?

And this is it: you always run into the wall. Or, more accurately, Kate Manne's electrified fence, which somehow seems to get tighter as the women's game itself gets deeper and denser. Every step in the right direction suggests more barbed wire to come. It's our aforementioned eyeballs, the attention, and then it's the idea that the game is constantly on trial, constantly having to prove itself: a massive game of snakes and ladders, and the snakes keep moving. I mean, we're trying to grow the game here, which means just playing it may not be enough. Men have all the money, all the power and all the time(s).

Looking in the mirror and falling short; looking at the plan of a book and falling short; looking at the Anfield turf about to explode and drench six-year-olds in expletives and fury – i.e. falling short.

Women in football are there, yes. But do our actions really, in truth, show that men want them to be? Do we reveal ourselves to be unable to change? Which of us would really pay a price to share with women some of the cultural power and strength of the men's game? If we try to answer that question honestly we see how far away we are from the PR and the rhetoric. This is not a counsel of despair. It is a counsel to look truth in the face.

Take a medal if you think you deserve one.

Television Is Not the Enemy

If you are reading this book I am prepared to gamble that of the football you watch, somewhere between the majority of it and the vast majority of it is watched on television.

It's a question of simple mathematics and behaviours. I am lucky enough to go to every Liverpool game at Anfield every season, and somewhere between ten and twenty games away from Anfield depending on progression in cups, and so on. There is a quiet irony that my job makes away games hard from time to time: I need to either ensure I can do some form of a show on the road and get it transferred back quickly – which can be tough given the ongoing war on bags – or ensure we have cover back home to sort it.

Let's stick with me as an example. Let's say Liverpool are the half-twelve on Saturday at Anfield and Manchester City are playing Brighton and Hove Albion in the half-five. Away. I reckon I am still out in town to watch the half-five with mates. Then the next day Everton are playing at two and Manchester United at half-four. I reckon I am watching at least one of them, one way or another. Already the majority of the football I watch on a given weekend is on television. Manchester City match-going supporters may have watched us in the half-twelve or may watch United the day after. We all may have watched *Match of the Day* on Saturday night if we've won – which is, by the way, where the majority of people who watch football watch the majority of the football they watch.

My point is that there isn't a clear delineation between people who watch football in the ground and people who watch football on television. Some people may loudly proclaim they only watch their team, which is fine but isn't inherently admirable. If it has to have any value judgement placed on it – and it doesn't – if anything, it's a bit ignorant. Don't you want to know how other sides are playing? What they are up to in their approach to the game?

Furthermore, the majority of people who care about a football club in this country, most weekends don't watch any football in person. Away allocations are very low as a percentage of capacity: how many tickets could Liverpool sell for away games in London, in Manchester, *anywhere*? It would be in excess of five figures almost every time, but Liverpool tend to only get around 3,000 allocated in most grounds. To be clear, therefore, only 3,000(ish) Liverpool supporters can legally watch their side in 2024 in the United Kingdom when they play away in a 3 p.m. kick-off or at an unscreened midweek game.

As a position it doesn't feel particularly philosophically sustainable, and yet it is the third rail of televised football in this country. All discussions of the professional game in 2024 need to understand that television is a massive part of it: for those administering, playing and watching the game. This doesn't mean that match-going supporters aren't important, and it doesn't mean that match-going supporters should be ripped off or inconvenienced. Indeed, if anything, it means the opposite: in the Premier League and the EFL the crowd and the fan culture is part of the global offer. But match-going supporters are not separate from the viewing public. They are a key part of the viewing public.

For Klopp, at times television was the enemy. He hated the Saturday 12:30 slot, and hated the frequency with which Liverpool got it. What never seemed to have been explained to him was that Liverpool, as the country's biggest European draw, and the 12:30 kick-off was controlled by the network on which the European football would be shown. Did we have hard lines with it? Yes. Was/is it a cost of being Liverpool? Unfortunately, yes. Klopp's was a sporting gripe, and one which was unique to Liverpool, as the disproportionate selection of Liverpool's games for that slot showed.

However, the Saturday-3-p.m.-versus-television-as-the-enemy trope has taken on a life of its own and become an avatar for change in the game being negative – along with any change in the FA Cup, VAR and, in the fullness of time, PSR regulation. Every kick-off move comes with complaint regardless of its merits, and every ill in the game, whether actual or perceived, will end up being thrown at television's door.

What absolute nonsense the gilded impression of Saturday 3 p.m. is. The handwringing around it. The notion that something about football is lost if a game doesn't kick off at 3 p.m. on a Saturday. That it means something deeper and more significant. Three p.m. kick-offs are sacrosanct, enshrined in law to protect the noble game and the noble time from the ignoble broadcast.

I don't particularly like Saturday 3 p.m. as a kick-off time. It allows you to neither stick nor twist. A laid-back post-match interlude knocks your Saturday night off course. It's now 7 p.m., you're five post-match pints to the good and whatever you were doing that night now seems a long way off. Saturday half-twelve is great if you win. Go hard and heavy from 11, or ease into the ground terrifyingly sober, but then the afternoon opens up. So much room, so many choices. Saturday half-five, wowzer! Town. Match. Town. Dancing. The best. I doff my cap to the half-five. I quietly reckon half-six might be better again, give you more afternoon to play with, but, whatever. Sunday half-four: you can build a weekend towards that. Creates an event.

But, listen, it's personal preference. I could be wrong, or, more accurately, you may rank the options differently. It's not so much the idea that Saturday 3 p.m. is dreadful, but that it should be sacrosanct, that it is the perfect time and, further, that a kick-off time is worth going to the mattresses for. Ticket prices, access questions, safe standing, policing, stewarding – Christ! – being able to take a bag in – even the actual price of the games on television themselves . . . Forget all that and focus solely on the when. 'What about the tradition? How have we let money men come in here and make me have more fun and enjoy three games on a Saturday which pertain to Liverpool's season rather than just one, like the good old days?'

Saturday 3 p.m. exists and holds sway because of the way working patterns used to be: people worked Saturdays and got a half-day off from time to time, and football, as an entertainment, something for people who work to go to to take their mind off things, scheduled itself accordingly. Three o'clock on a Saturday was perfect. Get on The Kop, they play the top Top Ten (they don't don't do that any more, which is a greater blow for traditionalism), have a sing and a dance, watch the game and then off you go into town, have a night on the ale. Enjoy. Be entertained.

But collective working patterns don't happen like that any more. They aren't as homogenous. A huge number of people still have to work Saturdays, and many of them work in the sort of industries where you don't have a lot of job security or money. For some people a Monday night may be the perfect time to go to a game.

It is instead this idea that the game has to work around one type of person – his memories, his nostalgia and his wants and needs – and you can very easily draw a picture of him. He's quick to join organisations and fast where surveys are concerned.

And then, because humans are humans, what it then often equates to is an argument that television isn't real. That it is a false experience and nowhere near the holy grail of experiences, a pale imitation. Of course it is different, but saying to a whole swathe of supporters that the main way they can share an experience with you is just a false simulacrum is wholly unnecessary and wrong. It goes against the essence of the collective and the essence of what being in the ground is. The eleven represent us all. The ground or the end represents this feeling of whatever 'us' is – and then there is the wider us, the greater us. Being there is a privilege. Never forget it, and certainly never act superior about it and act as if it should cater to our every whim.

Not least because it is important to remember we watch the majority of our football on television ourselves, and in order to do this other people need to perhaps be inconvenienced, but then I may need to be occasionally inconvenienced too. That's OK – I don't have to go to every match if it doesn't work for me. The world will continue to turn.

The biggest issues football has from the point of view of those going through the turnstile are to do with price and accessibility and availability for all. The price and difficulty of being in the ground. That and the impact it has in terms of people being priced out is by far the biggest problem the game faces. It's television and shifted kick-off times which can help save us with that. Let's win the next argument rather than chunnering on things aren't what they used to be, not least when they are actually better in so many ways.

We don't get many Saturday 3 p.m.'s any more. Good. Because we don't get tickets for twenty quid either, and I know which one I want sorting first, and I know where the money is coming from to perhaps help sort that – if we have the right argument.

Principles for a Different Kind of Blueprint

Before getting stuck into the principles themselves, let's tackle two tough acknowledgements.

1) Acknowledging the Realities

The Premier League Has Been and Remains Successful on its Own Merits

Saying 'this is the best league in the world' has become something easily derided, but it was gratifying when Jürgen Klopp said as much in one of his final press conferences when musing upon why no English side had made any European finals in 2024, and only Aston Villa made a semi-final. The quality through the division has improved markedly during Klopp's time at Liverpool, and is now visible by the sheer brilliance sides who finish mid-table have across the pitch. It is the place everyone wants to coach. The money has been very cannily invested in playing staff and facilities over the past ten years.

The money the league makes is massive. We can (and will) argue it should be shared differently, but that money is a signifier of its success. Sport is a leisure activity people pay to watch either in person or via a screen. The Premier League is a successful version of that by that metric. Not acknowledging its quality, its popularity with people who play, coach and watch the game, and its financial success is petulant.

Furthemore, its internal financial split of TV revenue is, by the standards of its peers, quite egalitarian. It is worth pointing out though that it is less egalitarian than the NFL which splits fees evenly.

The Premier League is a TV Product First and Foremost

This is the truth. The Premier League is not alone in this. Formula One is a TV product first and foremost. So is golf. So is snooker. So is cricket. So is basketball. So is kabaddi. (Go and check kabaddi's viewing figures.) The sports that tend not to be TV products first and foremost get their high point of exposure through the Olympics, where all those sports are bandied together for a period and people enjoy them and then probably don't go and see them in person or watch them on a screen again until the next Olympics. That's fine.

You can say you would like there to be less money in the Premier League – and that's an argument in its way – but removing its lustre as a TV product would mean removing money from the game at the exact moment lots of branches of the game could do with more. You can argue you'd like television to work closer with supporters around kick-off times. You can argue you'd like better trains, but the reality is: if you actively support a Premier League club, what we do is televised to the world.

Unless There are Remarkable Circumstances We're Not Changing Who Owns the Football Clubs Without the Clubs Being Happy to Do So

That stable door was open and the horse ran out. Premier League administrators come over like a terrible crew in almost any public appearance since 1992, but I have some sympathy with the current crop in terms of what they inherited and its direction of travel.

State-controlled football teams are in existence, and without their consent it would be a practical nightmare to change the current situation. Processes can be designed to stop there being any more state-backed purchases. Similarly, who runs the clubs and the parameters they run in can be changed too. But the owners, including Liverpool's, are the owners. You can argue it could have been better to have never allowed overseas controlling ownerships, but such a notion probably never occurred to Richard Scudamore.

2. Acknowledging My Biases

Football is a Liverpudlian Export Industry

This is my biggest bias and I make no bones about it. 'It means more.' That slogan was much mocked when it was Liverpool's marketing slogan, but in many senses I believe it does. That it makes people cringe, I understand (I have had this argument with people who actually work for Liverpool). I don't believe Liverpool's away end celebrates last-minute winners more than Nottingham Forest's does. But I do think that football is far more of a day-to-day force and economic driver in Liverpool than it is in Nottingham. I do think that Liverpool's last-minute winner locally, nationally and globally is of far bigger consequence. Football creates more jobs, and could create more were the circumstances right. Football gets Liverpool bigger hotel provision. Football gets Liverpool Taylor Swift. And football literally pays my bills in a way that it wouldn't if I were doing all this about Luton Town.

In terms of how that hits a discussion here, it is worth saying that if LFCTV were able to screen Saturday 3 p.m. kick-offs as part of their subscriber offer then that would lead to at least 50 media jobs, predominantly for young people either from Liverpool or those choosing to study in the region. The same could be said for Manchester or Newcastle. Such thinking never enters into any conversation when we discuss football and the media – what is lost out on without even being acknowledged in 2024.

Bigger Club

I support a big club. All of this is about supporting a big club, a club that wins: a club that doesn't finish below eighth. This cannot and should not be forgotten. Experiences become different, on the whole, but the flipside of that is that I speak to a lot of people who don't support big clubs due to the work I do with *The Anfield Wrap*. My favourite weekend of the season, both in terms of work and sheer enjoyment, is the third round of the FA Cup. Doing the build-up shows is amazing, and the thing everyone wants is the adventure. It's like talking to people in the queue for Nemesis at Alton Towers.

Liverpool are Rationally and Broadly Well Run – But That Hasn't Always Been the Case

Given all the controversies Liverpool's ownership have been at the centre of, this doesn't feel possible, but, in terms of the core task of running Liverpool, Fenway Sports Group have been calmly successful. The previous lot had us flirting with administration over a three-year slow burn: we saw what it was to be unstable and to entertain being unsustainable. Across the park at Everton, all that, and the chaos it can cause, has been fully apparent.

Our guiding principle, then, is taking what there is now, the reality of it, looking at the likely shape of what is to come and placing as much sheer enjoyment at the heart of it as possible. Football is a leisure activity. Playing, spectating. It is meant to be, more than anything, something that makes the soul soar and something which constantly provides hope and excitement.

But you can't have a soul soaring if you are constantly worried. Worried about owners. Worried about relegation and the attendant impact. Worried about going out of business. We need to remember that. The joy of football needs to be able to resist malign forces and sustain inevitable defeat. Everyone has to get beat at some point, but nothing should ever be terminal, and hope should always be around the corner.

Football is for everyone. No ifs. No buts. Its playing, its spectating, its discussion, its coaching, its administration shouldn't ever close any door. It's a spiralling game with enormous cultures attached to it, and those cultures need to be open and will only strengthen by being open. The adventures of football should be open to everyone too.

The core principles we will view potential change through are:

- The why of football (which comprises the vast majority of this book): to give people every chance of happiness.
- Every club needs to be sustainable, which means sustainability is an interconnected framework throughout the pyramid and beyond.
- Because winning is incredible, it has to happen, which means we need to make it OK to lose.
- Hope must spring eternal – the adventure is everything.
- The best possible English football, which has to include the best possible Premier League.

The game belongs to everyone. Which means the money has to continue to flow, but has to be made to work better.

A Blueprint

English football reached a point of crisis during the pandemic; it was a crisis that would always have happened, but Covid arguably brought forward the point where clubs outside the Premier League came to be in financial meltdown and the clubs inside the Premier League could no longer co-exist. That further intensified on a Sunday night in April 2021 with the announcement of plans for a breakaway European Super League. Klopp's Liverpool had a game against Leeds United on the Monday, which became a bit of a circus. After the game the manager said, 'I cannot say a lot more about it because we were not involved in any processes – not the players, not me – we didn't know about it.' This has always struck me as the key issue with all the grand plans: the clubs never even spoke about them internally, let alone consulted any of the key stakeholders – from key leaders in the field, like Klopp, right the way along to the fans.

In this moment that still has ramifications for how football views itself, let's start turning our principles into suggested courses of action.

'Every club needs to be sustainable, which means sustainability is an interconnected framework throughout the pyramid and beyond.' The fallout from the Super League controversy led to the *Crouch Review*, which in turn led to the Football Governance Bill. If we want to imagine a future for football which is engaged with the game as it is now, that government bill (scrapped due to the General Election of 2024 but confirmed as returning in July 2024's King's Speech) is a good starting point.

The bill proposed promoting the sustainability of the game by creating an independent regulator to grant licences to owners and officers of clubs in order to bring about real-time financial transparency and information flow to supporters, all the while protecting aspects of football's club culture.

One of the most striking things about the bill is that, for the first time, football clubs will be defined in English law. Football grounds and football supporters are enshrined in law, but clubs themselves aren't. What this does make clear is that football clubs are not the same as other businesses. Different rules apply. We should soon be able to say that with certainty because it will be there, in law.

The biggest danger of the *Crouch Report* and Football Governance Bill is that the establishment of an independent regulator for the game will be seen as the end of the matter. It won't be: an independent regulator cannot start to delve into competition rules and structures – and it is within those rules and structures where the future game can be made genuinely sustainable on its own merits.

The PSR (Profit and Sustainability Rules) controversy that intensified post 2022 with the docking of points, most recently for Everton and Nottingham Forest (both for breaching the threshold of allowable loss) is striking because, for years, there were grumbling complaints that FFP (Financial Fair Play, PSR's predecessor) had proven toothless. The distinction between the two is a little more than semantic, but that semantic difference matters: 'fair play' was always a misnomer in both practice and intent; 'sustainability' on the other hand is a clearer aim. It isn't always going to be 'fair', but the stated desired outcome is clearer.

Transparency is an important starting point, but should not be the end point. Other than during occasional appearances at Select Committee hearings – which have tended to reflect badly on everyone involved, not least the showboating MPs – and in broadsheet interviews that appear very curated, Premier League figures won't go public to put the Premier League's case on matters around PSR and beyond because of a desire to allow panels to appear to be independent, to try to remain above the fray. There is public silence and private wrangling. It dissolves trust.

The Premier League *is* the clubs. It is important to remember that, but it appears that the clubs would be better served to agree some general principles and then devolve responsibility to a commissioner's office led by one individual able to be a public face and explain decisions and choices both publicly and privately for a set period of time, thus removing the need for the clubs to vote on everything bar the very biggest, existential decisions.

That commissioner's office should work beyond the responsibilities the clubs will have after the Football Governance Act is passed – around the fitness of their officers and ability to demonstrate ongoing sustainability – and also be able to look into matters that pertain to everything public: PSR rules and punishments, scheduling discrepancies, refereeing questions, ticket price guidelines, signing off on club sponsorship agreements and any other rule changes.

Further, the commissioner's office should have a counterpart in the women's game and the two should work closely together to forge a set of principles to allow resources – primarily space but also money – for the women's professional game to grow and similarly be made sustainable over time with additional investment from the collective.

The frequent gripe around PSR now is that the owner should be free to spend his/her/their money as they please as long as they can afford it and can demonstrate they're not imperilling their club. But football is an ecosystem and we have seen repeatedly – Jack Walker, Roman Abramovich, Sheikh Mansour – what happens when that ecosystem gets disrupted. Furthermore, the Premier League is now so dominant within the whole of world football's ecosystem that we always need to bear in mind that changes made in this country will be felt across the continent in the medium term and globally in the long term. This is also a reason not to just turn the taps off or add any additional levies on English club transfers. Clubs across the continent end up benefiting from Premier League largesse.

Any proposed sustainability rules beyond legislation should not just protect clubs on an individual basis but protect every bit of sustainability right down the pyramid and across the women's professional game too. The punishments for breaking them should be more onerous and will need to taper right down the pyramid through the EFL: deductions should be mandatory and transparent all through the game. It looks likely at the time of writing the Premier League will replace that calculation with one closer to UEFA's sporting costs as a percentage of turnover model. Wherever it ends up, an agreed scale of punishments should be made clear prior to any breach.

Everyone would know where they stand.

The commitments to the women's game also need to be seen through and made public – any failure to do so should lead to mandatory punishment. If clubs won't make commitments to the development of the women's game at professional or grassroots level they should have to state precisely why.

What did we say? 'Every club needs to be sustainable, which means sustainability is an interconnected framework throughout the pyramid and beyond.' That has been sketched out. The more interesting changes I'd argue for concern how radical structural reform can release clubs from excessive fear of losing and offer constant resurgent hope – and brilliant adventures.

By the time the 2026 World Cup kicks off more years will have passed from the start of the Premier League and the Champions League than between 1992 and Bill Shankly walking through the gates at Anfield. The game doesn't look forward; it hangs onto scraps of its past while seeing money men pick off its future. We're looking to find a way forward that satisfies all of our principles (which include our acknowledgements of reality). Jürgen himself said that 'change is good' when he left Liverpool.

To square this circle from here everything needs to be considered holistically – we are now in thought-experiment territory. The above is perfectly able to just occur if the will is present, but from here we need the reimagining. It's the difficult part of re-envisaging how the game *could* work. What appear to be small tweaks would have massive consequences for clubs; but what appear to be massive changes would, in real terms, not impact the future for any club were the game as a whole to be bold.

Too much of English football is complacent in every single way:

there is always some hand-wringing when a club like Bury hits the wall, but, equally, very little action to bring about any financial redistribution. Furthermore, there is little actual exploration about ways to make the football better, to protect the footballers more, to increase and intensify the spectacle. What could it look like if we wanted to break the mould while protecting the clubs right down to the base of the pyramid? Many supporters are too desperate to hang onto the status quo up to and including simply having ongoing community vehicles. Mid-table Premier League sides don't want to risk touching the goose that has laid it so many eggs. The very best sides simply eye UEFA and FIFA riches and are charmed by the dangling of a carrot of things like a 39th game played abroad. It's led to inertia, an inability to wonder how it could be better, more exciting but more secure for everyone.

Along with the 20 clubs who actually make up the Premier League, at any given moment there are around 15 clubs in the country that still now (or did until very recently) view themselves as Premier League clubs; at any given moment at least 20 clubs outside the Premier League have big grounds and big fan bases. There is a massive issue with parachute payments – what they do and will continue to do. There is an enormous cliff face on either side of the Championship. In short, while the enormously wealthy Premier League is the problem, the hugely popular Championship is the graveyard of hope. Wages-to-turnover is out of control and has been for some time, while the Premier League is just at the top of that mountain.

It's time those cliff edges disappeared.

Similarly, the Premier League holds too much of the money: currently around 92 per cent of all TV money that English football generates. And what it redistributes down the pyramid it does so in a way that, because of the parachute payment system, massively benefits erstwhile Premier League clubs. What I'd argue is that it's time for a shift to a Premier League 1 and a Premier League 2, made up of two divisions of 16, with three divisions of 20 below. A potential new league structure would look something like:

Five-division pyramid: 92 clubs in total

Premier League 1 = 16 clubs
Premier League 2 = 16 clubs
Championship = 20 clubs
League 1 = 20 clubs
League 2 = 20 clubs

That would, in one stroke – if the existing money covered 32 teams rather than 20 – remove the cliff edges before even wondering about further redistribution. We will do more, though. The Premier League 1 and Premier League 2 format could be structured along the lines of:

- 30 matches per team per season in each division (15 home, 15 away).
- An additional ten matches to be played at neutral venues between the five sides who finish first to fifth in Premier League 1 to decide the final standings and confirm Champions League and Europa League qualification; in short, each team plays four additional matches. Points won from these additional four matches per side are added to the totals already amassed over the course of the normal season to decide the final placings. This isn't a playoff but instead simply four more games per side. So if a side starts these games with 66 points and wins three and draws one they end with 76 points. The league table gets updated with the results of the additional four games.
- In the same way, an additional ten matches to be played at neutral venues between the five sides who finish between 12th and 16th in PL1 to decide relegation, similarly with the points added to the final totals. Sides who finish in the bottom five cannot finish any higher than 12th, but the bottom three go down.
- In Premier League 2 the top two come up automatically, with third to sixth playing off as happens now in the

Championship, but with the playoffs taking place in neutral venues as one-off games. The bottom five in PL2 get relegated every season. Keeps it fresh and keeps the money circulating.

- The neutral venues for all games at the end of the season should have capacities greater than 60,000. Attendance for these games should guarantee 45 per cent of tickets to be sold by each club in each match, leaving only 10 per cent for the league and venue to distribute. Let's get atmospheres bouncing here and create events.
- All of these matches leave each side finishing first and fifth and 12th and 16th in PL1, having played 34 games.

Imagine those big games at the top and bottom of the table. What this does across the two Premier League divisions is remove the idea of the mid-table game played out at the end of the season; right through both divisions games should have a lot riding on them. The additional games themselves should be completely imbued with meaning, and being at neutral stadia would have the feeling of 23 rollicking cup semi-finals. They'd be the hottest ticket in town, and a worldwide television audience would flock to them. Having suffered the Michael Thomas moment in 1989 it is worth pointing out that the sheer vitality of that is part of what made the Premier League seem viable. This structure offers the chance of that sort of drama every season, while also adding another layer of sporting trial.

The idea of end-of-season games at the bottom of the table scares the life out of people – not least my editor – but this is the reason all this is meant to be holistic: relegation shouldn't mean the end of the world (and we will get to redistributing the money better soon), it should just mean new teams to play next year.

Leagues aren't handed down on pillars of stone by God. We're here to enjoy them and not just our own side – remember we watch the majority of our football on television.

Additional games at the foot of the table do sound terrifying: imagine you'd scraped 13th and there was more to do. But everyone goes into any season knowing the rules. The current Championship reality is that you can finish third and not go up. But those games are events that everyone watches at both ends of the table. We're in it for the drama. The Championship and leagues beneath should be five up and five down. Keep shaking it up, keep adding the drama.

There should also be hope, though. Hope of silverware and hope of European adventures. The FA Cup, competed for by every side in the country, would lead to a Europa League spot. The League Cup should only be contested by sides outside Premier League 1, with the winner receiving a Europa Conference League place. This would offer more chance of success to more clubs and also reassert the FA Cup as the primary cup competition, while adding the potential of Europe for more sides; you'd expect a new side to qualify every season. The EFL Trophy winner would be the recipient of a Europa Conference place (after negotiations with UEFA and the removal of Premier League under-21 clubs). For too long in England European football has been the preserve of only the biggest clubs. The idea of a different side every year from across the EFL getting a European place would be genuinely romantic and genuinely egalitarian. All the bigger leagues should look to do this.

The major thing we haven't actually addressed here, though – during all the drama and massive games with loads riding on them – is player welfare. It was a constant refrain of Jürgen Klopp's. At one point he compared it to climate change: 'When I start talking about it, I get really angry . . . It is like with the climate. We all know it has to change, but nobody is saying what we have to do. There must be one meeting where they all talk to each other and the only subject should be the most important part of this game: the players.'

Reducing the number of games per club in the top two divisions would protect the Premier League as a brand while maintaining the idea that it's the place to play your football. But the end-of-season games would mean there were an additional four massive clashes in big stadiums like Wembley for the players, the match-going supporters and the worldwide audience. Putting the players first would be a selling point to players from around the world.

But there's more that could be done around the schedule, having reduced the load. We've talked about the tours, about being Champions of Everywhere. Getting to go out and see supporters from across the world is great. Going to see your team abroad is great. And, endlessly, there is debate about playing games abroad. A Premier League cup played abroad every four years in August in an odd-numbered year, between 32 teams in a World Cup group with a last 16 format, would end a lot of debate and offer a lot of adventures for supporters here, be great again for the Premier League globally and, frankly, make more money. The room would be there due to the curtailed domestic season – down from 38 league games to 34 as a maximum.

The winner would be awarded a Champions League place the following season. (Of course, there would need to be controls on ticket prices for this because, well, have you met the Premier League?)

The reason this has to be holistic is that all of the above should come at a cost to Premier League clubs. Parachute payments should be scrapped in full. The two 16-club leagues could take a split of 86 per cent of TV revenues to the 60 clubs sharing 14 per cent. While a shift to 86–14 doesn't seem like it would make that much difference to the sides lower down the pyramid, in fact, the club that currently finishes 80th and receives around £1.35 million TV share would find they'd be in receipt of approaching £5 million if you worked it on 80 per cent equal share and 20 per cent merit in Leagues One and Two – almost quadruple their current sum by virtue of shifting what Leagues One and Two get, from about 1 per cent of the total pot to just a bit over 3 per cent, and eradicating parachute payments.

The Premier League currently splits revenue on season merit (i.e. league finish), facilities fees (i.e. how often teams are screened and grounds are used) and straight share (i.e. a split of the rest of the money). They should move to season merit, straight share and three-year merit (i.e. the performance of sides in the two Premier League divisions across the previous three seasons). That'd see most sides of the current 20 take a haircut of around £20 to £30 million a season depending on how you balance it, but sides that currently finish from 21st to 32nd in the pyramid would be far better off, while the gap between club 32 and club 33 would be about £12 million rather than the £95 million between 20th and 21st. No more cliff faces, and previous good performance would soften the blow due to the three-season merit payment.

The clubs that play in UEFA or FIFA competitions should be compelled to give 7.5 per cent of their UEFA/FIFA TV revenues to grassroots development. They are part of the pyramid, and what is good for them should be good for the game. This frees up the idea of removing the Community Shield, but Wembley would still get plenty of use with our neutral venue games.

What else? We'd need a weekly game on free-to-air television, and once in every eight weeks the terrestrial channel should get first pick – but they should also have to promote the networks with the paid games on.

Premier League ticket prices – both general sale and season tickets – would be brought down across a four-year period. For stadia over 50,000 capacity: year one (general sale, maximum price) would be as before. Year two would be £50 per ticket; year three, £40; year four and holding, £30. For stadia under 50,000 capacity year four would be fixed at £40 to avoid a competitive disadvantage. These figures could be adjusted for inflation at seven-year intervals, but rounded down.

Have we hit our remaining principles? 'Because winning is incredible it has to happen, which means we need to make it OK to lose.' Relegation would hurt. Failing to get promoted would hurt. But the idea it is a disaster that needs a massive parachute has gone. Prize money should be set in the Premier League so that 13th in PL1 would receive the same share and merit payment as fourth place in PL2. And then there could be a League Cup to win the following season too.

'Hope must spring eternal, the adventure is everything.' Everyone would have the chance of starting an adventure every season that led to the holy grail of European football; and removing the B-teams from the EFL Trophy would means more pleasure in that competition.

'The game belongs to everyone. Which means the money has to continue to flow, but has to be made to work better.' The free-to-air television and the reduction of ticket prices helps here. More flow of money into grassroots helps. The obligations to the women's game help. Is it perfect? I'd say not; you can always do more. But it is better.

'The best possible English football, which has to include the best possible Premier League.' This protects the players, keeps the Premier League clubs as the richest in the world, and opens up new potential income streams with the best run-in in the world. There are fewer games in general, but fewer games which have nothing riding on them, so the spectacle remains.

'The why of football (which comprises the vast majority of this book): to give people every chance of happiness.' Compromise is needed, something needs to give, but this offers the chance for so many seasons up and down the league to be exciting.

Can something like this really happen? The issue is always the holistic: it needs the lot, no cherry-picking; no liking in principle the end-of-season games then saying, 'Let's keep the 20-team league and play four games abroad that decide the top of the pile.' Because that's what happens when ideas are untethered from principles. For years it has been clear that more televised games should lead to cheaper tickets, and yet it hasn't. Getting very rich people to agree to share a little has proven to be a lot to ask through centuries.

But the wider point here is that fighting over the small stuff just means continuing to win some and lose some – the drift will be in the same direction. Finding a big push and pull, though, could change that direction. It will need bold moves to satisfy everyone, but the status quo appears to have undermined everyone's confidence. Clubs stepping back and running their own smart consultation process in the aftermath of the *Crouch Review* is what ought to have happened but, instead, egos and posturing came to the fore. It's time for that to stop; some combination of complacency, greed and holding onto the past have killed many a goose that has laid many a golden egg, and the Premier League and English football in a wider sense has all three in abundance.

Second Half

Timeline

14 August 2021	Norwich City 0 Liverpool 3. A capacity crowd at Carrow Road looks on at the return of Premier League football in front of crowds. I wasn't there. I had Covid.
19 August 2021	Jürgen Klopp does a recorded interview with Kop Outs's Paul Amann to address homophobic chanting. Klopp says, 'I'm not sure if people listen to me, but it would be nice. I don't want to hear it any more for so many reasons. Obviously we live in a time where we learn a lot in the moment. I'm 54 now, and when I was 20 we said so many things which we didn't think about and meanwhile, thank God, 34 years later we learn it's just not right to say, even when you didn't think what other people think is behind the message.' Klopp adds, 'I think it's easy – it's easy to decide [upon] not singing the song any more. Obviously, meanwhile, I heard it. It's from no perspective the nicest song in the world, so it's not necessary. It obviously makes people uncomfortable of our own fan group. For our supporters' group and for me, that means: done, let's go for another one.' People pretty much listened to him and people pretty much went for another one.
12 September 2021	Leeds United 0 Liverpool 3. While Harvey Elliott is down injured a small but audible number of the Leeds supporters begin to sing that '96 was not enough'; it had long been well over 96 but this, now, was legally as well as practically untrue and morally abhorrent.

3 October 2021	Liverpool 2 Manchester City 2. Manchester City dominate the first half, Liverpool the second. Mo Salah scores one of the greatest goals of his career to make it 2–1. He picks the ball up in the inside-right channel outside the box and befuddles five Manchester City defenders, leaving three on the floor in his wake before rifling it home. It is a big-game moment from a big-game player. It is Salah, in all his glory. Sadly Kevin De Bruyne's deflected effort evens the score. Liverpool unbeaten in seven from the start of the season. Great game. Two dropped.
15 October 2021	Conservative and Unionist Party MP David Amess is murdered by an Islamic extremist.
16 October 2021	Watford 0 Liverpool 5. Mo Salah scores the same goal again.
24 October 2021	Manchester United 0 Liverpool 5. Liverpool dismantle Manchester United at Old Trafford. The lead is four by the break. These events lead to Manchester United supporters funnelling out on the hour mark, and more Manchester United Football Club chat on the television than anyone can handle.
7 November 2021	West Ham United 3 Liverpool 2. First defeat of the season.
24 November 2021	The *Crouch Report* is published.
4 December 2021	Wolverhampton Wanderers 0 Liverpool 1. Liverpool have dominated the second half. The goal hasn't come. Diogo Jota has missed an open goal against his former club. The clock hits 94, Virgil van Dijk sends it 70 yards to Mo Salah. Salah surges and squares, and there is Divock Origi to turn and finish, and the elongated Liverpudlian contingent in Molineux loses its collective mind. Origi's massive moments-to-goals ratio is off the charts. He isn't finished yet.

19 December 2021	Tottenham Hotspur 2 Liverpool 2. Covid has hit the Liverpool camp. The season was always on this sort of knife edge and there have been legitimate concerns, league-wide, that there may need to be a pause. Liverpool won't win another game until 9 January 2022 and by that date will be 11 points off league leaders Manchester City.
2 January 2022	*Anne*, the drama about Hillsborough campaigner Anne Williams, written by Kevin Sampson and starring Maxine Peake, is screened on ITV. Precisely what ITV is brilliant at.
20 January 2022	Arsenal 0 Liverpool 2. A Diogo Jota brace sends Liverpool to the League Cup final.
30 January 2022	Luis Díaz signs for Liverpool.
16 February 2022	Inter Milan 0 Liverpool 2. An excellent win in the Champions League last 16 first leg means Liverpool will progress to the last eight.
24 February 2022	Russia launches a military invasion of Ukraine in a steep escalation of the Russo–Ukrainian War.
27 February 2022	Liverpool 0 Chelsea 0. Liverpool win on penalties through Caoimhín Kelleher's winning penalty and substitute goalkeeper Kepa's missed effort. Your correspondent went through all stages of penalties that won't end: pen nine: 'COME ON, LIVERPOOL.' Pen 16: 'Will anyone just miss? We've all got homes to go to.' Pen 21: 'COME ON, LIVERPOOL. FUCKING HELL, WE NEED TO WIN THIS.' Anyway, Virgil van Dijk also scored the best penalty anyone ever scored, and in so doing broke Kepa's brain.
3 March 2022	The UK announces sanctions against Alisher Usmanov.
10 March 2022	The UK announces sanctions against Roman Abramovich.

16 March 2022	Arsenal 0 Liverpool 2. Two early second-half goals mean Liverpool have won nine consecutive games and cut Manchester City's lead to just one point.
5 April 2022	Benfica 1 Liverpool 3. An excellent win in the Champions League last eight first leg means Liverpool will progress to the last four.
10 April 2022	Manchester City 2 Liverpool 2. Liverpool snatch a point after being dominated first half by Manchester City. The second half is more open but Liverpool can't find their way home.
16 April 2022	Liverpool 3 Manchester City 2. FA Cup tie. Three first-half goals and total Liverpool dominance take the tie away from Manchester City.
19 April 2022	Liverpool 4 Manchester United 0. Thiago bossed them.
24 April 2022	Liverpool 2 Everton 0. A valiant rearguard action from relegation-threatened Everton falls to Andy Robertson on 62 and Divock Origi on 85. It would be Divock Origi's last goal for Liverpool. Origi scored 41 goals for Liverpool: 32 in second halves; 15 in the last 15 minutes of games. Six came against Everton.
27 April 2022	Liverpool 2 Villarreal 0. Liverpool will progress to their third Champions League final of Jürgen Klopp's tenure. They will face Real Madrid.
14 May 2022	Liverpool 0 Chelsea 0. Liverpool win on penalties. They were the better side over 90 minutes and ought to have won in normal time. Kostas Tsimikas joins Alan Kennedy in the left-backs-who-have-won-penalty-shootouts-for-Liverpool category.
22 May 2022	Liverpool 3 Wolves 1. Needing to win, and Manchester City to fail at home to Aston Villa, Liverpool are level at 1–1 with 15 to go. Manchester City are 0–2 down. Mo Salah thinks he scores the goal that wins Liverpool the league. But City have made it 3–2 and they will be crowned champions.

28 May 2022	Liverpool 0 Real Madrid 1. The fan park was brilliant, their keeper was man of the match, UEFA nearly killed loads of us and lied about us before the delayed kick-off. Coming out was horrendous. Nothing has changed. Also Sadio Mané's last appearance for Liverpool.
14 June 2022	Darwin Núñez signs for Liverpool.
23 June 2022	*The Bear* premieres on American television. It is something exceptionally difficult to pigeonhole but is one of the finest realisations of the fact that ordinary people are capable of extraordinary things. A hymn to humanity.
7 July 2022	Boris Johnson resigns as Prime Minister.
29 July 2022	*Renaissance* by Beyoncé is released. It is enormous.
30 July 2022	Liverpool 3 Manchester City 1. Liverpool win the Community Shield in a great game between clearly the two best teams in the country, full of the usual *joie de vivre* we see in this fixture. Darwin Núñez seals the deal. This will be as good as it gets.
22 August 2022	Manchester United 2 Liverpool 1. Liverpool have won none of their first three league games and deserved to win none of them.
31 August 2022	Liverpool 2 Newcastle United 1. Fábio Carvalho scores a 98th-minute winner at Anfield. It feels like normal service has been resumed. It hasn't.
6 September 2022	Liz Truss becomes Prime Minister.
7 September 2022	Napoli 4 Liverpool 1. Napoli are brilliant. We are terrible.
8 September 2022	The Queen dies. The nation loses its mind, nobody wants to end up on the front pages, and national anthem discourse is on the horizon.

1 October 2022	Liverpool 3 Brighton and Hove Albion 3. Brighton go 0–2 ahead, Liverpool get it back to 3–2 with a barely celebrated own goal to edge into the lead. Finishes 3–3. Post match, Ben Johnson on our show says Liverpool look poorly coached, and it is hard to argue with the facts.
16 October 2022	Liverpool 1 Manchester City 0. Are you messing? You can't trust football.
20 October 2022	Liz Truss resigns as Prime Minister. The Turner Prize exhibition opens in Tate Liverpool. Veronica Ryan goes on to win it.
25 October 2022	Rishi Sunak becomes Prime Minister.
29 October 2022	Liverpool 1 Leeds United 2. First defeat in front of humans in the league since April 2017 and Liverpool get what they deserve.
8 December 2022	*A Spy Among Friends*, starring Damian Lewis and Guy Pearce and directed by Nick Murphy, is released on ITVX. It is the day that ITVX is launched. Quality television of scope being free to air has never been more important or more of a challenge.
10 December 2022	Grant Wahl passes away in Qatar. Not dissimilar to SOPHIE, in that the sadness comes because while there was so much brilliant stuff done, there was so much brilliant work to come. His writing always won the right to play and then played brilliantly, with love and care and the sheer conviction this thing of ours is for everyone.
26 December 2022	Aston Villa 1 Liverpool 3. First league game back after the World Cup in Qatar. We look all right.
30 December 2022	Liverpool 2 Leicester City 1. We're not all right. We're dreadful. Two Wout Faes own goals give us a victory but we are ruining the fun of beating Leicester now.
3 January 2023	Cody Gakpo signs for Liverpool.
14 January 2023	Brighton and Hove Albion 3 Liverpool 0. The Nadir.

4 February 2023	Wolverhampton Wanderers 3 Liverpool 0. The Nadir, no, really.
6 February 2023	The Premier League announces charges against Manchester City of breaching the rules on more than 100 occasions over a period spanning 2009 to 2018. Charges Manchester City strongly deny.
13 February 2023	Liverpool 2 Everton 0. The *UEFA Independent Panel Review Report* is released into the final, offering Liverpool supporters absolute vindication around the conduct of their behaviour and reaction to horrendous organisation. In short, a terrible situation would have been a lot worse if not for the Liverpool contingent. Having this confirmed is more important than winning Merseyside derbies.
21 February 2023	Liverpool 2 Real Madrid 5. Liverpool go 2–0 up and then lose their minds.
5 March 2023	Liverpool 7 Manchester United 0. Liverpool, in this season of all seasons, inflict the joint biggest ever defeat on Manchester United in their whole history. Roberto Firmino makes it seven having confirmed he will leave Liverpool at the end of the season.
11 March 2023	Bournemouth 1 Liverpool 0. Grow up, Liverpool.
24 March 2023	*False Lankum* by Lankum is released. It's a tremendous album and the best iteration to date of Lankum's ability to take from the past, respect it but update it, creating something vital through the process. What was gives way to what is and helps the now fly rather than tethering it by the neck.
9 April 2023	Liverpool 2 Arsenal 2. Having been battered at the Etihad and terrible at Stamford Bridge, Liverpool go two down to Arsenal before the team and Anfield decide collectively that we are mad as hell and we are not going to take it any more. Liverpool then batter Arsenal, should win, get the draw and go on to win the next seven. But it isn't enough to get Champions League Qualification.
6 May 2023	Coronation of King Charles III.

13 May 2023	Final of the Eurovision Song Contest in Liverpool.
20 May 2023	Liverpool 1 Aston Villa 1. Roberto Firmino's, Naby Keïta's, Alex Oxlade-Chamberlain's and James Milner's last home games. And so too, it would prove, for Jordan Henderson and Fabinho.
8 June 2023	Alexis Mac Allister signs for Liverpool.
2 July 2023	Dominik Szoboszlai signs for Liverpool.
8 August 2023	*Prophet* by Helen Macdonald and Sin Blaché is published.
18 August 2023	Wataro Endō signs for Liverpool.
27 August 2023	Newcastle United 1 Liverpool 2. Virgil van Dijk gets sent off. Anthony Gordon gives Newcastle the lead. But Liverpool hang in and Darwin Núñez scores two from the bench to give Liverpool the win, seven points from nine and make crystal clear Liverpool aren't in this season to make up the numbers.
1 September 2023	Ryan Gravenberch signs for Liverpool.
30 September 2023	Tottenham Hotspur 2 Liverpool 1. Curtis Jones gets sent off on 26 minutes. On 34 Luis Díaz scores for Liverpool but is flagged offside. The VAR consult and say it is a goal but the wrong information is relayed to the referee. Two minutes later Son Heung-Min scores for Tottenham. Cody Gakpo equalises on the stroke of half-time. Diogo Jota gets his second yellow on 69. Liverpool are still trying to win the game on 90 despite being down to nine. It takes a 96th-minute Joël Matip own goal to settle the contest. Good process, boys.
23 December 2023	Liverpool 1 Arsenal 1. Liverpool start poorly and concede first, a pattern in this season. They then should take the game away from an excellent Arsenal side between 45 minutes and 70. The air comes out of the balloon when the excellent Trent Alexander-Arnold hits the bar when he should score.

1 January 2024	Liverpool 4 Newcastle United 2. A genuinely spectacular attacking display from The Reds, similar to Liverpool 5 Nottingham Forest 0 in 1988. But Mo Salah is about to go to AFCON.
26 January 2024	Liverpool release a video of Jürgen Klopp confirming his intention to leave the club at the end of the season. It is the top story in the country.
21 February 2024	Liverpool 4 Luton Town 1. This shouldn't be here but yet it has to be. An incredible night to be part of. But Liverpool should always be three goals better than Luton.
25 February 2024	Liverpool 1 Chelsea 0 (aet). Liverpool – decimated by injuries – win the Carabao Cup with Virgil van Dijk's injury-time header. Bobby Clark, Jayden Danns and James McConnell, with fewer than ten starts between them, all finish the game for Liverpool.
2 March 2024	Nottingham Forest 0 Liverpool 1. The 99th minute and Liverpool need a win. Mac Allister hangs it up and there is Darwin Núñez to nod home and send Liverpool into delirium. It is Liverpool's latest-ever winner and keeps them top of the pile.
10 March 2024	Liverpool 1 Manchester City 1. The last of the best games you have seen.
18 March 2024	The Football Governance Bill is introduced in Parliament.
7 April 2024	Manchester United 2 Liverpool 2. Liverpool have 18 shots first half at Old Trafford and conspire to get beat 2–2. They have given way in the title race.
11 April 2024	Liverpool 0 Atalanta 3. Jürgen Klopp's final European game at Anfield ends in an emphatic defeat.
12 April 2024	'The von dutch remix with skream and benga' is released by Charli XCX as part of the brilliant rollout of *Brat*. It is important not to get carried away but it could be the best piece of pop music since 'You Keep Me Hangin' On' by The Supremes. *'Cult classic. Still pop.'*

14 April 2024	Liverpool 0 Crystal Palace 1. Arsenal 0 Aston Villa 2. Liverpool and Arsenal give way to Manchester City and suddenly Liverpool are snookered.
18 April 2024	New agreement between the Premier League and the FA announced which removes replays from the competition proper, shifts the fifth and sixth rounds to clear weekends while moving the final to the second to last weekend of the season and sees the Premier League offer £33 million more a year to the grassroots game. No one appears to have spoken to the EFL or an EFL club about it.
24 April 2024	Everton 2 Liverpool 0. You have to take your medicine. Everton get the three points they richly deserve.
13 May 2024	Aston Villa 3 Liverpool 3. Jürgen Klopp's last away game is a frankly bloody stupid affair but Jürgen is acclaimed throughout and is clearly moved afterwards.
19 May 2024	Liverpool 2 Wolverhampton Wanderers 0. Jürgen's last match in charge of The Reds. The crowd is on its feet for the last ten minutes singing his song on repeat. He doesn't cry. He chants the name of his successor, Arne Slot.
	He says, 'People told me that I turned them from a doubter into a believer. That's not true. Believing is an active act, you have to do it yourself. I just said, "Do it yourself," and you did it, that's a big difference.' He says, 'I saw a lot of people crying, and it will happen to me tonight as well because I will miss people, that's clear. But, as well, change is good and just you never know exactly what to expect, but if you go with the right attitude into that, everything will be fine, because the basics are 100 per cent there.' He says, 'I'm one of you now. I love you to bits. Thank you for that. You are the best people in the world. Thank you.'
20 May 2024	Liverpool announce Arne Slot as the next head coach.

Key Game 10
Manchester United 0 Liverpool 5
24 October 2021

You pick your key games and then realise there is only one against Manchester United. If you'd have told 2012 me that 2024 me would be writing a book about Liverpool and there would barely be a mention of Manchester United, he would never have believed you. But the fact is: they just haven't been relevant. What Klopp has done by being the one man prepared to aggressively chase Manchester City down is leave United in our rear-view mirror.

I've tried. You can make an argument around the 7–0 home win of 2023 because it equals their all-time record defeat, including when they were Newton Heath. It's important to think about that: their joint heaviest-ever defeat. Two of the other three 7–0 defeats took place when Stanley Baldwin was Prime Minister. However, if anything, that fact actually makes me annoyed referee Andy Madley didn't give a nailed-on last-minute penalty for a rash challenge by Luke Shaw out of human decency. It's always worth surpassing a Baldwin. Stanley, Mike, Alec.

You can make a stronger argument about including the 2–1 defeat in March 2018 when the whole of our end celebrated that Liverpool team, leaving the Mancunians bemused as they packed ten men behind the ball and hung on for dear life. 'Aren't we winning?' 'Well, this one 90-minute battle, yes. But the war, that is moving our way. We can see it. Can't you?' I'd even considered the 2–0 in the Europa League in 2016 at Anfield, but Dortmund somewhat steals its thunder. Because even then Manchester United, even in 2016, they were weirdly ceasing to be our business.

But I settled for this one. Part of the reason why is the context of it being the first big win – the first big away win – after we were all allowed to be together. The other reason why is that one of the best things about being brilliant across these seasons was the realisation that sides would quickly cease to be your business apart from when you played them, and when Liverpool played Manchester United on 24 October 2021 they ceased to be our business by half-time, as we were 0–4 up, and instead became Manchester United Football Club, and emphatically their own business.

In the list of things that just don't happen, in the list of football miracles, being 0–4 up against Manchester United at Old Trafford at half-time is pretty high. In a way, the 0–4 at half-time is more damning than the 7–0 final whistle in 2023. You could kid yourself that just gets out of hand, and you can tell yourself, 'Anfield.'

For years Manchester United were competing for the biggest honours when we weren't. But not once did they come to Anfield and score four goals in a half. Not once did they come to Anfield and make a show of us – the one time they threatened it, we got out with a 3–3 draw. That isn't to say they didn't win, or to say they weren't better. It's just to say they were humiliated around the world in the biggest game in club football by Jürgen Klopp's Liverpool.

By Mo Salah's Liverpool.

Salah's attitude to Manchester United has been consistently wonderful. He's treated them with absolute contempt and scored goal after goal against them, received a series of bookings for taking his top off and, on this day, on this occasion, he bagged a hat-trick yet came off frustrated because Liverpool stopped playing. They just stopped. Chose to stop. Because they could. For Mo this was inconceivable. There were more goals to score, there was more embarrassment to inflict, more world stage to strut on.

The Salah of this period could well be the greatest one. He played his best football, scored his best goals, scored as heavily as he did (with the exception of his first season) in the first half of 2021–22. He was in his element, at one with his teammates, and unplayable.

In a number of ways Salah is perceived to be quite inscrutable. The smile, the hair, the fact he doesn't do many interviews – and when he does he seems especially thoughtful and careful with his words. His unorthodox agent. Even his faith, and its public nature, gives him an air of difference to other players.

But the truth of the matter isn't that he is inscrutable through his actions. Instead, look at all those actions and find simplicity. For me, it's that he is very straightforward. He loves playing for Liverpool. He loves scoring goals for Liverpool. He loves seeing the chaos he causes. He loves being Liverpool's Mo Salah, and nothing in his professional life has ever given him more joy. He loves his teammates. He loves training. He loved signing a new contract for Liverpool, and had even had jokes in the video.

It's hard being Mo Salah. Your world-stage identity is constantly up for grabs. You are one of the world's most famous Arabs and Muslims, which too many in the West see as the same thing when they very much aren't. You are the world's most famous Egyptian in a post-Arab Spring world. You are African. You are a very public father of daughters.

But when he pulls our shirt on he is Liverpudlian, with all that that entails. We love him, we loved him quickly, and we won't stop. Because he scores all the goals, all the different type of goals, and because we see beyond all the reasons he needs to be careful, and we see the man delighted to play for the team we are lucky to watch.

Even when he shows his faith and his humility after he scores for Liverpool, I love it when he turns back to us and gives it one more, gives it a little bit of 'get on me', as the other thing about Mo Salah the Liverpudlian is we've watched him grow from a lad in his mid-twenties who fancied himself to a man in his early thirties who knows he's incredible.

The year before we had gone away, been separated, we hadn't been there to be with him and this whole period, 2021–22, felt like him making up for lost time. Jürgen Klopp's team needed a crowd, but so too did its maestro and that is what we got that October day.

Mo Salah loves beating Manchester United because he is one of us, and he gets to show that to the world when we play them – and he gets to show it to us too.

They walked out when he made it five. Walked out because the show was over, the humiliation complete, their cameo in this book done and dusted. Jürgen Klopp had delighted Kenny Dalglish and destroyed Alex Ferguson. At the point this game ended there was no overriding sense that Liverpool could be 45 minutes from a title by May. Optimism abounded – how couldn't it? – but the magic of 2021–22 was that there was always just about to be another gift, another moment to cherish. There was the satisfaction of this job being done, of them not being our business, of them being so far away from us, and the sheer visceral delight that we went to their place and made that crystal clear. It was a gift to the Liverpool-supporting world. In a way, it was the follow-on from those scenes of celebration and defiance in March 2018 when we lost. We knew then that this was us, this right here. We knew that day they wouldn't really be our business for a good long while.

That October night, town was staggering. Every pub had people spilling out of it. As I have said before, I don't have many photographs of me at the match, but I do have videos. That night we made a video in Pogue Mahone's. Me, Fuad Hasan and everyone I could get my hands on. We did it as a live thing, with the backing of a directional microphone we loved. Fuad shot our Jürgen documentary 12 months later. He is very good at rolling with the punches, and this was something I just wanted to do, something I could just imagine.

It looks like an advert with a half-a-million pound budget. An advert for a pub, perhaps. An advert for a beer, maybe. It was meant to be an advert for a podcast. But, ultimately, it looks like an advert for being alive, for being part of something shinier than you are and it making you shinier still. It looks like an advert for visceral living, an advert for the promise of the greatest night out of your life. It is, in many ways, in one quick capsule form, the purest gift of what it all has been.

It looks like being back, knowing you've been away, but finding your way back: to the greatest little boozer and to 'Sally MacLennane'.

Man kann nicht auf allen Hochzeiten gleichzeitig tanzen

When Liverpool were still in three competitions, as the winter of 2022 began to turn to spring, Jürgen Klopp made reference to a German phrase in one of his press conferences: '*Man kann nicht auf allen Hochzeiten gleichzeitig tanzen.*' 'You can't dance at all the weddings at the same time.' In my head this became 'dance on too many dance-floors', which is the same thing but neater.

There is a reason no one has ever done the quadruple. Essentially, it boils down to one of these two: a) you need to be perfect and lucky; b) it is impossible. Because no side can be that perfect and that lucky.

In recent years, in different ways, both Liverpool and Manchester City have come close – Liverpool closest in 2022 when a change in two results, or perhaps only 50 minutes of football, would have awarded them a staggering achievement. In 1999 Manchester United did the treble but lost in the quarter-final of the League Cup to the eventual winners Tottenham Hotspur.

There is a very clear hierarchy in terms of how competitions are viewed in English football. The Premier League and the Champions League are the big two. In general, the game is making its peace with other forms of European football as being good, not least because of the sheer unbridled fun West Ham United and Aston Villa have had recently. Then there is the FA Cup, the primary purpose of which is to make everyone mad that the world has changed since their 11th birthday. Lastly, there is the Carabao Cup, which has become this fabulous tyke of a cup, a Wednesday night out which you enter into knowing it may just be a quick one or an evening which may get out of hand – and before you know it it's shooters at 1.15 a.m. despite (or perhaps because of) work in the morning.

The way sides prioritise the cup competitions is a source of constant ire and debate. Some feel the bigger sides take the early rounds too lightly. Others feel they take them too seriously – it's the league and the Champions League that should be the priority. But this stretches down the division and even into the EFL now. The nature of football is that few league games can be written off: in January everyone has something to play for. Even if that is nothing to play for.

My view for Liverpool is very much that the league and the Champions League should be the priority. I am in camp two. But, increasingly, I am in neither camp, out of sheer pragmatism: there is no longer any need for camps because of the reality of the way football now is. The sheer pragmatism thing is that sides that play European football build squads capable of playing European football and Premier League football at the same time. Therefore, those sides have somewhere between 16 and 25 brilliant and/or multi-functional players. And they are increasingly experienced. A key reason Manchester City make the late stages of domestic cups is that they have brilliant players used to doing it. It has become part of the rhythm. What that means in practice is that the bigger clubs progress, unless they meet a top ten Premier League club, probably away.

The old-school idea that a Premier League side doesn't like it up 'em has simply disappeared (for the most part). In 2023–24 Newcastle went to Sunderland and physically dominated them. Newcastle are an extreme example, but the Premier League is a remarkably intense league: game after game, on top of all the technical ability. Throughout his time at Liverpool Klopp's principles around the domestic cups demonstrated such thinking. He had no interest in seeing a side embarrassed in the early stages of a cup; he wouldn't send a Liverpool side out that he didn't think could compete – but he also used those games as opportunities to rest, rotate and, crucially, get some game time into his squad players. He wasn't desperate to win but was comfortable picking a team he thought would. We could see that from his selections against Everton in January 2019, when he was comfortable to trust Adam Lallana to bring it home, and the difference in his selections from Arsenal away and Norwich City at home in 2024 when he started ten who looked first XI(ish) against Arsenal in the third round but was prepared to have a look at 18-year-old James McConnell in the fourth round.

As Liverpool's squad improved under his tenure this meant in practice that Liverpool were likelier to progress. The 2021–22 squad was probably the greatest Liverpool FC have ever had: by the February Liverpool's sixth- and seventh-choice forward options were Takumi Minamino and Divock Origi, the former very good, the latter a strong candidate for greatest living Liverpudlian. Liverpool's reality shifted, and they began to be in a position where they were going to get invited to a load of weddings.

A pattern became clear:

2015–16: lose the Carabao Cup final to Man City; lose in an
    FA Cup fourth-round replay to West Ham United away.
2016–17: lose in the Carabao Cup semi-final (over two legs) to
    Southampton.
2017–18: lose in the Carabao Cup third round to Leicester City
    away.
2018–19: lose in the Carabao Cup third round to Chelsea at
    Anfield; lose to Wolves in the FA Cup third round away.
2019–20: lose in the FA Cup fifth round away at Chelsea.
2020–21: can't remember. Who knows? Not even written down
    anywhere.
2021–22: Win both domestic cups. Nearly get embarrassed
    against Leicester in the Carabao quarter-final; play Norwich a
    lot.
2022–23: lose in the Carabao Cup fourth round to Man City
    away; lose to Brighton in the FA Cup fourth round away.
2023–24: win the Carabao Cup; lose to Manchester United
    away in the FA Cup.

There are four oddities in terms of Klopp's behaviour and the outcome. The first two are the fourth-round FA Cup games at Anfield in 2017 and 2018 (the former against Wolves, the latter against West Bromwich Albion). Wolves were a side about to finish 15th in the Championship (they won the Championship the following season, after a takeover) and Liverpool went really weak and walked into one trying to save it from the bench. In 2018 Liverpool went so strong against West Brom you wouldn't believe it. Sadio Mané, Roberto Firmino and Mo Salah all started, as did Virgil van Dijk. It was the first game at Anfield with VAR, and it was an absolute mess. I watched it in a nightclub in Dublin without sound and on a projector where the score was outside the projected image. We didn't know what the score was for long stretches, and Liverpool didn't seem to either. It was a mess. The other two already discussed oddities are Liverpool's games against Aston Villa and Shrewsbury Town in 2019–20 when they were weakened to the point of a youth team. Villa whacked them; Shrewsbury remains one of the all-time great nights of our lives.

Because in 2021–22 and, to a lesser extent, 2023–24, Liverpool were involved in all the cup competitions, the suspicion was that something had changed. Liverpool were trying to dance at too many weddings. They risked the big two for the lot and lost them both. This could be reasonable – after all, we don't get to see the road not travelled. They did have to play three more Carabao Cup games and one more FA Cup game than Manchester City in 2021–22, and in 2023–24 Arsenal definitely benefited from losing away at West Ham in the fourth round of the Carabao Cup and to Liverpool in the third round of the FA Cup.

It is worth emphasising that Mikel Arteta treated those two games exactly as Klopp would have done, picking nine of his ten outfield starters against Liverpool and rotating good squad players in against West Ham.

This kills the debate – if you are Liverpool, Manchester City or Arsenal, or indeed any of the sides in the top eight. Unless you send a youth team out to be whacked, as Liverpool did against Aston Villa in 2019, unless you overlook squad players who aren't getting starts in league games and go one rung down (which for squad harmony you shouldn't and can't), you are almost certainly going to progress until you hit a good side away. Your camp in the debate no longer matters.

You can also think more than one thing at once. The Carabao Cup wins against Chelsea in 2022 and 2024 are among my favourite ever days supporting Liverpool. They were incredible – 2022 because we never got to be in a ground in 2020 for the league, and 2024 . . . well, read on.

But I would give them both up for a 10 per cent greater chance of having won a 20th title under Klopp. Being in those moments in that stadium, watching Virgil van Dijk dance to The Real Thing with a trophy in 2022 or hugging Sky Sports's Harriet Prior as she sobbed uncontrollably in 2024 (Virg and H – the big two) are such special memories. However, one more title would have meant days of dancing to The Real Thing and weeks of sobbing.

So, no: you can't dance at all the weddings at the same time.

Not all weddings are created equal.

But, done right, all weddings are good and special and all weddings should be danced at. And, most of all: there are people/Evertonians who would give limbs to be invited to half as many weddings.

Key Game 11
Liverpool 3 Leicester City 3 (League Cup)
22 December 2021

So come on. Have you had the best night out of your life yet? Is it to come? What about when it sneaks up on you?

This night, this rambunctious night against Leicester City, should have been one you get through, one where you don't really care, one which comes out the other side one way or another and is easily forgotten or its redundancy celebrated.

There are a few games I remember fondly while Klopp was manager because they didn't feel like your life depended on them. The 5–5 League Cup game against Arsenal in 2019, or the AC Milan away dead rubber in 2021, or the Community Shield against Manchester City in 2022. Games you got to enjoy like they were just sport. Like going to the cricket. A lovely day had by all, and everyone acquitted themselves well.

This was supposed to be one of them – leaving aside the fact it felt dreadfully timed, a League Cup quarter-final with Christmas on the horizon, with a to-do list long as your arm, a hectic footballing run, a life up the wall, and all with the addition of a pandemic banging on.

Liverpool picked a team which suggested they just wanted it out of the way. But a struggling Leicester picked a strong team. They picked a Jamie Vardy team, and Vardy had a ball around Billy Koumetio, a brace in the bag by the 13th minute. Liverpool kept giving it away cheaply and suffered, carrying too many vulnerabilities. The whole right side couldn't cope and the stress test was too much.

But Roberto Firmino and Alex Oxlade-Chamberlain were not to be cowed, and both remained bright and linked up well. When Liverpool grabbed that one back you just began to wonder.

A James Maddison drive ten minutes before half-time made it 1–3 though, and took the wind out of any and all sails. There was a sudden concern we were going to be made a show of on our own pitch, and the atmosphere shifted from this being a nice one to get out of the way and say 'Merry Christmas' to one another to being one where we just weren't standing for it. Their end helped matters enormously, with their poverty chanting. So deeply, needlessly obnoxious you went from being interested in a nice evening to idle away the time to feeling the whole thing deep in your gut.

The manager made three half-time substitutions. Ibrahima Konaté, Diogo Jota and James Milner who all, in their own way, weren't going to stand for this shit. You can build houses on James Milner. Build eras on James Milner. And, in a way, Jürgen Klopp did. On this night, you built a comeback on him.

They weakened as we strengthened but, weirdly, unexpectedly, during the game which was meant to be just got through, we suddenly needed more than wanted, and wanted for all time. We wanted the story, the adventure. Naby Keïta strutted on and was the best version of his inconsistent self. Joe Gomez was yet again present and correct when required, and the temperature went up and Ibrahima Konaté made Jamie Vardy an absolute irrelevance. Liverpool were the better side and first to everything. Leicester were bemused and wasting time and feigning injury. They didn't want to know. Liverpool wanted to know. Liverpool wanted the whole kit and caboodle, and suddenly Diogo Jota scored a very Diogo Jota-like goal, full of shark-like instinct – fin visible – and suddenly this was the best night out of my life. Anfield became bedlam, became pandemonium, because of loads of good reasons and also a dollop of fuck everybody, and now Leicester were neither here nor there, and, my God, have you ever seen 6,000 people bottle it at once?

The truth became that eternal one: this is 2–3 on 88 and they go. The ball dropped to Takumi Minamino and he grabbed his most glorious Anfield moment, his endless attacking tidiness leading to the messiest explosion. He forced it home from 20 yards and the comeback was complete. Penalties were immediate, and despite Minamino missing one Liverpool got through eventually via Diogo Jota. Jota then told their end to fuck off because it was that sort of night and it was fantastic to see. 'Feed the Scousers'? We'll water our glorious golden crops with your tears.

We bounced out of Anfield. Bounced into our evenings, into Christmas. It was the sweetest kiss on the forehead, the hand on the arm, the glint in the eye, the shake of the hips, the bite of the lips.

It was a night when you remembered how you can just get carried away, and getting carried away is the best way to travel, especially from a standing start.

The National Anthem

The worst thing about getting to a load of domestic cup finals wasn't the idea of dancing at too many weddings but, rather, the amount of national anthem discourse that it created.

And the Queen died. Which meant that, unless there had been a violent overthrow of the existing political system, there was also going to be a coronation. Which, in turn, meant more airing of the national anthem, and an even more febrile atmosphere for national anthem discourse.

Liverpool supporters booed the national anthem at the FA Cup final in 2022 and it was front-page news in the *Mail on Sunday*. The speaker of the House of Commons, the endlessly pompous Lindsay Hoyle, decided to stick his oar in and get stuck into Liverpool supporters in conjunction with the *Mail*. Liverpool had sung over the national anthem in the 2022 Carabao Cup final in February with 'You'll Never Walk Alone'. Liverpool supporters had disrupted the national anthem consistently through previous decades.

It should never have been front-page news. It was as dog bites man as it can get. But this was Britain, in the time of Jürgen Klopp, where every year got madder, where someone or some group needed to be privy to a bloodletting by someone like Lindsay Hoyle every Sunday – but also a Britain where they put Klopp last, at the end of the radio news, because his was a rare, public, rational, optimistic voice in the nation. And on this, when pushed, Klopp said of Liverpool fans: 'They wouldn't do it if there was not a reason.'

The reasons are many. It's not about one thing. Let's run through a non-exhaustive list:

- It's political and social and cultural, and a thing that happens at the connection of those things.
- It's about Irishness and the historic anti-Catholicism of the establishment.
- It's about Hillsborough and being told you are the enemy within.
- It's about being failed by the state because you are seen as the problem and never the answer.
- It's about class.
- It's about geography.
- It's a simple act of identity and it's about us, and if that's not you or not for you, well, OK, but you don't get to tell us who we are or who we get to be.
- It is defiance.
- It is sometimes light-hearted.
- It is sometimes from the heart.

And it is about our space. Football's space. The choice of playing the anthem is one which makes the space theirs. The choice to play the anthem is the first political act. And the choice to disrupt it is the second political act.

There are endless political acts at football. Any large gathering of people is inherently politically charged. Remembrance Sunday being commemorated is political. It's a political action everyone is broadly all right about, but it is a political action, regardless.

Part of the key point, the key pushback across the last however many years, is that Liverpool and places like it – i.e. English cities – have had a lot done to them. Not done with them, not done with their consent, but done to them. Something had flipped by the time of the coronation of the new king. It was a strange time, one of forced bonhomie across the whole of the country that seemed to clash with lived realities. There was pressure to conform everywhere, but people seemed to have begun to have had enough. Liverpool FC were put under pressure to play the anthem prior to the game against Brentford on the day of the coronation at 5.30 p.m. and released a statement that read, in part: 'Before kick-off and in recognition of the Premier League's request to mark the coronation, players and officials will congregate around the centre-circle when the national anthem will be played. It is, of course, a personal choice how those at Anfield on Saturday mark this occasion and we know some supporters have strong views on it.'

When it was played there was an emphatic rejection from the Anfield crowd – and the national reaction to that wasn't overtly critical. It felt like, instead, there was the idea: 'At least somebody said something.' The alternative view on the coronation, albeit the minority one, had been given so little airtime it needed something like Anfield spontaneously making its point in a way which couldn't be muzzled.

Ultimately, I don't like the notion of 'Scouse Not English'. That isn't because I don't think Liverpool is different from the rest of England, but precisely because I think it is. Merseyside has a lot to offer the rest of the country, and it would be good if it would listen too from time to time. Though I do think it has begun to listen, on a cultural level, due to there being more unmediated interactions with the place.

Similarly, Merseyside doesn't get to pretend it isn't part of the rest of the country, isn't subject to its politics, and shouldn't wilfully turn itself away. Only by making common cause with Essex or with Southampton, only by listening and seeing their similarities to us do we manage to make positive change collectively – and we need collective change.

They need to hear more of us, and we need to have the humility to speak to them. Weirdly, that day against Brentford, I think they heard. I think they heard this bit most of all: it's a simple act of identity, and it's about us, and if that's not you or not for you, well, OK, but you don't get to tell us who we are or who we get to be.

I think we, in that maelstrom of what passed for coronation fever, got to speak for some of them. Stop trying to force that palaver down our necks. Real life matters more. And this is our space so we get to decide.

Key Game 12
Arsenal 0 Liverpool 2

16 March 2022

In the teeming rain in north London Liverpool were scratching around as half-time approached. Nil–nil, and they weren't quite value for it. On 62 minutes Roberto Firmino made it 0–2 and Liverpool would cruise from there. After the game, Jürgen Klopp was asked what was said at half-time: 'We reminded them that they enjoy it when it's hard.'

It defined that team, that squad, that season. In one sentence it defined Liverpool, the city and the entire worldwide notion of Liverpool. And it defines Klopp.

We reminded them that they enjoy it when it's hard.

With Klopp it was nine years of having to take the high road, or nine years of choosing to take the high road when there was choice – or, instead, nine years of getting stuck into the high road comically, like Sideshow Bob stepping on rakes.

It's who Klopp is. For all the smiles, the hugs, the one-liners, the tactical insight and the charisma, he is a grafter. When in doubt, you work. You work for the people around you. You put one foot in front of the other. And that's who we are.

Christ, it was hard that day. Arsenal were good – you could see the trajectory they were on. Martin Odegaard was, for 45 minutes, an absolute nuisance; the stadium made a racket when it could be heard over the rain; and Mikel Arteta had them well organised.

But the rain wouldn't stop, and the rain blew directly into our end. It remains the wettest I've ever been at a football match – including when playing. Plenty of our end gathered from row 18 back but, along with Steve Graves, I stood relentlessly on row 5 because you couldn't get any wetter, so why step back?

Another thing that happened for nine years was the manager talking about weather and people being annoyed by it. It's striking that even as much as mentioning one of the biggest variables in a football match is deemed to be making excuses. The weather matters. If it is windy, it matters. If it rains heavily, it matters. If it is hot, it matters. In England it is often two of those things. Walk on through . . .

The rain was relentless and Liverpool had clambered up the mountain: they had been 14 points behind Manchester City and, since beating Arsenal in the League Cup semi-final second leg in January, had played twice as many games as the Gunners. This would be their ninth consecutive league win. Second half they were sumptuous. Andy Robertson right in front of me in row 5 was incredible at such pace. Everyone should have to do a game a season close to the front row to see the speed and what you can't see when you are at eyeball level. It's terrifying how good they are.

That second half they had crampons for the hard road, and they took every twist and turn brilliantly. Diogo Jota finished from a moment of sublime pleasure out of Thiago Alcântara with a minimum of fuss before Robertson took the smallest breath, savoured the slight peace in the rain and the tumult, and found Roberto Firmino who settled the argument before celebrating like Kenny Dalglish in north London in 1978. The football played in the south doesn't truly matter until Liverpool turn up. Firmino into our end behind the goal and the belief tumbling out of them.

We were 14 behind, we won a cup and turned it into one point when we went on the march. We enjoy it when it is hard. Does it always have to be this hard? Shut up. You'll enjoy it. Promise.

Dogme 95 versus The Studio

They've barely said a bad word about each other, or to each other, but the last 15 years of elite-level football has been defined by the rivalry between Pep Guardiola and Jürgen Klopp.

They've taken from each other's football and driven one another to exceptional heights. Guardiola won the 2023–24 league season, and on the same day had a cry in a press conference about Klopp leaving. Klopp seemed slightly more conflicted: he won less, and the shadow of what built Manchester City sits over it, but he couldn't be, or have been, more complimentary about the man himself over and over again.

And it wasn't easy for Guardiola either. Nothing is easy in the world of football. These days, only about 0.004 per cent of players who enter the academy structure in England get a professional career. Nothing is easy.

What's striking about Jürgen Klopp though, in the context of his rivalry with Pep Guardiola, is the difference between the two in terms of background. By this I don't mean their lives growing up; trying to understand the complexities, differences and commonalities of seventies and eighties culture in areas as different as the Black Forest and Catalonia is beyond our remit. But it is worth pointing out that at the age of 11 Pep Guardiola went to La Masia de Can Planes (Barcelona's youth academy) – and he sort of never left. The rest of his football life, with the possible exception of some late-playing-career experimentation, he carried and created La Masia with him as he went. He had six seasons playing under Johan Cruyff, one of the all-time greats of the game. His entire career has been spent in elite environments with elite colleagues.

Klopp gets amateur football: Bundesliga 2 in Mainz, under Wolfgang Frank. These are massively different environments and also massively different life experiences. For their respective decade or so at Liverpool and Manchester City there will have been some degree of parity of salary between the two (it could be possible that Klopp earned more), but by the time Klopp was 32 his life, while equally as immersed in football as Guardiola's, was one containing a lot more of what we'd be able to reasonably call 'normal' experiences – before he was thrust, with a minimum of preamble, into the Mainz manager's job.

Guardiola had a season to cut his teeth as Barcelona B boss back in La Masia before ascending to the throne. Klopp experienced two heartbreaking failed promotion bids at Mainz, where the prize dangled was pulled away in injury time on the last day. Twice.

Even Klopp's career break, post-Dortmund, was cut short in a way he wouldn't have planned, whereas Guardiola's cruised on into a lovely time in New York after feeling he needed to leave Barcelona prior to arriving at Munich. The differences between the journeys and experiences are genuinely stark, and it is possible that Klopp will be one of the last of his types, owing to football's general academisation.

None of this is to state anything is better or worse. For instance, the idea that to prove something in some way Guardiola needs to coach at a lower level is just a false one. Guardiola's proven this: he is the best coach of elite football players the world has ever seen. It is just worth pointing out that his life has been that elite environment.

People have hinterlands. At the biggest clubs you get to see both footballers and managers change and form something new of themselves, but that metamorphosis comes from somewhere; it has to, they have got themselves to here. But it is those hinterlands which form people, which make up their real story. Part of why Klopp versus Guardiola was always so compelling on some unspoken level was encapsulated precisely in all of this, with its further mess of contradictions: that

Klopp was a more polished media performer; that Guardiola was more hard-bitten in the final reckoning. There was a richness which transcended the idea of media spats – just there, just out of view – and the mutual respect made both the rivalry and the football all the more compelling.

Key Game 13
Manchester City 2 Liverpool 3
(FA Cup Semi-Final)
16 April 2022

The week prior to this game Liverpool had played at the Etihad and drawn 2–2. First half City had been brilliant and Liverpool did well to sneak one to keep it only 2–1 at half-time. A marvellous moment from Mo Salah, who fed Sadio Mané, made it 2–2, and Liverpool then had 20 minutes to win it before City righted themselves. Riyad Mahrez missed a great chance to win it at the death. Two each didn't feel enough for Liverpool, but we'd have all taken it on 40 minutes given the way the game had gone.

To then have Manchester City again the following week in the FA Cup felt enormous. Both sides were still in the Champions League; they were a point ahead of us in the league, and then there was this.

But because Liverpool were going for everything, I had to have a holiday somewhere, and so we had long ago chosen Easter weekend because the FA Cup semi-final felt like the least significant from some way out. It was a Saturday afternoon. We were on BBC1. And I wouldn't change a thing.

Not simply because of the result but because of how I got to experience it. Jürgen's players flew into Manchester City that day. There was a real desire to push them back and get on top. Ibrahima Konaté scored the opener from a corner with a majestic leap.

FA Cup semi-finals at Wembley tend to generate better atmospheres than FA Cup finals, mainly because there are more supporters in. This day was no different, but what added to it was the idea that it was Klopp's Liverpool up against their fiercest rivals in Guardiola's City, and

– for the only time in a game which wasn't a Community Shield – it was on neutral turf.

When we went 1–0 up the Liverpool crowd, which had started the more boisterous, put on a show: one half of the ground was a sea of red, the noise unbelievable and constant. One long Liverpool roar when The Reds had the ball, cacophonous boos and hisses when they didn't. The noise added to the second: Zach Steffen dwelt on it before Sadio Mané tackled the ball into the net – the ultimate pressing goal; Mané was desperate to make it happen.

The period from 2–0 to half-time is why I wouldn't change a thing. I got to experience the game as the vast majority did. You couldn't look at the red smoke, shirts and noise and not want to be a part of it – wherever you were in the world. I was amazed at how cinematic it looked that day on BBC Television. It was free-to-air, this great slab of marketing for Jürgen Klopp's Liverpool. They were on the front foot, they were playing brilliantly, with Thiago Alcântara metronomic, Trent Alexander-Arnold spraying passes and Sadio Mané so direct. The third goal saw all three of them involved, Trent more than once, playing a big ball from one flank and linking with a touch on the edge of the City box. Mané piledrove it in with aplomb, and the half Liverpool had dominated was reflected in the scoreline.

Just getting to see it, experience it through the screen, have Steve Wilson commentating on BBC forced to acknowledge it, was awesome. This is us, who we want to be, who we are. This is it: the best version of ourselves and, watching it with my friend and *Anfield Wrap* stalwart/ spiritual godfather Rob Gutmann, we concurred that this is what Klopp wants us to be, what he wants to see, on and off the pitch. Guardiola and Manchester City were just reduced to a supporting act, which almost wasn't fair. It was our day, our party political broadcast.

It was purest Klopp. Because it was the journey and it was the moment; and there was no trophy to be won (though we would go on to win the competition). We'd failed to win the week before but we weren't cowed. The players had grown at the Etihad – not enough to win but enough to salvage the point, and they took that into the game six days later and used it. The greater we, that crowd, that end, was determined not to look a gift Wembley in the mouth, determined to make the most of the time together, determined to make memories, sing songs, be Liverpool in all its flaming glory.

In so many ways it was the most Klopp day: a display of intensity, learning and courage; an eventual brush with jeopardy; a chance to show off; and a game which brought the crowd into it and made them its central feature for a long period. Watching abroad I was so proud of them – of us – of the journey. How could your heart not be captured by it, if your heart was available for capture?

Red resplendent. Look what we did together.

Brooklyn Graffiti

'Football without Origi is nothing.'

Brooklyn graffiti

This appeared in February 2022 as we approached the end of Divock Origi's time at Anfield. It's one of my favourite bits of global Liverpool supporter culture. It's not a complicated bit of street art. It just sits there, black text on white paint background behind an iron fence. (My favourite is the Indonesian flag of Anne Williams which shows her face in relief with 'Iron Lady' written beneath it. It was created by the Indonesian Supporters Club in 2013 and flown at pre-season friendlies. It now has a home on the Kop. To know enough of British political culture and of Anne's specific incredible struggle to get justice for her son Kevin, who was killed in the Hillsborough disaster, and make that reference is genuinely mind-boggling when you pull it all together – it reinforces what this thing transcends.)

After Origi scored his late winner in 2021 against Wolverhampton Wanderers Klopp said, 'He is an incredible striker and for different reasons he did not play that often, but I hope one day he finds a manager that plays him more than I do. He's one of the best finishers I've ever seen in my life. In this great team, with our [front] three, he doesn't play all the time, but he is a very positive boy, loves the club, wants to contribute and he did in an incredible way.'

Divock was indeed to go in the summer of 2022, but he is still yet to find that manager at the time of writing. Origi, beyond his iconic, legendary status, is an intriguing piece of management. He didn't start anywhere near enough games at Liverpool after the summer of 2016 but was always near the periphery from December 2018, about to emerge for a big moment. After Klopp left the club in 2024, he discussed Origi on stage in Liverpool:

He played, at Borussia Dortmund, a game I never saw from a striker, honestly. It was absolutely insane. Then things happened. You get knocked down – really bad tackle – and then he comes back for the Europa League final. He rushed it a little bit – because it was a final he tried to get on the pitch – didn't work out properly.

And in a really important phase of his career, he couldn't keep getting confidence, couldn't learn how good he actually is. So we used him in the way we used him. He had a few too many injuries, unfortunately, but we still used him. You just have to be honest and reliable. If you say something, it should happen. If I tell a player, 'You will not start this week, but you will start next week,' and they don't start next week, then you have a problem.

It's about that. It's about respect, and the role is to improve the players. It's my job, so I cannot let them hang alone in the corner when they are not well. I have to get them out of there. I have to try to help them. And for that, again, you need real energy. I have to make that step, players don't come to me immediately after he doesn't do great [but] for me, it's important that I can catch him as early as possible in this kind of situation, so I can help him early and not let him go far in the wrong direction. That's how I understood the job. Other managers do it differently, they are more successful, and stuff like this. I just never knew another way. That's it.

The moments when Divock Origi emerged in a big way for Jürgen Klopp's Liverpool could be seen as lucky. And I'm all right with that – it's a game, after all. Things pertaining to luck happen in all games that are worth anything. A lot of what has happened to Ben Stokes playing for England in cricket has moments of the most outrageous fortune about it. The key isn't to focus on that fortune but instead the brilliance that surrounds it, that is perpetuated by it. In sport, in games, you create the conditions for luck to emerge. You create the circumstances. And then you also have to possess the ability to ride that luck.

Origi became who he was for Klopp because of what Klopp says above. In team sports, you create the bond, look after the person, and be honest with them. You never know when you will need them. Each individual is their own person, and, in Origi's case, his own temperament meant he stayed cool, which was valuable in potentially big moments – but then you also need to be in big moments for it to be valuable. The Origis of the world need to be got there. They won't be Mo Salah and be able to get everyone there. But once there, you never know . . . Is it chemistry? Is it alchemy? Is it luck? Is it a trick of the light? Is it magic?

It is football. The purest football. The way the game has always been and will always be, season after season. Our Brooklyn friend knows it. Football without Origi is nothing.

Partnerships

In 2021–22 the crowds came back and that helped. Liverpool seemed determined from the first whistle to put on a show. Liverpool went from being a side who couldn't properly construct a game when 2021 started to a side who dominated so many through the campaign that followed. Against the teams who finished in the bottom ten they played 20 and won 19, the miss being a weird, emotional 3–3 draw against Brentford in the gloaming.

By comparison, in 2020–21 they only won ten against the bottom ten, and the same was to come in 2022–23. Furthermore, in 2019–20, when they blew the league to pieces, they scored 37 goals in 15 games against the bottom ten prior to the league shifting behind closed doors – a perfectly respectable 2.46 goals a game. But in 2021–22 that figure was 56 in 20 – moving to 2.8 goals per game. Essentially, any side that faced Liverpool in 2021–22, outside the top four, could reasonably expect to concede three, probably at least two. That's no way to start a game of football. It felt like the desire to put on a show was everything. 'You're here, we're here, and we never got to finish it together. Let's go now, together, in harness, and let's wring the life out of every minute.'

Virgil van Dijk came back from his long-term injury, and that helped too. More than any defensive player, it had long been van Dijk who epitomised Klopp's reiterated idea that everyone attacks and everyone defends, that it can only work if the team is entirely in harmony. Van Dijk, from the moment he arrived, helped Liverpool defend higher. The introduction of VAR helped that further – van

Dijk being generally vexed by late flags became a theme. His return in 2021 helped the pitch be compressed, on the one hand, but also his calm and his distribution helped Liverpool build the play better in all phases. Van Dijk gets you through the thirds.

What he also brought was the return of partnerships. After the chaos of the previous season, at the back Liverpool tended to be van Dijk plus either Joël Matip or sole summer signing Ibrahima Konaté. Matip was also back from long-term injury. Partnerships had grown to be so important under Klopp prior to the pandemic hitting, and the injury crisis of 2020–21 had seen them dissolve. Suddenly they were back with a vengeance everywhere.

Beyond the centre-backs there was the issue of how they'd operate with Fabinho, the latter doing a little bit more of splitting the centre-backs than we had seen. That was, in part, because of his relationship with Thiago Alcântara. Those two were a bedrock Liverpool could rely on and create with. It streamlined Fabinho's role, but Alcântara loved a scrap as well. Fabinho could progress without the ball knowing Alcântara could sit, but Alcântara would arrow passes forward.

Alcântara also loved playing with Andy Robertson, happy to watch him go then cover – and Robertson, in turn, delighted both Sadio Mané and Diogo Jota. Robertson would make the run they needed, overlapping or underlapping, and could be used by using him or, to paraphrase the great Barry Davies, you could use him by not using him. Mané and Jota themselves were in harness together much of the time in the space between the opposition's right-sided centre-back and right-back, until the signing of Luis Díaz in January 2022, and both carried an unerring threat with ball-carrying, pressing and heading ability.

On the other side, Trent Alexander-Arnold, Mo Salah and Jordan Henderson tended to be a three that worked as we'd seen before, though Harvey Elliott only lost his place due to a broken leg in September. Salah was often starting wider, which led to questions, but he was then electric getting between the posts, with Henderson being able to carry the water of both him and Alexander-Arnold when playing that advanced right-sided midfield role.

Liverpool had lost Gini Wijnaldum, and over the course of this season Roberto Firmino would struggle to get on the pitch. What we were getting was reminiscent of what had been, but it was new, and, as we've shown with the goal return, it was destructive. It was never quite as inevitable as the 2019 crew, but was oddly more irrepressible.

This was, in part, because the depth was mind-blowing. Divock Origi was Liverpool's seventh option in attack by February, with Alex Oxlade-Chamberlain able to feature there too. Naby Keïta supplemented the main midfield three expertly, arguably having his best season for The Reds and showing why everyone had been so excited to sign him. Yet behind him and the senior three were Curtis Jones and James Milner, as well as the aforementioned Oxlade-Chamberlain and Harvey Elliott. If you clicked into the side, the players around you had such understanding, you'd be carried along with the tide.

It wasn't just Klopp's best squad on paper, it was his best in practice: for instance, away at Inter Milan when Liverpool found themselves suddenly under the cosh in the last 16 of the Champions League, Klopp was able to swap Díaz, Henderson and Keïta (on with Mané, Fabinho and Elliott making way) and suddenly Liverpool went up a gear and shifted the scoreboard away from the Nerazzurri, winning in the San Siro 0–2. Klopp was excellent at ensuring everyone had connections: no rotation or substitution ever saw a dip in everyone knowing their roles – where in the previous season players had got lost a little in the maelstrom, that never happened this season because it wasn't a maelstrom, it was mostly in the palm of the manager's hand.

That was also in part visible when teeny storms struck: the attack lost a little something when Jota got an injury he never quite seemed to shake off in February; his ability to score key goals was unparalleled in the side. Yet the attack did march on to three finals and breaking 90 points. The goals didn't stop coming.

Everything, though – the ability to rip sides apart, the constant victories, the ability to go again and again – stemmed from that box of four made up of the two centre-backs and two midfielders: van Dijk the main constant, then Fabinho with Konaté, Matip, Alcântara, Henderson and Keita all doing their share. Formations have become ever-more slippery, and while Liverpool did tend to select three players you'd call midfielders, there was a consistent and visible pair in front of the back four playing as a pair.

Partnerships. Everywhere you looked. Making it that bit easier for one another, and making it easier to enter into. It was a wonderful, vibrant season. It was what we'd been missing.

Key Game 14
Liverpool 3 Wolves 1
22 May 2022

There is an image taken after the final whistle of this game that I find deeply, grimly comic, of Mo Salah on the Anfield turf receiving a golden boot for joint top scorer in the league while crying. At the moment the ball hit the back of the net, Salah thought he had scored the goal that won Liverpool their 20th league title. Another grimly comic moment occurred on the outskirts of the celebration of that goal when Joël Matip asked someone in the crowd the score in the Manchester City game and was visibly devastated to be told it was 3–2 to Manchester City.

There is something about these games which is rare: the crowd, in a way, is closer to the meat of the action than the players. They hold both games in their hands, whereas the players only hold one. It makes the experience discombobulating. These games have perhaps been the ones I have least enjoyed, for the same reason: the action that matters isn't happening before my eyes, it is elsewhere.

This was the second of these days against Wolverhampton Wanderers under Klopp, the first having been at the end of the 2018–19 season. Perhaps precisely because it was the second one, perhaps because Aston Villa got themselves a 0–2 lead against City, perhaps because they didn't go on to win in Paris, it stings more, remains closer to the gullet despite getting fewer points over the course of the campaign than in 2019.

Perhaps it stings more because it suggests a fatal flaw somewhere. Or possibly because the wider context exists, with all their charges versus our hard road, and it just feels fundamentally unfair. But it does sting more.

Kelly Cates says to the manager post-match, 'That points total would have won you the Premier League in pretty much every season.' He replies, philosophically, 'Story of my life. I'm still record holder for not getting promoted from the second to the first division in Germany with the highest points tally, with the second-highest points tally as well, so, yeah, but it's OK.'

Falling short better than anyone else is quite something. But flaws are as much reasons as we love as strengths, especially flaws like that. Perfections can belong to the uncanny valley. Flaws we can share, falling short we can share – they become balm to ease stings. The sting of 2022 is more when I am in the quiet room, because on the day we had the people, we had each other and we had him. Story of our lives, so, yeah, but it's OK.

We'll Always Have Paris

The second most important thing to remember, because you can never cherish it now, is that until 5 p.m. on Saturday 28 May 2022, Paris was brilliant. Everyone you saw, everyone you spoke to, was having a ball. We'd been there since the Thursday, having taken a busload of our usual people, which included Dan Austin, who'd been working with us for years, speaks fantastic French, and who had been our tour guide tasked with herding cats (especially me and John Gibbons, who kept having to run off to do media) around the city. I remember the landmarks and the cocktails and the bistros and the chats. Paris felt like the exclamation point on the most magnificent and, in a way, the most punishing season you could remember.

They took the cherishing and the magnificence off us. They let us keep the punishing part.

Shevchenko Park in Kyiv in 2018 before Klopp's first Champions League final had been one day, one moment; not that many people in not that big a space which we absolutely filled. It was glorious and it was the template for everything moving on from that point. It was an enormous celebration, and there is a version of this book which starts there and then ends in Paris on 28 May 2022: another book which is underpinned by world events and battling against a world outlook that ordinary people are to be stepped on at the convenience of power.

That day in Kyiv, in that unlikeliest of locations, Liverpool agreed to enjoy it, to revel in every moment, to not be complacent about a thing ever again, to make every single time our time. The manager would not have known about Shevchenko Park before it happened, but it happened because of the weather he had made, the feel he put about the club. It was his gift, in a day.

Paris was that, was Shevchenko Park, was our time, but for three or four days, a sprawl across the most beautiful and romantic of cities. It's the second most important thing to remember. Everywhere you turned Liverpudlians were revelling in it. Parisian Liverpudlians were revelling in it; we did an event the night before with the Paris supporters' club and they loved every minute of the party being in their place.

They took that off us. Off them.

The next morning we went to the fan park early because we were on first, and it was being very, very oddly policed outside when we tried to gain access. It ought to have sounded the first alarm bell, but going to football you get used to odd policing. Then the other thing: people started messaging that they couldn't get access to the fan park when it was meant to be open, that they were being held in areas. Maybe that should have been the second alarm bell.

John Gibbons, Mo Stewart and I went on for *The Anfield Wrap* when there was no one there because they weren't being allowed in, an absolute contrast to Madrid in 2019, but we welcomed people in and by the time we finished there was a decent crowd – but I was starving, so a few of us slipped out the back entrance and went for something to eat and saw Parisians dancing to the sound of the fan park, despite all the fencing, which maybe should have been the third alarm bell: everything really rather locked down in an odd way. But the people of Paris were loving being part of it.

They took that too. They took that from Paris – took the sheer unadulterated fun of what should be hosting a party – away from the Parisians. Why do you want to host these events if not to throw a party?

We went back into the fan park to hang out backstage. It was really hot, and there wasn't really enough water or enough places to get water, now I think about it, but everyone was making the best of it, having a ball. The high point for me and Dan Austin, and just about seemingly everyone, was the three Sense of Sound singers: three black Liverpudlian women singing Scouse dance anthems in front of over 50,000 people.

It was overwhelming, and when one shouted out, 'We haven't come here for fucking nothing, have we?' it felt like a battle cry into the next stage of something new, something this had needed to be but we had only just found the way to do it. They were brilliant.

They took that off us.

Before the fan park had finished, Dan and I went to meet with our friends Phil Blundell, Paul Senior and Kris Walsh (and whoever they were with) – a ten-minute taxi drive away, so we could see them and then get to the ground sharpish, because you never know about getting in. We had a couple of drinks in a lovely bistro where they'd been hanging out all afternoon, got a photograph altogether. They said goodbye to the people running the bar and off we went to the ground.

We began to get held, over and over, for no apparent reason on the walk from the crammed train to the stadium. Weirdly, we began to lose one another, until finally we were stopped in an underpass and Dan asked a member of the police force how long we were going to be held there. 'Could be a couple of hours,' came the response. Dan made the point that it was hot and no one had any water. No response to that. Around me, about 20 metres to my left, I thought I saw Billy Hogan, Liverpool CEO – but I thought that couldn't be right.

There's a picture of the crowds in the underpass with me front and centre that was put on social media and ended up in David Conn's coverage in the *Guardian* and I hate it. After the *Guardian*'s minute-by-minute visual breakdown of the events of Paris came out loads of people sent it to me, thinking, I don't know, that I'd be happy somehow? There I am, enormous, in my big daft yellow tracksuit top that I still wear, in the underpass, which is getting increasingly busy and, crucially, filling up from behind, and I have already lost Paul and Dan (fascinating how quickly that happens) and I am looking down at the floor and I am pretty much sure that photograph is the moment that I am thinking to myself, 'There's a solid chance we die in here.'

I remembered Seville, going back to the start of Klopp's Champions League journey, how dangerous it was outside the ground, but that every Liverpool supporter just repeatedly said to each other not to push, just to stay calm, that it was only a football match. It's only a football match. We've all seen football.

I wish they hadn't put that photo in the coverage. But then I wish a lot of things. I wish they'd not put it in Paris. I wish this didn't have to be a part of this book. I wish they'd planned it properly. I wish the people who ran football cared about football supporters. I wish I cared about the result and I wish I wished to change it. I wish police forces didn't see themselves as armed branches of the state. I wish I'd never written for the *Observer*. I wish people told the truth at the first time of asking and that our people didn't need to go to the French Senate to get a proper record. I wish the British media didn't take the word of any establishment figure at any place at any time ahead of anything ordinary people say.

Yet here, on the day when it was all falling apart, one aspect of the British media, the majority of football journalists, did get it right and sided with ordinary people in real time and as a result we got a wonderful case study contrasting with those who didn't.

Part of why remembering all the hugely enjoyable aspects of Paris matters is because it was part of how the argument – insofar as it matters and will ever matter – was won and won fast. The thing was this: the Parisians – the journalists, the club officials – had spent days seeing Liverpool supporters love it. Love and relish the moment. So going from the French Authorities'/UEFA's version of events – from that to this – made no sense. It made *no* sense. Kaveh Solhekol and his Sky Sports camera crew had been brought onstage at the fan park by John Gibbons not because of some Machiavellian plan but because John wanted to share the party with the world . . . so they knew it made no sense, as did so many others because they'd spent time with supporters and knew the ropes, or because they'd been influenced by the Liverpool journalist and former Football Editor of *The Times* Tony Evans, or some combination of the above. Conn, Kay, Delaney, Reddy, Draper and so many others.

It was this which underscored the accurate journalistic coverage on the night by everyone who wasn't part of the core mainstream broadcaster, BT Sport, who did the thing that usually happens in Britain, in conventional journalism, and sided with power, sided with the author-itative voice that said the delayed kick-off was due to the late arrival of fans. BT Sport disseminated UEFA's authoritative voice without ques-tioning it for a second; they hadn't been among the people in the way others had because they had that most wonderful of things for their coverage: access, and being on the ground. They didn't need to go to fan parks or to hang around with the supporters. They could interview the teams instead, and at the key moment they were found wanting, in a way that others who didn't have their access simply weren't. BT weren't in the bit of the ground that mattered, and in disseminating as they did, they were harking back to Hillsborough.

Anyway, the underpass. Nothing moved until it did; they just opened the ground and we were in the perimeter of the ground without having had to show a ticket. Every single turnstile I just walked past. I had now lost everybody, was rammed, but I began to bump into familiar faces, friends and listeners; we got chatting about how this was a mess and we needed to get in now despite there still being an hour to kick-off, given the size of the queues and the chaos. I was pretty much the last to get in through my turnstile before they closed it, and got into the ground and sat next to a mate who had been part of organising the fan park. We saw the UEFA message on the scoreboard, blaming the late arrival of fans, which Jake Humphrey shouted from the rooftops across British TV, and it very much angered people who had been around the ground for about three hours who could see scenes of tear-gassing on their phones, who were getting messages about what it was like, who were worried for their friends, and getting messages from people back home worried about them. So too were the Liverpool players, whose friends and relatives were among the crowds.

The game kicked off when it did. I don't really remember much of it. Another couple of friends who had been at the fan park arrived just after kick-off and sat the other side of me, and the lad to my left starting asking loads of questions of the two on my right. One was very shaken and just kept saying he wanted to watch the game.

But they'd taken that from us too.

The game still feels like something which never happened because:

was everyone all right? We conceded, had it chalked off, felt the better side but conceded again, and none of it felt real: it all seemed to be happening if not on screen then through one, just over there, away from us all.

As the final whistle approached they placed a battalion of riot police at our end, with no extra police at the Real Madrid end. We were one goal behind in a Champions League final and I wasn't watching the game. I was watching the police and the reaction to them, hoping against hope that nothing happened, not hoping against hope we'd equalise.

The final whistle went.

Me and Timo Tierney, lead singer of Tea Street Band, got a dart on the whistle. We went down and tried to find an exit away from the stadium in the dark, but it was chaotic outside. We went down a different underpass to the one pre-match. There were lights overhead, coloured lights, and we went down into it to see it narrowed and at the end there were riot police blocking the exit. We didn't like that, turned around and left, and said to people coming out not to go down there. Later we found out the police dropped teargas down there, hitting a crowd which included a pregnant woman I'd spoken to pre-match. People came back up, blinded, and were mugged.

Me and Timo kept circling the ground, among the chaos, wondering if we could climb over a fence, a wall or a gate and get away. Timo was a natural climber; me, a natural faller. It's hard to put over what it was like, and how unprepared we were for it, but, regardless, we ended up back in the original underpass. We needed to meet with everyone who had been on our bus from Liverpool but we just urged everyone to get back separately. We couldn't meet. Missiles were being thrown coming out of the underpass, right the way along the road, a row of coaches just there to the right blocking a view of the road and where the missiles were coming from. We got back to the train station, saw the police guarding it, saw what it seemed like inside, with what appeared to be figures running everywhere, another lodestone of chaos, and decided that it wasn't for us and walked on by.

Suddenly, it was all right. This is the bit which got me then, and still gets me now, and which people who don't know what the dark side of being policed is like will never understand. We moved away from the area being policed, the area which was UEFA's, into what should have been considered a dangerous spot – but it was just that: a dangerous spot in a European city at night. Me and Timo, we knew that. We had lived that before. It wasn't what we had had around Saint-Denis. It felt safer not being policed.

There are people who spend their lives being policed, people who aren't white men predominantly, who will know that feeling all too well. But it remains, for me, an ever-present of being a football supporter too. However, I had never known it as keenly as that night in Paris. Authority figures everywhere and you feel terrified; no authority figures and you feel fine. Suddenly, the environment was just a bit ropey. It wasn't actively loathing you in every single way and making things less safe at every turn.

Weirdly, we bumped into a lot of our crew on our journey back; they had done the same thing in terms of eschewing the station. Everyone was pretty much all right, we had a bus to get and then a ferry to catch and Francophile Austin was marching ahead, burning with fury, as we headed back.

Christ, was he. By 5 a.m. he'd written his first piece for *Metro* and shown it to me for an edit on the ferry. It started thus:

Children trembling with fear, their eyes streaming from an arid yellow wave of tear gas billowing through the barriers. An elderly man crumpling in on himself as he suffers a panic attack in a crushing crowd and cannot move. Women being kettled by state-employed bullies with reinforced shields.

No, not in a riot, a brawl, or a war. This was the UEFA Champions League final in Paris on Saturday evening.

It was published at 8 a.m. It's because he loves France, loves the French, loves Paris that he burned.

Everyone's phone wouldn't stop: how it had been around the ground, who had seen what, how everyone had supported each other, shouted over and over for everyone to stay calm, what had happened afterwards. Everyone sharing. Phil Blundell did the first interview the morning after for the BBC and nailed it, relentless and accurate.

We were getting media requests from 6 a.m. John Gibbons did two different radio interviews from the motorway; someone from Liverpool City Council asked if we had anyone who could speak French. Dan was nervous but agreed to do it. Days later he would do an hour on French television live with a presentation worked on by me and an *Anfield Wrap* contributor called Philippa Smallwood, which pulled apart the lies of the French government about – among other things – policing and counterfeit tickets. Dan spent the summer on everyone's case, saying yes to everything and demanding more.

I spent the afternoon after we got back (having not been to bed) on Sky Sports ostensibly talking about the parade but continually coming back to the events in Paris. The unspoken idea was it mattered to be normal, it mattered to be a football supporter, mattered to be inclusive. While doing Sky I managed to interview Joanne Anderson, then Mayor of Liverpool. She'd been there and called for an investigation. It still wasn't 24 hours since me and Dan had left the fan park.

By halfway through the following week Spirit of Shankly, the most mature supporters' body in the country, were getting stuck in. I had West Derby's MP Ian Byrne in the studio, Tony Barrett, too, from Liverpool FC. Both looked shattered, but there they were. Liverpool FC responded brilliantly, institutionally and individually. It had been Billy Hogan I'd seen in the underpass, and, in the days following, he looked straight down the barrel of the camera and said what it was the club wanted to see happen and what they were going to do, and the first thing was they were going to stick with their people. This was the logical end of them having backed their people since 2018, since Shevchenko Park, but given some of the club's history it remains deeply gratifying they were clear from day one.

Unspoken, though, was the thing. There wasn't time for any of this to be co-ordinated because we knew that everything had to happen immediately, before mindsets were allowed to settle. The nearest I got to co-ordination was seeing Steve Rotheram, Mayor of Liverpool City

Region, on the central reservation outside both of our offices and us shouting at each other for 90 seconds about what we could do.

What could we do? We pushed people forward, pushed ourselves forward. What was the point of being elected, of working for Liverpool, or for us of owning the means of production, of having done this daft podcast for ten years if you couldn't use it and its people now? Everyone had done their 10,000 hours, and there were things that needed to be said as loudly as possible. I had long had this line that 'you think you are doing podcasts about football but you are running a civic institution by accident'. So fucking run it hard, dickhead.

That comes with responsibilities and it comes with pressures. That week, and in the months that followed, everyone stood up and was counted over and over. About a week in, one morning on my way to work, I bumped into one of our contributors, Damian Kavanagh, on Old Hall Street. Damian had done great work as a Hillsborough survivor with so many, campaigning and putting their case for decades. We chatted and he said, 'Anyway, I'm glad I bumped into you, the lads in the Stanley WhatsApp group said you are all doing great, and I couldn't agree more.' We went our separate ways, and he never knew but I burst into tears just then. None of it was for approval, not for a second – not least because doing this weird thing there is no one's approval, not really, other than people's general warmth to what we do – it can't work that way. But that moment meant a great deal – like away goals, the lads in the Stanley WhatsApp group counted double.

I lie awake at night staring at the ceiling concerned that we are occupying space that could be better used by others; that we're the mediocre independent cinema blocking the space that a genuine arthouse institution could better utilise. I get terrified of getting it wrong, of being old, of being finished – God, am I scared of being finished – of not being able to be the thing we need to be when called upon. But this, around Paris, this we could do. This we did.

There was to be an independent report convened but not conducted by UEFA, and my endlessly bleak soul was sceptical, but everyone reassured me – Austin, Amanda Jacks, Emma Johnson, Barrett, Alison McGovern, Susan Black – that it was worth doing, and its report

dropped on the day of the Merseyside derby in 2023, leaked out deliberately to scupper plans around the proper publication, because
everything remains malicious. But the report was complete and utter
vindication, in black and white, and reinforced the idea that your friends
and mine saved lives and your friends and mine won righteous arguments and spoke better than anyone else. There were recommendations.
Loads of them haven't been followed (ironically, including updating on
the progress of them), because power is as power does, and Manchester
City supporters got fucked the year after because who cares about
ordinary people? Because the endless bleakness will always win in the
end. But, still.

I dream once a month about coming out of that ground. I only
spoke to Timo about it the other day – in part, because of this writing
– and he's the same: those lights overhead down into the police kettle,
he said, he thinks of it all the time.

The second most important thing to remember is that we'll always
have Paris. We'll always have those Parisians and those days before that
day, with its pâtisseries and its landmarks and its art and cocktails and
that chateaubriand steak that John Gibbons shared with Paul Senior
which I can't forget and I only watched them eat. You see, none of this
is allowed to spoil Paris. Because to spoil Paris is to spoil the world.

The most important thing to remember is that we were there for
each other.

And they couldn't take that.

The Toll

Summer after summer it was predicted Liverpool would come a cropper. Predicted by the outside world, but also by a fair number of our people too. The idea was that they couldn't sustain, they needed to buy, the midfield wasn't good enough, wasn't creative enough, wasn't strong enough or deep enough.

And that idea was wrong, repeatedly wrong. Until suddenly it was right.

Eventually, it was always going to be. It was like going to a casino and putting half your money on black and it coming up red. Then half of your remaining money. Then half your remaining money. Then half your remaining money. Eventually all plots move deathward. Eventually you spin red. And then you get double your money on that final stake.

But it happened. Liverpool suddenly looked shot, and looked it fast. The toll had been too great. And the toll was also too great.

The toll that had been put on was the 2021–22 season, which had seen Liverpool play every single match with everything riding on every game, a shortened summer due to the World Cup on its way in the winter but, as much as anything, the impact of both failing to win the league, failing to win the Champions League and the reality of Paris as a whole. The burden was on the whole football club. The whole football club had been caught up in the ineptitude, and it was still weighing on the club through the pre-season, news breaking while we were on tour.

Ultimately, though, the manager thought his squad was in good nick: he was going to be proven very wrong indeed. The first game against Fulham they started slowly – as was going to be the case across the following two seasons – got punished, recovered, but then van Dijk conceded a soft penalty. Still, they recover again to 2–2.

There still remains one of those moments, though, in that first game against Fulham when Jordan Henderson hit the crossbar in the last minute from distance. If that had nestled, then Liverpool would have won and gone on from there, despite having had a tough day. Instead, they drew, then drew the first home game of the season against Crystal Palace, when the manager picked the wrong team – Nat Phillips starting at centre-back, in for a resting Joe Gomez, only for Gomez to come on and look great. They then lost at Old Trafford.

This is the other toll. By dropping seven points against poor sides in their first three games, Liverpool's players already knew that their chance of winning the title – even if they could hit the previous season's form (which they could not) – was gone. They knew the pace you needed to go at, and they knew they were even then so far off it. They never recovered that intensity all season, which opened up a whole heap of issues quickly, and the idea of Gegenpressing for the third or fourth or seventh consecutive season for some became both physically and mentally too much. They could do it in spurts but were never right collectively. The manager changed the shape over and over, and said he was doing so to change the message, but he wasn't helping because he was picking bad teams that were leaving too much onus on his best players to both carry the piano and play it. Players repeatedly wouldn't start games for fitness reasons, but be on the bench and then be turned to out of sheer need when matters had got away from the side.

It spiralled quickly into a mess – despite putting nine past Bournemouth. Liverpool's rhythm was disrupted by the death of the Queen. They played only one league game in September: a Merseyside derby they could have lost but could have won in injury time – it finished 0–0. They were actually good in general at Arsenal for about 50 minutes but utterly appalling in the first and last minutes of the first half and for a penalty they conceded. They no longer liked it when it was hard, which was crystal clear by virtue of the fact they didn't win a domestic away game until 6 November – the last before the World Cup break.

By then it was all over: they were a mile off the pace and couldn't pick up the pace. The manager was having murder with Fabinho during games when he just wasn't where he was supposed to be; Henderson looked confused by events; and the pressing was dreadful up top. Everyone was exposed. It was a season to mitigate the damage, but then that had been the case weeks earlier, and they couldn't get a collective grip then either. There are a fair few examples of this through the last 20-odd years of top-flight football: a lot of sides who dipped after big seasons – and, indeed, barring Manchester City, and that only to an extent in this one given how far off the pace they were by Christmas, everyone who had had a lot of games and had European football in this compressed season struggled.

For Liverpool, though, the crisis seemed more existential. The plot had moved deathward. But the thing was this: no one was going to rant and rave about the manager, even when he wasn't great. He'd earned that, earned it 100 times over. He was our man, and so it just hurt.

Key Game 15
Brighton & Hove Albion 3 Liverpool 0
14 January 2023

Post-match press conference, post-hammering press conference, on the idea of Liverpool not winning challenges, Jürgen Klopp said, 'It's my job to organise it so they arrive there in the right moment. It's my job to make the right line-up, all these things, set up the right tactics . . . I can't remember a worse game. I honestly can't. All. Not only Liverpool, I can't remember. And it's my responsibility, and that makes it a really low point.'

Brighton & Hove Albion away in mid-January was Jürgen Klopp's lowest point of this season, making it high in the running for the lowest point of his Liverpool career. Liverpool lost the game 3–0 but it could have been any score by the end. Coming into it, Liverpool had abandoned their usual shape. There were injury issues, but Liverpool had been poor in their previous three games and Brighton were a side who were playing some of the best football in the division – certainly some of the most interesting football.

Brighton completely dictated terms for the game. They made the pitch big. Normally, when we say that we mean that a side made the pitch wide, but here they made it deep, prepared to bait a press right the way back to their own goalline. This wasn't the first time we'd seen that, this wasn't new, but it was the purest, most committed iteration of it, and Liverpool had no answer: they weren't set up to do what they'd normally do regardless, so instead they did nothing.

There was a game against Pep Guardiola's Manchester City at Anfield in the October of 2018 which suited both managers at the time to be a bit of a non-event. Within it Guardiola had his goalkeeper taking goalkicks backwards. This was before the rule change on goalkicks, so his players needed to be out of the area but behind the goalkeeper. It was Guardiola finding space where Liverpool wouldn't press, or where if they did press they'd cease to be compact. It was the first time I'd ever seen anything like it.

You'd come across tactics here and there which would work against The Reds in snatches. Carlo Ancelotti's Napoli response to Klopp's approach had always been to have his players occasionally miss a player out in build-up, play a 25-yard ball when normally a ten-yard pass would suffice, flit between a back three and a back four in the build-up, drop an extra man deeper, find something, find some space. Villarreal had invited Liverpool on cleverly in the Champions League semi-final when Liverpool went away to Estadio El Madrigal and earned themselves a 2–0 lead, but Klopp's men were full of confidence then, and Unai Emery's side couldn't sustain it. Luciano Spalletti's Napoli had done something similar in Liverpool's 4–1 hammering in the autumn of 2022: they'd used the length of the pitch to their own goalline, baited Liverpool in, and had then been able to find clipped balls into the spaces created 35 yards from their own goal and started playing from there. That day they would then look to go quickly vertical, with running or direct passing. Space, you see. The halfway line dictated the size of the pitch due to not being able to be offside in your own half, which in turn dictated Liverpool's line, which in turn dictated how compact Liverpool could be, which further discombobulated their pressing game.

Brighton, on this day, was the ultimate iteration of opposition sides having a better conception of space on the field seen so far. Worse, it was domestic, a side that would finish sixth, but a side who historically shouldn't have been giving Liverpool all these problems.

The issue with all of this is that these were instances of teams setting up in a way which was a direct reaction to the football that Jürgen Klopp played. Gegenpressing had, in a way, become a response to the Iberian football of Guardiola and the Spanish national side. But this stuff was intended to defang the press. It worked. Liverpool were in a dreadful moment but it worked plain as day and, post-match, Klopp went to the Liverpool fans with his hands pressed together in supplication.

In his press conference he was asked if the players were listening. In response he said something fascinating: 'If you face a team full of confidence and joy we need to have key moments as well . . . No moment in the game where we could [clicks fingers] get a little lift, and go from there.'

Brighton were full of joy, and made the absence of which we had felt keenly for at least three months feel even more stark. Nothing was sparking, and this manager needed his football to spark joy, to feel emotional. Liverpool were stuck playing football from the pit, the football of the abyss. We'd seen this before. In 2002–03 Liverpool didn't win a league game from 2 November until 18 January and, my God, did they play a lot of them.

In a sense, in 2023 it would get worse before it got better: Liverpool would lose 3–0 at Molineux before the turn came, but that defeat to Wolves could be far easier explained by shocking individual errors and sloppiness rather than looking like a robot from a 1970s sci-fi film. Liverpool would then win four of their next five league games before hitting a mini-slump, come out of that and attack the run-in.

We went back to Brighton the following season, in Klopp's last, and the game was like a psychological thriller. We'd learned and responded under Klopp, but that meant great stretches where both sides were trying to bait each other. Liverpool started poorly – a recurring theme not going anywhere – but had grabbed a 1–2 lead by half-time and ought to have made it three, being much the dominant team after the break.

This is key because it would be easy to depict Klopp as an old dog unable to learn new tricks, easy to depict him as yesterday's man by the time he decided to stand down, unwilling to compromise. The truth was far more complicated than that: he could indeed change and adapt. He had been changing, compromising and adapting for some time, and what was killing him in 2022–23 was as much the lack of energy and joy in his side than anything else.

Possibly though, being able to learn new tricks isn't the same as wanting to, isn't the same as having the energy and enthusiasm to go through a whole new cycle knowing that the kids are coming up from behind. There is wisdom in knowing that you are just about to lose edge when edge is precisely what is needed. If you are over 50 and you aren't self-aware, you are doing it wrong. You shouldn't be so certain. That day in January was a day that certainties ebbed.

Build It Around Bobby Firmino

In the end Roberto Firmino leaving in the summer of 2023 almost felt like a warm-up for Jürgen himself leaving. The week it was confirmed he scored the seventh against Manchester United. In his last home game he scored against Aston Villa. Away games became opportunities to serenade him. His song was constant and he was sheepish, not least because he was out injured for some of it, but that didn't stop anyone.

When Jürgen was asked as part of his own farewell tour in 2024 how to build a great side, he said, 'Build it around Bobby Firmino.'

It was both completely sincere and him blowing the question off. He didn't want to do an extended pulling apart of it all when he possibly can't entirely undo the alchemy from the coaching himself. There is both alchemy and coaching around Firmino. And the enormous sincerity is that Firmino is the player Klopp would build in a laboratory: technically incredible, tactically brilliant, committed to winning the ball back like a demon, and a laugh.

Each of these factors is hugely important for a Jürgen Klopp football team. There needs to be within it some irreverence, some sense of mischief. But there also needs to be so much intelligence and so much graft and guile. Firmino had it all and he was, more than anyone, his manager's talisman. When he left the manager said, 'We will stay friends for ever, definitely. I will be grateful for ever for everything he did for us, for me, and he will go down as one of the Liverpool greats. What can you wish more for in a footballer's life than that?'

Why this is interesting is that it speaks of Klopp's skewed relationship with football history. Klopp, since his arrival, had wanted to minimise the idea of the weight of Liverpool's history while continually urging his players to write their own page of it. It was him, his players and the club who put massive significance on the idea of the sixth European Cup, but immediately wanted to take positive experiences and build on them, as he told me when I asked him about the Champions League win in 2019. For him, in that second, that was to be a building block – but in the distant future a glorious memory. This was what he wanted: in the moment right up until the time of his own departure. Greatness is just there, but the memories are for the future, never for the ever-moving now.

There hasn't been some fantastic litany of success from Klopp's departing players. That success was there for them at Liverpool, and with him. Everything else for them, with the possible exception of Emre Can, has seemed like returning to the ordinary world after leaving Toontown in *Who Framed Roger Rabbit?* – all a bit grey and drab.

But he also wants to part friends with everyone. Somewhere in his mind in all of this there has been the notion of some future catch-up, some moment forever ten years hence when drinks are drunk, backs are slapped and 'we sure did something there, didn't we' is said to the echoing sound of cacophonous laughter.

Michael MacCambridge, author of, among others, *America's Game* and crucially *Red Letters* (with me), observed that the title celebrations of 2020 in the stadium could well prove to have been the last time ever some of the people who delivered so much joy would ever be in the same room together. That is the nature of sport: it is constant but it stops and restarts with the same shirts but a slowly different crew. And it cripples me as an observation. I hope they get one or two more nights together, and if that does happen – when that happens – in my head, at the centre of it, is the manager, of course it is, but there, right next to him, is Roberto Firmino.

Eurovision/Coronation/'You'll Never Walk Alone'

I've long had this theory that the city of Liverpool tries to impose its own bank holidays. These things culturally rise up, unbidden. Today, we are, to all intents and purposes, off. Today is not normal. Not like those other days.

Mothering Sunday, while obviously a day without work, is spectacular in the city. It was something I wasn't aware of until I lived slap bang in the centre of Liverpool and witnessed roaming cross generations of women determined to have a brilliant time at all costs. The Grand National festival is similar: the city grinds to a halt and is entirely defined by this one event. It's a Goldilocks thing: Liverpool is big enough to cater for something like the National but not so big it subsumes it and adds it to its portfolio of things to do this weekend. There is one thing. That thing. This is why Liverpool gets caught up in things, gets carried away.

They gave us Eurovision.

And we took Eurovision.

We took Eurovision to the extent that even though in 2024 it was in Malmö, we were still putting events on. We became a Eurovision overspill city. We got carried away.

God did we. In 2023 it overwhelmed the city, resulting in packed bars, commissions around public art, and eight days of live music. The BBC relocated. Rylan was everywhere. It was, for a week, all everyone talked about and obsessed over. The village was right by our office. How right by? We had a view of the urinals. Some would say too good a view.

226

When the whole extravaganza hit, when the big night happened, there was a celebration of Liverpool on the main show broadcast across Europe, and it closed with all the main cast singing 'You'll Never Walk Alone'. It was quite something, an arresting moment, not quite as quintessentially Eurovision pure as Daði Freyr singing 'Whole Again' by Atomic Kitten, but a genuine, deep moment of affection and warmth towards the city that had played host and given Europe another reason to fall in love with Liverpool. With added Hannah Waddingham. It was hard not to be moved.

A couple of weeks before, at the King's Coronation Concert, Andrea Bocelli and Bryn Terfel had banged out 'You'll Never Walk Alone' too. It struck me as odd. 'You'll Never Walk Alone' is obviously a show tune but, as our Evertonian friends and neighbours observed on the night of Eurovision, it is synonymous with the football club. The football club which famously disrupts the national anthem and belongs to this weird, odd place which has deemed itself separate from England and which England has been happy to be separated from.

I have a theory that because of social media everyone was, at most, two degrees of separation from Liverpool's trophy parades of 2019 and 2022, that everyone saw over a million people welcome Liverpool FC home with the noise and the drama, the colour and sheer outpouring, and everyone saw it unfiltered, not refracted through tired old media. They saw it on the Facebook and Instagram feeds of their friends and relatives: everyone was just two degrees, two clicks away, and people liked that and saw it anew.

I have a theory that, since 2008, since the European Capital of Culture, people have been coming to Liverpool in their droves and having a great time. Whether for that event, its follow-ups, the football, a stag do, a hen night, a weekend away, people have come. And when they have come they have mostly had a good time. And then they have told people, either in person or online. And then more people come, and the nighttime economy takes care of them all, and they go back telling their stories and posting their pictures, and then more people come, and the restaurants get better, the bars more varied, the nights out more memorable, and then more people come, and they take more pictures and tell more stories.

People tell stories.

The unmediated view is what has driven the shift in perception in the city across the nation.

Then there are the parades and the football and the emotion. There is Barcelona at Anfield and everyone in front of the Kop and 'You'll Never Walk Alone' playing, and then that is everywhere as well. Then there is Jürgen Klopp at the end of every Greatest Hits Radio bulletin in soundbite form, or his resignation press conference live on BBC and Sky News at once; there is Liverpool front and centre, and everything Liverpool equals in the popular imagination, which is no longer the jokes but the good times and the togetherness, because Andrea in number 23 went for a weekend and she put the pictures all over WhatsApp and they had a ball, you know, Andy. We should go when we get a spare weekend.

Bang. 'You'll Never Walk Alone' at the centre of two different cultural, nation-defining events because everyone wants a slice of that action, everyone craves some semblance of what we have; everyone wants in. Everyone wants to get carried away. Getting carried away is the best thing.

Klopp 2.0 – Brief Encounter

In the summer of 2023 Klopp backed himself. He backed his coaches. He backed his players. He backed his football. He backed his way. And he backed that he had our backing. And he was completely and utterly vindicated.

He himself called it 'Liverpool 2.0', but it was massively based on his own ideal lines. The stats showed that Liverpool ranked strongest for opposition passes allowed per defensive actions, for counterpressures, for counterpressure regains in the opponent's half, for opposition passing percentage completed. What all these added up to was that Liverpool were horrible to play against. You had the ball, they wanted it back like men possessed. And when they got it, well, they were highest ranked for forward passing (On Ball Value) and by a substantial distance for xG created. They moved it more directly than anyone and created more good chances than anyone.

Forget the stats, though, the eye said the same thing. He built a team that would attack and attack and attack until their legs fell off. They wanted the ball, they wanted the points and they wanted to dig each other out. From the start of the 2023–24 campaign a new vibe struck: aim to be the best. No excuses whatsoever allowed. That stayed in every press conference, every post-match interview, every performance, every player. No one felt sorry for themselves, whereas the season before it had felt as though everybody had felt sorry for themselves.

That idea that every game could be won, every challenge overcome, came from Klopp and from the sense of there being a fresh start. Players left and four new midfielders arrived. The leadership group reconstituted itself, and players who were viewed as young moved into the class just below that, became seasoned professionals who had been around the block despite being firmly in their twenties.

He gave everyone confidence in themselves but, crucially, in both the plan and in one another. It was that which had eroded for 28 league games of the season before. You couldn't run because the man next to you might not, might not be willing or able. Furthermore, it had been unedifying to see the manager's own frustration with Fabinho, with slanging matches from the sidelines a prime example, or James Milner's frustrations with his own teammates after goals had been conceded. They'd grated on each other, not least because they'd known each other for so long – but not like this, as the world fell apart.

Immediately, in pre-season in 2023, things were visibly different. Liverpool were higher and happier, determined to win everything, because it is only with joy and confidence in your work can you achieve what you need to. Klopp had spent a lifetime not looking for hiding places. It went wrong, he'd want to fix it. He gets asked a question? Answers it to the best of his knowledge. Doesn't like something, thinks something unorthodox? Says so. The whole essence of him was to grasp the nettle.

But he wouldn't be human, which he very much is, if he hadn't had doubts approaching (and during) the summer of 2023, and therefore this must have taken some grasping, if somewhere in the back of his mind was the idea that he wasn't long for this footballing world. It must have been there, but he looked into himself and found the way he sees the game at its core and gave it to those players anew, whether or not they were new.

But also at his core is that idea of backing and trusting. He backed himself. He backed his coaches. He backed his players who remained. He decided that they could still press as he needed, follow the instructions, and he looked at the younger lads and put his faith in them and knew they could do the hard yards he needed. He didn't compromise his methods, he doubled down on them. And he trusted us, knew he could give us what we wanted and that we'd love him and them for it: a Liverpool team that crawls off the pitch if it has to.

No excuses. Trust the people. Be the best version of yourself.

Key Game 16
Tottenham Hotspur 2 Liverpool 1
30 September 2023

Some games of football end up with far too much on them. Tottenham Hotspur 2 Liverpool 1 at the end of September 2023 was one of them.

It was the game which Jürgen Klopp suggested should be replayed, in that way of his, that way being: 'when asked a question at a press conference, answer it honestly', which caused havoc. It was the game that gave us, 'Well done, boys, good process,' which, in many ways, was a gift. It was the game where we got to wonder why on television when normally every contentious refereeing decision is played over and over, this one in real time hardly got a second glance until there was a statement from PGMOL ready to go. It was the game where, afterwards, we found out more about Premier League referees spending their spare time doing some additional games in the Middle East – quite something.

Ultimately it was two things: 1) the best defeat in Liverpool's history. Strange that, but true. It was a defeat that made you believe they could win, and for the longest time in Klopp's final season that held. Spurs away, along with Newcastle United away, became statement performances for this new team of Klopp's. And, 2) the game which nailed down the story that the officiating in England is on its knees.

Basically, it was hard lines that Curtis Jones got sent off – a red, broadly, but one where you feel for the player. Liverpool had an opening goal checked and found to be onside by the VAR but the referee misunderstood and didn't give it while saying, 'Well done, boys, good process,' and then nobody did anything about it because of 'protocols', Tottenham scored, Liverpool equalised, Diogo Jota got two yellow cards where perhaps one of the fouls given might have been a free-kick. Liverpool were then down to nine but kept trying to score like maniacs, Tottenham ran out of ideas, and then one ricocheted in off Joël Matip to give Spurs the last-minute winner.

They then celebrated like they had won the league, but were eventually going to finish 16 points behind The Reds, which was obvious while watching the game, but Gary Neville was going to say some mad stuff over the course of the season: that Tottenham could finish above Liverpool and Arsenal. In my match review I wrote, 'I'd rather have our lads than your win, and by Easter Sunday the table will make that undeniable.' Easter came early in 2024, but we'd take that win to the bank.

Liverpool showed so much quality, togetherness and courage that you knew from this game they could challenge for the title. It went from hoping to knowing in one afternoon. Just at the point Jones got sent off they were beginning to run the show, on Tottenham's pitch. Then they were still better, until it became eleven versus nine.

It was a statement defeat. Another oddity of the era. It also set Liverpool on a course of us versus the world, which isn't the worst thing for a football team to have. What set Liverpool on the path of us against the world was the officiating.

Writing about this in a book is interesting because my argument, really, is that the key issue officiating has in the VAR era concerns language. The language around what needs to be done, and when, is a constant movable feast. In the season 2023–24 errors that needed the video refereeing intervention had to be 'clear and obvious'. But across the campaign what that actually meant was, in and of itself, never actually clear and obvious. There was a lot of conversation about thresholds.

But what there also is, when the television screens are brought into play, is the need to deny the evidence of your own eyes. When, at Anfield in December 2023, Martin Odegaard looked more like a basketball player than a footballer in the penalty area the video referee had the ability to see the same footage the whole TV audience could see. But whatever he looked at, he considered it insufficiently clear and obvious to intervene, which blew the mind of the viewer, left the people in the ground confused and the players both gobsmacked and increasingly lacking faith in the whole process.

An even better example came in the FA Cup semi-final at Wembley between Chelsea and Manchester City. Chelsea had a free-kick, it hit Jack Grealish in the wall on his arm, which may or may not have been in an unnatural position, and the referee Michael Oliver gave a goalkick. This was then checked by the VAR for about 60 seconds. In the end the VAR went with the onfield decision and the goalkick was taken.

The problem was that for 60 seconds everyone could see it was a corner. The very notion there was something to check meant it hit someone in the wall. But also, Michael Oliver presumably hadn't seen it hit anyone. If he had, then he would have given a corner. So it becomes reasonable to assume that Michael Oliver hasn't seen the incident properly. We can establish that. At no point, though, did the VAR offer him the opportunity to look at it again, because to do that would suggest he had made an error which may need to be overturned. But we all knew that he had made a quite significant error – if an understandable one – which a worldwide TV audience was being shown the nature of repeatedly. The final outcome was the one thing that all the evidence of our eyes told us it shouldn't be: a goalkick. Play on.

A truism has come in around VAR that it suits the TV audience more than the in-ground audience. I don't think that holds. Watching that Grealish incident on television burnt my head out to the point I had to turn the TV over. It became philosophically untenable. The contortions that incident meant you had to go through were just too much for my brain to handle. Football resisting reality makes it feel intensely like this post-Baudrillard small-scale experiment.

Every club ends up with hard-luck refereeing stories – it has been forever thus, up and down the country. Watching Liverpool get refereed in the recent past at Anfield has been infuriating. A series of the same fellas sent by PGMOL (Professional Game Match Officials Ltd), turn up and demonstrate they won't be swayed by a partisan crowd on any number of mundane decisions.

It is also worth remembering that towards the end of the 2022–23 season a linesman appeared to elbow Andy Robertson in the back of the head after the half-time whistle had blown and had to apologise. That, of course, led to broadsheet discourse ('the footballers have had it coming', essentially) but no consequences.

For Liverpool, on this day in September 2022, it's worth emphasising that a failure to use language well robbed them of a legitimate goal. It is, as far as we know, a completely unique occurrence, and the broadcaster didn't interrogate the incident as they usually would until PGMOL had made its statement. Then all hell broke loose.

After the Spurs game Liverpool weren't on their knees. They stood tall. The same can't be said for the officiating before, during or after, and who knows where that will end up.

The Day He Said He Was Packing in

I received a text from Neil Jones, who covers Liverpool, at 10.58 a.m.: 'Side door.' He was on his way to the studio to do our *Press Conference Extra* show at 11, as the manager had done his press conference prior to the Norwich City FA Cup fourth-round game the day before. All leisurely. I hadn't had breakfast, had a lovely afternoon planned of a long lunch while scheduling before easing into the weekend. I opened the side door and saw Neil staring at his phone slack-jawed. He looked at me and said, 'He's gone. The manager's gone.' I turned right to see Josh Sexton, our editor, coming out of the studio. He shook his head. I barrelled past Josh into the studio and got my phone out and saw the start of the video. I presumed immediately that it was a deep fake. Then I checked the publisher. Saw it was Liverpool FC. Presumed they'd been hacked. Everyone is very sophisticated these days.

I watched the video, staggered.

We did the show, the three of us, now about the fact he had gone – was going – that everything had changed, that the whole thing was a shock. Our phones blew up. Friends, families, WhatsApp groups, media requests. We were trying to do this show and I, for one, was trying not to cry, and the whole thing felt, immediately, so overwhelming. Only the other week I had been saying I expected him to sign one more contract till 2029 and then leave in 2028, his work done, Liverpool 2.0 boxed off.

We said yes to everything because you do. You just do. The stipulation was they had to come to the office on the waterfront by the

Museum of Liverpool. We have a great office, but so many people always want you to get to Anfield, and the public transport links, they aren't great. The point where I realised this was different was when Sky and BBC were both trying to get me pinned down for after his press conference. Why was this different? Because it was news teams not sport, and it was for immediately afterwards.

I checked the messages – many were from friends who had no interest in football. I checked the websites, and this was top-story news. Klopp going was front-page news.

It seems obvious now, but I had never really computed it. Doing Sky News (they asked first) straight after the press conference – like, he finished, got up and walked, and they threw to me for 15 minutes or so – I really didn't feel equipped, really didn't feel like I had it in my back pocket. I didn't want to become a meme, blubbering (and thankfully didn't), but he had meant the world and felt just so very present in everything.

The day wore on, a twirl of shows and media, and it ended with us doing our 20-minute free video show, sponsored by Erdinger, as an hour-long live chat with a revolving cast. But what it did was get it all out. Get it all clarified. Get your mind straight. And the point started to be made: there will be a next thing. We need to get ready for the next thing. We have had this wonderful thing but we decide when it stops, not him, and, anyway, he doesn't want it to stop.

So then I did 5 Live on the street outside the pub with Darren Fletcher and others, and it was all Richard Attenborough voices. It was all black tie and try not to disturb the neighbours, and I remember enjoying, revelling in every second of that – not maliciously, not the idea that they all hate us, but precisely because it was front-page news, as significant as it gets without being genuinely tragic. Sport in a suit, but me on Slater Street. There was a Liverpool Friday going on around me and, irresponsibly drunk for radio, I remember thinking, 'Fuck this.' All plots tend to move deathward, but the point of sport and the history of Liverpool FC, at the very least since Shankly turned up, was that of renewal. I was looking around at the youthful faces in the city on a Friday and feeling my own eternally youthful outlook bristle. I was thinking about him and what he would want and I was – how do we put this? – full-throated in rejecting the Attenborough tone, the black tie and the difficult day.

We get to choose. We get to choose what the day is, and we get to say that we are going nowhere, not now, not ever. We get to choose, and that was precisely what he reminded us of all that time ago in 2015 when he first turned up. We decide when it is over. Between 82 and 94 you can make eight goals, if you like, and that moment on 5 Live it was important to remind everyone listening, with us, against us or non-combatants, of that fact.

Because, if not, he had wasted his time. We weren't having that. And we still aren't. The next thing started that day. He said so.

Key Game 17
Liverpool 1 Chelsea 0
(League Cup Final)

25 February 2024

Injury-hit Liverpool at Wembley. More injuries picked up through the game. Every substitution making Liverpool younger and less experienced. But you must never, ever forget: Football Miracles. On a weekly basis. Season after season. You must never forget Jürgen Klopp. Mainz. Dortmund. Liverpool. We can all say this: *He came to this place. He found these people and he changed this football club for ever.*

And it was that belief in miracles, that idea that we were lost and had been found, that change he made in all of us . . . it was that you could hear precisely at the start of extra time against Chelsea.

At the start of extra time, for ten minutes, when Liverpool had been under the cosh at the end of normal time, was something else entirely. It was an entire end of supporters saying, 'We're with you. Be brave, and if the worst happens we were with you anyway.' It was support in its rawest, most active form, the raw verb: not fandom, not celebrating brilliance you can see – Manchester City at Wembley in the semi-final in 2022 – but urging on your own people to be the best versions of themselves at exactly the second they need you.

You saw, in the ground, Liverpool grow and Chelsea shrink. You could see what it meant at the moment you heard it, and suddenly the whole game was Liverpool's despite the injury crisis, despite the substitutions, despite the variety of young players right the way across the pitch.

At the very centre of it, though, was Virgil van Dijk. The game's responsible adult. As the game wore on there was this thing eating away at me as we traversed the highs and lows – Virgil van Dijk is going to have something to say about this. Virgil van Dijk will have other ideas.

He had had one disallowed in the second half, but deep in extra time, when the very essence of being Liverpool, being Jürgen Klopp's Liverpool, rose to the occasion, so did van Dijk. He swept across the front post, and it was overwhelming.

He at least had the good grace to be overwhelmed himself. Grace. He is made of grace, grace and steel. The man of the match. He didn't just win it for us with his head, he won it in defence. Chelsea needed Raheem Sterling to be lucky, or for Trevor Chalobah in the final moments to get the better fall of the ball. It never came for them because Virgil van Dijk marshalled Liverpool's defensive play with calm. Nobody panicked for 120 minutes, no matter what. Because there was Virgil.

This was the manager's last final, possibly of his life; this was a final where Liverpool's young players were needed, and the support was needed more. This was the culmination of nine years of saying to people, 'Go on, believe. Go on, enjoy it at all costs. Go on, take every last chance to live.' But, more than all and any of that, this was both the van Dijk final and the manager's ultimate occasion.

It was to be his last Liverpool final and he and all his coaching staff were moved to tears in front of the stand after the trophy had been presented. It was an enormous emotional display that exhausted everyone: the most crying I had seen since Madrid.

Liverpool had wanted it throughout: every battle, every tackle, every push forward. Liverpool wanted this and, in the stands, every hand lifted a scarf. A sea of red from beginning to end, relishing it, wanting it in what became an exceedingly long game. For every minute everyone – every spectator, every player, every player not playing but spectating – craved it, young and old.

Young and old sort of became Harvey Elliott in a game like this. He has so much experience for one so young, and he ended the game exhausted through having given every ounce of energy. He showed constantly and was so brave with and without the ball. Seeing him with the trophy at the end was perfect.

Caoimhín Kelleher produced a man-of-the-match performance, if not for his captain being the whole fucking show. He smothered everything, was quick and smart, leapt to his feet after every save and kept his cool admirably.

In many ways, the manager had turned the injury problems into a young legs solution. To keep going without goals for 120 minutes is hard. But this young, inexperienced Liverpool, in part, managed it precisely because they were young and inexperienced. But they were also excellent. James McConnell came on and was as good as Alexis Mac Allister, which was useful as Mac Allister was excellent. Bobby Clark won everything in the first 15 he was on. Jayden Danns did the running of two. Jarrell Quansah again was calm, the essence of unruffled. This was their magic. Across the board, whether Kelleher from seasons prior, Quansah from the start of the campaign, or Conor Bradley as it wore on, what was most impressive about this crop of youngsters was their temperament. They all kept their cool in all circumstances.

It was, though, to be the week of the academy. Young players were also going to excel against Southampton, Nottingham Forest and, in Clark's case, Sparta Prague. Danns had made his debut only four days before and would bag a brace against Southampton in three days' time before being on the pitch for the 99th-minute winner against Nottingham Forest.

All the way through the campaign, the whole season, not just this day, the thing was: no excuses, no regrets. Yet also: no blame. No negativity. The remarkable thing Klopp, his coaching staff, van Dijk and the whole leadership group of players nailed in 2023–24, after everything that had gone on in the year before, was that they got everyone to buy into motoring relentlessly forward together and never, ever feeling sorry for themselves under any circumstances. Everyone bought into what this was, on the pitch, in the dugout, in the stands: a set of footballers making you proud, precisely because they didn't feel sorry for themselves, whether senior or junior. They kept backing themselves, and one another, kept attacking, and kept trying to win because they were – and we were – that day in London, the most a product of what one man had been leading for eight years in his own inimitable way, which chimed with us, which was our inimitable way. To quote: 'You do what you do for yourself and your people and what the outside world thinks about it, I couldn't give a shit, to be honest. And you can write that exactly like that. This is for us and nobody else.'

His quote.

His football club.

His culture.

His revolution.

He came to this place. He found these people, and he changed this football club for ever.

Playground Football

When Liverpool played Manchester City on 10 March 2024 there was a moment right in line with me in the ground – the halfway line – when Harvey Elliott, Wataru Endō and Alexis Mac Allister fought for the ball with Rodri, John Stones, Erling Haaland, and one other City player – I want to say Phil Foden because, God, he's good – with Bernardo Silva in attendance.

A City player was on the deck and the players were all just kicking at the ball, trying to get it out and away for their side. Like eight-year-olds. I think City may have edged that contest, but I was agog at it. It reminded me of the game at the Etihad in January 2019 when it felt like Fernandinho and Vincent Kompany spent half the game on the floor, Andy Robertson steamed into challenges and powered up and down the flank. Or the game at Anfield in January 2018 when Emre Can harassed the life out of Manchester City.

Every single one of those games between these two sides (when they were good) had a stretch or a moment like this, often five or six of them, when a group of the best footballers in the world – the best-coached, best-educated, smartest footballers in the world – played playground football, like eight-year-olds scrapping for the ball; the players all of these probably once were, on small-sided games on tiny pitches.

In different ways part of the aim of the football of Jürgen Klopp and Pep Guardiola is that incidents like this should never happen. For Klopp, you win it clean and go. For Guardiola, you have so much control something like this never happens, you keep duels away, apart from specific moments on your terms.

Part of why the games between Klopp's Liverpool and Guardiola's City were brilliant was precisely because of moments like this: that, for all the principles, sports science, analytics, insight and, frankly, genius, that for all the seconds of unspeakable, breathtaking quality, you got to have this stuff as well, the stuff of far less refined managers' dreams, but precisely what they could not bring to bear when they played Klopp's Liverpool or Guardiola's City.

In short, it takes the very best to match up, to make every turnover feel heartstopping, to mean that rolling around on the floor kicking at the ball isn't just some meagre fleeting moment of pride in a local derby, an opportunity to drag them down to your level . . . but is vital, match-defining, the heart and soul of the contest.

This is so cheering. This book doesn't like nostalgia – things weren't better in the old days – but it is striking that the game played as well it can be, as well as you have ever seen it, takes us back to the eternal values of football. Win your battles. Back your teammate up. Earn the right to play. Make yourself available.

What's been incredible about such games is that the best way to earn the right to play has been to play and play and play: to find angles and space and cleverness; to ping the ball no one can see; to tempt the ball no one can play.

But every now and then you have to roll around on the floor and get your mates to come and help you out. Because this is the very highest level, and you've got to dance with the eight-year-old that brung you.

Key Game 18
Liverpool 1 Manchester City 1
10 March 2024

The last time. And when it kicked off we knew it was the last time.

What's become clear since Jürgen Klopp, Pep Lijnders and the whole coaching staff left the building is that they were so immensely proud and impressed with this Liverpool performance against Manchester City. Immensely proud and impressed.

So was I. Liverpool, for 60 minutes, after going behind, were genuinely excellent. At the point where Manchester City scored midway through the first half, Liverpool had only had two shots and the xG value was negligible. By the end of the game, which finished 1–1, Liverpool had had 19, should have been given a last-minute penalty, and the xG value was over 2.5. City hit the post late on, and Phil Foden had an excellent chance, but apart from that they had barely been in Liverpool's half after they scored.

But we didn't win.

As metaphors go, it's almost too strong: too strong in summing up a season, and too strong in summing up an entire rivalry. When they say 'you couldn't script it', in this instance what we actually mean is that the script editor rejected it for it being too on the nose.

It was dominance in terms of possession, territory and chances, which Liverpool had never quite managed for three-quarters of a game against Manchester City. Other teams had beaten Manchester City, including Liverpool, since Pep Guardiola took over. In this same season Aston Villa put a marvellous performance in against them as well. But Liverpool–City, Klopp–Guardiola was different; has been something else.

But we didn't win.

Pep Guardiola called the second-half combination of Liverpool and the crowd 'a tsunami'; called Liverpool 'the best team [he] had ever seen in the high pressing'. He said, 'At Anfield it is really different. It is the environment. We know it. Our players know it. I know it.'

He said this, in part, to praise his players. And he was right to. The constant context makes it so hard to just praise Manchester City, just say how good they are baldly. The constant context makes writing about the football hard. We know it has jarred and disrupted European football in a way which isn't good.

And we talk like we know Pep Guardiola, know his coaching credentials, know his genius mind, know how he revolutionised the game, know how he has only ever worked with elite players and only really spent his life in elite facilities.

What doesn't happen enough is to praise the battling qualities of his coaching, of his players. His ability to eke every last ounce out of them and get them to make one more step, one more run, one more pass. His ability to man-manage. His ability to get the maximum amount of fight in his players. That isn't praised enough, anywhere, perhaps because it often isn't seen; it doesn't need to be seen.

But I have seen it. Over and over. I have seen it because it was in those games, our games, where it came to the fore. I saw it in the 2–1 in January 2019, saw it in the Champions League quarter-final first half in 2018 when they were 3–0 down, saw it in the fastest game in Covid in November 2020 when the sides knocked lumps out of each other. Over and over I have seen it.

The reason why the Liverpool coaches loved this game on this day was the flip side. Liverpool passed the ball better than Manchester City, Alexis Mac Allister was full of touches, turns and, more than anything else, brains – and it was he and Wataru Endō who controlled the tempo more than Manchester City, who were better at managing space, at winning battles, at creating openings, at beating opponents one-on-one all over the pitch. Liverpool outdid Manchester City at all the things Pep Guardiola is meant to be good at. Pep Guardiola loved his players after this one because they did all the things Jürgen Klopp's players are meant to be good at.

The truth of the dominant coaching battle across the last 15 years is that the two of them constantly moved closer together, took from each other's football and created almost two hybrids. Pressing and counter pressing in Klopp's fashion intensified into a reaction to Guardiola's Barcelona. Guardiola kept trying to find ways around it, but in England ended up with an enormous team that pressed in his way. Klopp realised he couldn't spend a footballing life in transition so looked to keep the ball better and smarter, best signified by the signings of Thiago Alcântara and Alexis Mac Allister.

But we didn't win.

The difference between the two ultimately came down to risk. Guardiola's football was more risk averse, especially in the post-pandemic period. I'd argue it has cost him a little: 2023–24 saw his side fail to beat Real Madrid, when he had Manuel Akanji playing give-and-go balls around Real Madrid's box to Kyle Walker. He'd point at the treble in 2022–23 and that would be me told.

Klopp's much more open to risk, open to backing his players, to finding their solutions in games, having rolled the dice on his players being better when that moment hits. I'd argue it cost him a little in 2023–24 too: there were too many games in which Liverpool went behind and, while they so often turned it around in great tornadoes of attacking play and emotion, eventually the well ran dry. Klopp would point at where they were at the start of the season and tell me to put a sock in it, and that would be me told.

What was brilliant about these games was that both had to constantly risk it all. Klopp knew his players tended not to be better. Guardiola knew that his way of not playing, of removing risk through sterile retention and positional play, actually increased the risk against a Klopp side. So neither would ever play dead. They would instead play and play and play and play. Only by playing is there a chance of not losing. To not play would be to lose; you will lose if you do not play. Before every single game against Manchester City Klopp would talk about having to carry genuine threat, because if not you would get punished.

Klopp's football is the football which I'd die for. It won less, but it lived more. It had more singalong songs which became scripture, more beats per minute, more nights out, more controls set for the heart of the sun, more lusty little crushes, more 365 party girl, more running wild through the night, and more mornings after the night before. Massive highs.

But we didn't win. Crushing lows.

Except for all the ways and all the times and all the things that we won over and over and over again. Every last drop that we wrung out of it while he wrangled it out of them. All the things. We won each other. And I am immensely proud and impressed with that Liverpool performance.

You Can't Keep Going Behind

The post-Paris league period for Liverpool was defined by one trait across the two seasons: starting badly and conceding the first goal in games. These are the raw numbers of goals for and against in the first 30 minutes in the league across those two seasons for Liverpool, Arsenal and Manchester City:

Liverpool 2023–24 – F17; A14
Liverpool 2022–23 – F19; A18
Arsenal 2023–24 – F25; A8
Arsenal 2022–23 – F29; A11
Manchester City 2023–24 – F29; A8
Manchester City 2022/23 – F27; A8

The differences are stark and the underlying numbers back this up. The poor starts in games ultimately did for Liverpool in the 2023–24 season. While they didn't finish the campaign well, it is worth pointing out that this trait persisted all season long. They conceded in the first five minutes of their first home game of the season against Bournemouth. They conceded first against Luton Town at home. They conceded in the first five minutes against Arsenal at home. They conceded first against Manchester City at home. They conceded first against three of those four opponents away.

But the rub of it all: they only lost one of those seven games where they conceded first. Through the 2023–24 season they showed enormous resilience.

Until they didn't. Until they couldn't show any more.

You can test your resilience and strengthen it, make your shell harder, keep bouncing back. But the thing about an ever-hardening shell is that when it cracks it can shatter, and that is where the side ended up in a campaign pock-marked by refereeing madness, managerial resignation, endless injuries and an actual kidnapping. They ended up shattered.

All the way through Klopp's tenure there had been the glory of it being hard and emotional and tight. There had been the enormous celebration of the late winner, of hanging in and waiting for your luck to turn. But there had also been the cost of that: playing as hard as you can for 100 minutes over and over and over because you conceded a soft one early, and that means your 2–0 is actually 2–1 and the opposition know they only need one ball to bounce their way and they have an equaliser. That was 2023–24. It was a successful season on general merits. Any season where you win a trophy and still have something to play for in April is exactly that. You don't know you're born if you think otherwise.

Yet a combination of opportunity and romance left it feeling like there could have been more. Liverpool were alive in everything in March and top of the pile in April. It wasn't quite to be – the players returning from injury couldn't find rhythm. Liverpool ended the season with the feeling that only six or seven of the matchday squad were actually playing well. The rest were either scratching around for form or shattered by the endeavour.

In the final reckoning though it was a successful season for Klopp. There would have been times the year before when he may have considered going but found such a thing untenable. Jürgen Klopp wanted to leave Liverpool in the best possible shape, and through 2023–24 he managed that. He left a club in rude health with excellent players, most of whom are under 26 and most of whom have unbelievable experience(s). They have an attitude and an approach and a temperament worthy of him, and so worthy of us.

What needs fixing isn't that hard on the surface and, crucially, it appears to be only surface questions that remain. An example being:

you can't keep conceding first. Fix that, move those numbers to those of Arsenal and Manchester City, and you never know.

Regardless, Klopp discharged his final responsibility with both aplomb and care. You take your work seriously. You do the job as you see it and you enjoy it in action. You leave any place better than you found it.

We don't really talk about 'the Liverpool Way' any more, and that pleases me, but that final flourish, that pleasure in work, in life, in action, that responsibility to tomorrow, and joy in today, that'll do for me. It's as good a framework as any.

Post-Match Analysis

Nostalgia Will Kill You and Nearly Did Kill Us and We Must Guard Against It

Nostalgia will kill you.

Back in the heady days of 2014 John Gibbons and I wrote and edited a book about Liverpool's 2013–14 season. It was exciting, that season, and the writing of the book. The football team had been an absolute ride, and we had to turn the thing around really quickly.

When we had finished, when we released, there was this other book that we kept seeing displays for. It was on shelves everywhere, and there was a massive fuss. It was called *H is for Hawk* by a woman called Helen Macdonald. It was about her training a goshawk in the aftermath of her father's death. Us being us, *H is for Hawk* became something we would joke about. We turned it into the opposition.

Then I read it and loved it. It is a marvellous piece of work. So us being us, I then reviewed it for *The Anfield Wrap*, interviewed Helen for the show, and finally ended up hosting an event about *H is for Hawk* at Waterstones with Helen, whom I found great company. I remember that time being about working a lot out, a lot which has laid the groundwork for *The Anfield Wrap* today – and the hawk book, with its deep soul-searching building to a crescendo, helped. It is a piece of work about learning how to exist in the present tense while carrying the past rather than being weighed down by it. There was the eternal process of being yes to everything and then the victory that was the marvellousness of Helen and her excellent writing which helped create a philosophy and sense of deep enjoyment in whatever strange moment, and Helen and I have remained in touch since.

There is something odd about the idea that if it wasn't for, say, Daniel Sturridge's three goals in the three 1–0 wins in August 2013 then I wouldn't know Helen. Daniel Sturridge is a man who has made and will continue to make a number of significant interventions in making the universe a happier place, but the zigzags of all of our collective existences – the unlikely, fortuitous circumstances – matter, and what we then make of them matters.

I loved Daniel and still do. His brilliance and impudence is something I miss quite profoundly at times, and his being ravaged by injury hurts more than most. Daniel at Stoke. Daniel's outrageous lob at Anfield against Everton. Daniel at Fulham finishing one of the most aesthetically pleasing goals you will ever see. Daniel leading us to Helen.

Helen wrote a new book with Sin Blaché and it was an excellent sci-fi thriller that is not about hawks or nature in general. Its title was *Prophet*, and it is the absolute business. Its central premise is that nostalgia will kill you, will kill all of us. That where nostalgia is writ large it feeds into nationalism and becomes exclusionary and dangerous and turns people into yearning voids, trying to cling to simulacra of yore. It's marvellously written and has a glorious love story at its heart that left me begging to read about one kiss. All it takes.

The key thing about the past is how it plants seeds for the future, how we get to imagine living similarly but living anew. Or flip it: that these days could well be ones people choose to be nostalgic for later but these days, right now, are just part of a journey towards the ever-moving now, and that that now is the bit that matters. The good days are the ones where you're laying the groundwork for the next ones to be better again.

Prior to the start of the 2023–24 season, my concern was we were going to become nostalgic. Because we were going to be less relevant. That the heady days of 2013–14 would be something to look back on with increased headiness, precisely because headiness was lacking now: big wins, bigger nights out, a (Sound) city unfolded for delight.

Well, headiness most definitely wasn't lacking in 2023–24; Jürgen Klopp's New Reds saw to that.

Something began to happen, though, as the campaign unfolded, an odd frisson of immediate nostalgia for what had just happened and what hadn't finished. After the League Cup final 'we will never see the likes of this again' was the message – from the manager himself, for one. He himself began to oddly feel like a manifestation of nostalgia precisely because he was becoming a relic, an object clung to one last time. He wasn't a simulacrum but he would speak about his years knowingly, affectionately, aware of what was about to occur, and he couldn't help that, not least because he was weaponising it before our eyes, using his farewell tour as a call to arms.

I have an overriding concern for the era that follows this. Put simply, it will be less fun. Not that it will be less successful – it may be, or it may be more successful – just that it may be less fun. Less breakneck, less in need of football miracles because you just win the game you should in a normal way rather than needing the crowd rabid for Luton Town at home.

Then that feeling leads to nostalgia and eats away at it all. We can't let that happen – it would remove the lessons learned or reminders made and kill the core value, the one the manager believed in. This thing of ours is indeed ours. We make it and hold it and define it

There is an argument that if it wasn't for Daniel Sturridge's three 1–0s at the start of the 2013–14 season I may not be here now doing this at all, but enjoying and acknowledging what has gone before doesn't mean wallowing in it; wallowing in it traps us. We live in a time across the world where people want to wallow, want to return, want to rehash old arguments and then, finally, ultimately, be exclusionary. You can see it everywhere. It means there is a backlash to a perfectly reasonable referendum vote in Australia: recognising the original inhabitants of the land in the Australian constitution became full of reactionary rhetoric and spite, dragging backwards, excluding. It defined British politics across its frustrating spectrum: an inability to escape a yesterday that cannot come back. There is no route back to 1953, 1978 or 1997.

It cannot come back. Daniel Sturridge cannot come back as he was, but he can be a brilliant adjunct to our lives as he is. Jürgen Klopp was the remaking of us. But he cannot and should not stay for ever or come back as a manager. We need to take the best bits and make anew. It is the way cultures stay strong, and why ours felt weak in 2013.

When I was last in Las Vegas – a place I am far more fond of than you may think – I saw the B-52s. The B-52s! What was so striking about seeing them was how much their sound made organically – with conventional instruments often used unconventionally – made me think of hyperpop; that there is a line from them to SOPHIE or Charli XCX, or whoever, which would have alarmed a lot of the audience there who were enjoying the nostalgic wallow. But the B-52s' exact qualities persist, can be reframed, are continually redeployed. The B-52s were weird and different and the B-52s still ended up in Vegas, and the whole show was about that journey and about the value of still being weird and different done authentically, done with love.

When we played Brighton in the autumn of 2023 (rather than in the dark winter of 2023) the game made me think of all the eternal football values and how playing Roberto De Zerbi's Brighton made them weird and different, twisted closing down into a negative and turned space against you, but authentically so. The game was something that would have looked alien in 2013, or even 2019, but it was still Jürgen Klopp's Liverpool – indeed, part of why the game looked the way it did was because of Jürgen Klopp's Liverpool. We change and mould the world as we go.

Shouting, 'Nothing stupid, Liverpool,' as I did in the context of that game was both utterly ridiculous and simultaneously very much Liverpool's game-plan. Liverpool had to deal and live in the now, and it was thrilling and it was terrifying and it was part of a journey.

The journey was now, obviously, towards trying to win a league title. In among all of this – the memories of Helen and hawks, the rejection of nostalgia which underpins everything, the B-52s, the zigzags, the politics – the key question we should always return to, the key question this book posits, is: 'Have you had the best night out of your life yet?'

During the journey of Jürgen Klopp and Liverpool, people in their fifties and sixties who'd gone everywhere, seen everything, won the lot and thought they'd had it all found out they had no idea. Absolutely no idea. That it could be made anew and could be made better again.

That it could scale even greater heights. There is only a point it has all been downhill from if we acquiesce to that reality. Instead it winds its way towards a new peak. The old Reds and the old nights out lead to the new Reds and the new nights out, and may well lead to that one, the one we never truly had, the one where you won the league, the one which may well be the best one, the best League Cup final, the best European affair, the best comeback, the most critical save.

Learning from the past, enjoying its unlikely fruits in terms of connections made, all of that is different – taking yesterday's beating heart and adding it to today's pounding heart is one thing. Pining away empty and fading is another entirely. Nostalgia will kill you. Zap your spirit. Cheapen your soul.

The City's Best Photographer Was You

You told the story. You came and you saw and you posted pictures and you wrote captions and you spoke to friends and you told them, told them what was happening up there, what was going on. You told them there was this thing of ours and it was open to anyone who wanted to come.

You took the pictures, you shot the videos, you altogether in the ends, on the concourses, in the squares, in the fan parks. At the restaurants, in the bars, meeting people from all over the world, you depicted a life and a way of going about our business altogether.

You were on the parades and you documented the parades and you shared the being and the documentation with people you loved. You gathered everyone together and found your bit of concrete, your temporary bit of Liverpool, and you delivered the soundtrack to complement Calvin Harris as the buses went by. You became a snapshot of history and you delivered a snapshot of history. You did that.

You put the flags out, created the furnace they played in and gave them those reminders about what it means. You were the production designer and you were in charge of sound and you made it just right when they needed it.

You came over from your supporters' clubs and you went back and you told the rest of them that you simply have to go. You have to have a turn. Do what you can. Get over there and relish it, you said. You simply have to go.

You told your friends that it isn't like that. You represented us across a vexingly mean little country which doesn't like things that are different. You sent them up, trusted we'd take care of them, expected they'd get the best version of us because that's fair enough, isn't it?

You made everyone welcome. You realised that this place is at its best when the doors are thrown open wide. You realised it isn't where you are from but where you are at which matters most.

You made the place better, worked on small corners to get some victories which we know are also temporary, will need to be won over and over.

You told the story. You were the story, the point of the story, the only way the whole thing made sense. It had you within it and it was for you. Mo Salah looked into your eyes at Manchester City.

The city's best chronicler was you.

The city's best emissary was you.

The city's best photographer was you.

You were the best thing that could have happened. Maybe, just maybe, you just needed a nudge.

But when push came to shove, it was all you.

You Have to Lose Big

There's a working theory picked up from bouncing around the city, going to live shows across the world, speaking to everyone, listening to everyone, that there is a solid number of Liverpool supporters – of football supporters in general – who would be all right with a sturdy fourth-place finish in the league and a cup run.

Think about it, it's comforting: to come a sturdy fourth you have to win 22 games, draw ten and then lose six. That's not many bad days, really. Maybe there's a very disappointing defeat in there and a pair of daft home draws where you tut and say, 'That'll cost us in the long run.' But cost us what? A lot of heartache and stress about challenging at the top? That's the cost? Smoking cigars here, smiling from ear to ear like Mighty Red.

Plus a cup run. Not even a cup win, a run. Some good days, one big win, something to look forward to of a midweek from time to time. There. A season not on the brink but comfortably in the pink.

Jürgen Klopp's entire career is the counterbalance to this because – and, let's be clear – good God, has Jürgen Klopp been good at getting beat. He's lost so many finals, suffered four deep final day disappointments the likes of which could generate reams of epic poetry, and in general has made Icarus look unambitious and undercooked. He has chosen to lose big time and time and time again, and it still grinded on people who supported Liverpool, even in the time of his leaving, that he wanted to believe in everything being possible in all phases and was prepared to risk it all to win big, to win his way.

It feels like the whole of Trent Alexander-Arnold's career will be this too. Trent constantly tries to win big, in all phases of the game; Trent is almost the purest Jürgen Klopp footballer, and he has been, across the last five years or so, the most discussed Jürgen Klopp footballer. Not Mo Salah, for whom magnificence is constant, not Virgil van Dijk, who could be the best ever in his position, but Trent Alexander-Arnold, because watching and talking about risks generates the most controversy, and controversy equals clicks, and because Trent is never, ever going to stop trying to win big.

Sometimes in games when Trent is struggling you want him to keep it simple for 15 minutes, do bits and rebuild and then go. But no. Over and over he tries to bring it all to bear in one fell swoop, and this irritates some supporters. But Trent is prepared to lose big, prepared to risk making himself back-page news in the worst sense in order to be back-page news in the best sense.

You have to be prepared to lose big in order to win big. You have to be prepared to be called bottlers for finishing second, for making a mistake in a cup final the world is watching, to have your decisions micro-analysed on a Monday night. To try to be the team, you have to try to beat the team, and there's another working theory that, in 2017, a lot of football thought the smart move from English sides was to leave Manchester City to it. Let them crack on. Still now that feeling pervades. Still now there will be sages chin-stroking and saying, 'It's the hope that kills you,' when a side goes through a rocky patch, when settling for fourth feels like the easier road, the rational option.

There's a great tranche of storytelling history that runs through this whole idea of settling for the quiet life, of taking the easier option, starting with Achilles and Odysseus meeting in the Underworld. It's a well-ploughed, late-middle-aged man furrow – Homer was just the first to reap it millennia ago – but it so rarely examines the opposite path, whether or not it leads to people being let down and opportunity squandered.

In life the harder road can also be the much more rewarding road. It's hard to remember that when you can see the easier road, when you can see the path oft trodden, with its benches and occasional buses to move you along quicker, when you see the gleaming, polished, relaxed faces of those easy-road bastards in politics, in business, in media, in life, and, yes, in football. At times, losing big hurts so, so much precisely because you can lose to the easy road. You get knocked over by its buses at crossroads, swept away with barely a word. Klopp's been swept away time and again but has understood his options and engaged with them with the most serious work ethic to find the greatest glory.

We all have choices to make in life, constant decisions on whether we are prepared to lose big on this one, responsibilities to balance. It isn't easy.

But in football? Fuck that. The truth is that it's a game. At heart it is a game. Just a game. The best game, but a game. Football's constant albatross is that bit adjacent to the idea that it's the hope that kills you; that hiding away from potential ecstasy due to the risk of potential agony is in any way good or worthy or logical or mature is and always has been for the birds.

Marla Daniels in *The Wire* said, 'You cannot lose if you do not play.' But, flip it: playing is the point. It is why we are here. Jürgen Klopp lost big a lot, but I'll always want to be in his gang, whatever the price because you always get back up, ready to win big again, ready to lose big too, because that is what it takes.

Football Miracles

Anfield Wrap contributor John Milburn found a quote on an Everton forum a few days after Alisson Becker headed home against West Bromwich Albion to make it 1–2 to Liverpool: 'They can have more enjoyable moments in a week of football than we've had in 30 years. Everton are the most miserable club to support in this country. A combination of us being unable to have any high whatsoever compounded by them getting football miracles on a weekly basis season after season.'

When we do live shows I can read this out about five times. Different emphasis on different sentences or even words within there.

Unable to have any high whatsoever.

Whatsoever.

It's beautifully written, concise, poetic. We should probably find whoever wrote it and get him to write this book. It's been deleted now. They must have got wind of us talking about it all the time.

Season after season.

This is the prevailing Evertonian view of Liverpool going back years – I mean, Istanbul happened in 2005 – but it is something that Jürgen Klopp deepened and intensified.

There are miracles within miracles: some come from nowhere; some, actually, shouldn't be miracles or shouldn't need to be miracles. Luton Town at home, in his final season, shouldn't have felt like it had some magical energy about it but it did. It just did.

More enjoyable moments in a week of football than we've had in 30 years.

Every time you enter a football ground it is important to remember that it's always someone's first game, and so it's always potentially some-one's first miracle. I always remember when Gerrard scored to make it three against Olympiakos in 2004 on the journey to Istanbul, there was an American three seats down who lost his mind. That was his first time at Anfield.

If we think about that in the context of Jürgen Klopp there will be children for whom their first home game against Manchester United was the 7–0. There will be supporters who found the club in 2017 who think that Liverpool have a one-in-two chance of making a Champions League final if they qualify for the competition, or that any first leg can be overturned.

The best thing, though, is that all this fits who we were before Klopp – again, he didn't make us. He reminded us and let us do the rest.

This has been a book of miracles – the timelines are lousy with them – but I'm always taken back to West Brom at Anfield, to that moment when he stood in front of us and said, 'This is what we can do,' and there were a million different possible outcomes and we, you and me, we got this one.

'Life Without Emotions. Imagine That. How Boring It Would Be.'

There's a video of a young Irish wheelchair-bound Liverpool supporter, Dáire Gorman, being invited to the club by Jürgen Klopp and the Liverpool squad to meet the manager and the players and watch them train, and Dáire can't contain his emotion throughout. It's overwhelming. I know how he feels. It was a video of him unable to contain himself during a rendition of 'You'll Never Walk Alone' that drew the attention of the manager.

In May 2024 I was in Kirkby to do an interview with Pep Lijnders before he left, and we were hanging around in a room waiting when I went to go to the loo and there in front of me, waiting for the lift, was Mo Salah. I just veered right and hid until I thought he had gone. I'm 43. So poor Dáire has to meet everyone, and has Klopp wheel him through the training facility throughout, and he is understandably emotional, then Jürgen says, 'Life without emotions. Imagine that. How boring it would be.'

I've been lucky enough to meet him seven times. Six interviews, and once at an event. Most of the time our time is taken up by the actual interview. I'm only there because people listen, so you want to give them as much as possible.

But the last interview, the one conducted just before he left, was a pleasure – but, God, it was hard. We had time before and after, but all the way through that time my brain couldn't stop buzzing about this possibly being the last time to see him and it needing to be special in some way, while I had a job to do.

It was hard because I wanted to talk to him. At him. With him. I just wanted to list all these things he had been part of with us, but, of course, he is more interested in you, in your world. He asks so many questions, and is warm without being overbearing. There has to be a veneer of professionalism, but this throbbing in my head and gut just wanted to howl gratitude, which makes answering his detailed questions difficult and his deep thanks hard to process because, God, my thanks are deeper and may be the reason my knees appear not to be working.

Basically you (I) worry he thinks you are (I am) a weirdo.

That's OK, though, because the key point is that he understands emotion. In fact, he doesn't just understand it, he has harnessed it, weaponised it and been debilitated by it himself. Emotion was why he was a perfect fit. This place of ours wants to love and to be loved. It is the unspoken thing about the city. Liverpool is needy. It's proud and headstrong and certain of itself. It loves a half-joke which could be a full joke or could be serious. It wants to plough its own furrow. But it wants you to like it. Wants you to love it. We're not asking for permission or forgiveness. We're asking for acknowledgement.

At their core, Ferguson's Manchester United didn't care about whether or not you liked them or even acknowledged them. They didn't give a fuck. And nor, then, did that city, that place. It would do things as it wanted. You wanted a word, they'll see you outside. It's lost a lot of that now, Manchester (writing as an interested observer), stuck between a business-international vibe and a far too local one at one and the same time. But Ferguson fitted then, and they yearn for that understanding and perhaps even clarification now.

Klopp was right, and then matters unfolded as they did, and he realised as we did he was more and more and right. He was the right shape to fit the mould, but circumstances unfolded to mean the shape of the mould grew bigger, and with it he grew. This is the crux of why this is fascinating, and what we will never know is to what extent all this could have been anticipated. Did he turn up knowing he would need to show an emotional leadership style not just to a group of players and coaches but to a whole club? Did he turn up knowing that the whole club meant a diaspora of supporters?

That just doesn't seem true or plausible. Instead, this just became increasingly true, and he had the capacity to do it. It wasn't always necessary, but there he was every single time because he was doing the job anyway.

Emotional leadership is a difficult formula to crack, a tough tightrope to walk, and there will have been failings we won't know of yet – players left feeling disenfranchised from the process, or who may well have been better with a different type of leadership. Nothing is perfect.

But he was as close to perfection for us as this time and place could hope for. Precisely because he never wanted it to be boring (he never bought a player he had worked with before), always wanted it to be emotional, and knew it was about life.

The only non-interview time I saw him was at James Milner's Foundation Dinner in 2019. He came over at the start and said hello to the table and then disappeared off and was hounded all night. Finally, Craig Hannan, our head of marketing, being himself he went over to ask for a picture and Klopp apologised to Craig for not subscribing. Craig informed him it was only seven quid and he should sort that out. A big booming laugh. We did the picture as a group and left him and the footballers who were present alone, pretty much.

It was mad. Kaizer Chiefs were the band, and all these football people pretended they were at a proper gig (because how often do they get to go?), and the exuberance of it carried you along and as the night crumbled and the DJ came on and the responsible people went home we hit the dancefloor.

I was minesweeping a bottle of vodka from a table and he was a way off but for once not being bothered and he saw me and laughed and saw the *Anfield Wrap* crew behind me in their own world together. He gestured at them and mouthed 'good team' at me, I think. I smiled and gestured with the vodka. Great team. He laughed and toasted, he drank from a glass, me from the bottle. Great teams are worth toasting.

Key Game 19
Liverpool 2 Wolves 0
19 May 2024

The golden rule of post-match writing work is always never to write the report before a ball is kicked.

There was an urge before his final game to cheat. After all, what was going to happen, really? Game, palaver, Klopp. Take a medal if you think you deserve one.

But that urge was suppressed because of part three. Klopp.

He always has his own agenda, has his own ideas, has his way of being. And he always exists in and inhabits the moment. The moment is everything with him. It has been part of the magic.

Another part of the magic has been how he wants everyone to be the best version of themselves. He wants to create the circumstances where that is constantly possible. He wants that for everyone. For his players. For the team around him. And for us. The supporters.

He wanted that since the day he arrived, not just the best for us, but that we be the best version of who we can be. And that we help one another in being the best version of who they can be too.

That didn't stop against Wolves. So there weren't tears from him on the Anfield turf; instead there was an enormous call to arms. This does not stop. This cannot stop. Because if it stops then he has failed. We have failed, but he has too – his intention was always to bequeath the best possible club to his successor, and we are part of that. We are active, we have been active and we remain active.

He was right to point that out, that he didn't change us from doubters to believers, but instead created the circumstances which made that easier. We had to do that ourselves. We had to be active. We had to be alive and to make change.

Change isn't something inherently bad. It isn't something to be scared of. Part of why he chimed deeply with me, and presumably with you, is because his was a rare voice in this increasingly desolate country which chose to speak with optimism from a place of reason, chose to speak progressively and without fear. He backed himself and his people, and, crucially, he backed you and he backed me, and I can't think of anyone else's backing I want more.

Often in these scenarios – the immensely emotional – the game itself can be a challenge.

Not today, though. This wasn't hard going. Liverpool's possession game was very strong. The captain was being the captain and was having one of those games where he had decided he was going to roam all over the park and bollock anyone who didn't pass to him. He was a scream, Virgil van Dijk.

Wolves were defensively robust in the first half. After 20 minutes passed with no goals, you wondered whether this was a strategy that would again put Liverpool a goal behind, but then the daft challenge occurred, Nélson Semedo saw red, and it was likely to be all over bar the shouting.

The opening goal was a cracker. Harvey Elliott picked out Alexis Mac Allister, who headed home delicately before the scramble for the second. Second half, José Sá made some very strong saves. Liverpool players looked for a goal with both effort and abandon, knowing nothing turned on this result and that Anfield would love to see them score. Sá, though, did not oblige and Liverpool yet again failed to kill a game as much as you'd like.

That didn't matter, though. The game was theirs. By the time injury time was called, nobody cared. We were singing Jürgen Klopp's song for 15 minutes, us all together, and we knew we were all done. Good done. Happy grief. Sweet sorrow. A sign in the Lower Kemlyn unveiled in the final minutes just said, 'He said so.'

Yes. He said so. He did what he said. How rough is the world outside

Anfield that we feel someone achieving what they said is remarkable, is wonderful.

Children in Merseyside tonight deserved some people to deliver what they said for them. There are a lot of things that need to be done for people. But in our corner of L4 we applauded a man who delivered what he said, and this is why he sticks out like a sore thumb. Why he chimes in this era which lacks authenticity and decency and honesty. He wanted to change things and he did. He wanted us to believe in him and we did. Tonight he told Anfield that he believes in us. If we want to achieve things in the future, we can never forget that lesson.

It's hard to resist the bait-and-switch of 'the big man is the best of us', etc, etc, and then have it be about Joël Matip, but we shall resist by virtue of saying that Joël Matip was indeed the best of us. He has been an integral part of a team which won everything and those integral qualities have been everywhere around the place given the way his teammates and manager speak about him. It's been a truly great Liverpool career and therefore a truly great career and whatever happens next he deserves the very, very best.

Thiago Alcântara has in so many ways been my favourite. I want him to be happy. He plays football like a man who has jokes. I want smiles and laughs.

The heart swells at the sight of so many of the coaching staff leaving to start anew. It's sad, obviously, but I hope they are excited. I hope they are emissaries too, chatting about the way they do it in Liverpool, the way they love it in Liverpool.

But it all means we get to start anew too. New journey, new memories, new miracles. We get to put a show on for a new crew, a crew who should be excited because they are about to get to do the best thing they will do in their whole lives. Imagine being them, seeing all this, this thing of ours, and being about to take responsibility for it all.

Because it needs responsibility. It needed it throughout, needed the greatest care to have the greatest careless moments, needed responsibility to drive our hedonism, and needed them to need more than want and want for all time with their collective skills. They wanted to win the league more than me and that is why I got what I wanted more than anything – to win the league.

And now it changes. Now the guiding force and some of the supporting force has gone. But not really; we know that. We know how this works. Just because someone isn't here, doesn't mean they aren't really here. Just because only 3,000 can be in an away end or 60,000 in Anfield doesn't mean there aren't millions of us amassed together in a grand spiritual space, yearning and loving and wanting our players and one another to be the best versions of ourselves. That's how this works. How it has always worked. And how he has reminded us it has worked.

Just because he isn't *there*, just there, opposite me at Anfield, doesn't mean he isn't *here*. Because the way this works is that he always will be. You are always here, too. We are always here together, and that we now includes him – the greatest living Liverpudlian. All the best ones come from outside. Another part of the magic.

Go well, big man. Nobody could have asked for any more.

Acknowledgements and Thanks

I shall try not to be too soppy. There has been almost 300 pages of that. And I am convinced I will accidentally forget someone and if you are that someone then apologies.

You wouldn't be reading this book were it not for Kevin Sampson insisting I meet Jamie Byng and insisting to Jamie Byng he meets me. Kevin is and has been for years a source of ongoing marvellousness and can't be thanked enough and he worked out the best way to make this happen was to get me and Jamie on a big sprawling pint around Liverpool and see where we ended up.

Jamie is CEO of Canongate and has been the business since the pint in question, and I have very much enjoyed the whole firm and hope to enjoy them even more as we market this book and pull an audiobook, events and everything together too. So thanks to him and to Melissa Tombere, Vicki Rutherford, Caitriona Horne, Jamie Norman, Gaia Poggiogalli and Joanna Lord for all their work, alongside Gill Phillips who gave it both a legal read and a couple of neat edits. There will be others whose names I don't have. There are so many!

The editor himself was Ian Preece whose enthusiasm and forbearance with many idiosyncrasies and continual murdering of tenses was greatly appreciated. Any remaining errors will most definitely be mine. He was a godsend.

My agent is David Luxton and I adore him; the way I want to describe him to you is that he's a man for all decades and all situations. Oli Kay pushed him in my direction and Oli has done some good things in his time but none more so than that. David worked with Rebecca Winfield on contractual elements and I would like to thank her too.

There are a great many people named in the book who are friends and family of mine and I would like to thank them all. You know who you are. This is a love song.

But of the readers and sharpeners of some or all of this I want to make special mention. Chief amongst them is Michael MacCambridge, who has been with me every step of the way on this. I cherish his friendship and support both in general but especially through this process. Knowing he has gone through this for something as special as *America's Game* and knowing we had worked together and that he was there to read and examine any text and have multiple calls was such a boost and I hope we work on something together again.

Dan Morgan had his book about Jürgen too, but he was around for me through this and was there to call on when required. I think the two sit together as the best companions you could ask for and that sentiment goes for him too.

Steve Graves gave me the sort of late quality assurance I always wanted from him. Steve will always be viewed by me as the best of us.

I am continually a bit of a headcase and honestly not quite one to put myself forward so when I was wobbling about writing the book for any number of self-indulgent reasons Alison McGovern threatened me with a wooden fork in Anfield and then read and made suggestions to improve and sharpen a number of chapters even while sorting out an election campaign.

John Furlong has been similarly encouraging and a lifelong friend. He is continually in my corner whenever I need him and is in many ways the target audience for a lot of these chapters. You need a person in mind when you write sometimes, and he is quite often mine. Martin Fitzgerald is another like that and will always back an idea, back an ambition.

Steve Armstrong read a chapter and I am using that mischievously here in part to get a picture of Zion sent back to me but also to thank him for his decade of support in a myriad of ways.

In terms of helping with aspects of the book, well, I could go on for days, but specifically I want to thank Rafa Honigstein for the German and for general soundness and encouragement. Kieran Maguire, The Swiss Ramble and Greg Cordell were all of use on the financial aspects, Kieran with a phone call which was an enormous amount of fun. The numbers ended up not being used to any great degree but they were worked on and if they were worked on erroneously then the errors are most definitely mine.

It was pointed out to me that Rob Gutmann barely appears in the text. This is the work's greatest weakness because there is no man alive, including Jürgen, who helps me enjoy both football and life itself more. Any day with Rob in it immediately becomes a better one and because there are many early starts that means there is even more day to make better. I love him.

I'd like to thank everyone who has worked with *The Anfield Wrap* down the years. It's a lot of people by this stage. Gareth Roberts was basically the first person to get me to write about football and Josh Sexton the man who has had to put up with the most of it. He knows Ian Preece's pain. Andy Heaton's boldness changed my life.

Emma Johnson, Craig Hannan and John Gibbons have been the bedrock of so much good and I can never thank them enough. It hasn't always been straightforward; we have chosen many hard roads and I have shot many messengers but we got to wherever here is with an amazing amount of joy still at the centre of everything. The joy would have been impossible without them and I nearly dedicated the whole book to them at the start because it is the least they deserve.

As ever, Samantha Brocklehurst is mildly disappointed this book is about football. This one isn't dedicated to her, not least because she made it a little-known fact about her in a work thing that 'at least one book she has never read' is dedicated to her. There are in fact two. But there will one day be a third dedicated to her and her hopes it may not be about football could be realised. We shall pull it together in the fullness of time. And I cannot thank her enough for everything down these years described here.

Ultimately though the book was dedicated to Joan, my mother – it could just as well be for Eddie, my dad or David, my brother. But Joan, she never gets mentioned, you see. She reads like a demon. And I know where my bread is buttered.

All my love

Neil

LIVERPOOL
Standard Chartered
LIVERPOOL
WALK ON WALK ON
Carlsberg